HEALING DELIVERANCE

By Gene Moody

Deliverance Ministries
Gene B. Moody
14930 Jefferson Highway
Baton Rouge, LA 70817-5217
www.genemoody.com

Telephone: (225) 755-8870
Fax: (225) 755-6120

NOT COPYRIGHTED
This manual is not copyrighted
I encourage you to make copies and distribute them for the Glory of God.
You may freely use the lessons as God directs you!

HEALING DELIVERANCE MANUAL

TABLE OF CONTENTS – OVERVIEW

SECTION 1 - PREAMBLE TO HEALING DELIVERANCE MANUAL 1

SECTION 2 - OPERATION DELIVERANCE 10

SECTION 3 – DRUGS AND MEDICINES 16

SECTION 4 - PHYSICIANS AND MEDICINE 29

SECTION 5 - PSYCHIATRY 34

SECTION 6 - PRAYERS AND LIST OF DEMONS FOR HEALING 36

SECTION 7 - CHANGE YOUR BRAIN CHANGE YOUR LIFE 50

SECTION 8 - SPIRITUAL ROOTS OF DISEASE 56

SECTION 9 - GODLY PEOPLE STRICKEN BEFORE THEIR TIME 61

SECTION 10 - DIET & HEALING RECOMMENDATIONS 74

SECTION 11 - DRUG ADDICTION AMONG CHILDREN 76

SECTION 12 - CHILDREN'S DELIVERANCE 80

SECTION 13 – CURING AND HEALING THE BODY BY DELIVERANCE 86

SECTION 14 - CANCER AND ARTHRITIS DELIVERANCE 95

SECTION 15 - HEALING FOR KIDNEYS AND OTHER DISEASES 105

SECTION 16 - TESTIMONY - JESUS SET MARIE'S BROKEN ARM 114

SECTION 17 - FAMILY TESTIMONIES 116

SECTION 18 - BALDNESS - BEARDS - HAIR 150

SECTION 19 - DRUNKENNESS AND GLUTTONY 157

HEALING DELIVERANCE MANUAL

TABLE OF CONTENTS – DETAILED

SECTION 1 - PREAMBLE TO HEALING DELIVERANCE MANUAL 1
  PREAMBLE 1
    Normal Numbers 1
    Alternatives For A Changing World 2
  DANGER 3
  CHRONIC ILLNESS AND DISEASE 3
    Preface 3
    Skyrocketing 4
    Alarming Facts 4
    Alarming Statistics 4
    Astronomical Rates 5
  PROCEDURE 5
  SUMMARY 7
  REFERENCES 7
    Recommended References 7
    Health Books That Can Be Used To Minister To Others 8
    All Health Books By The Following Authors 8
    Other Health Books Which May Be Of Interest 8
    Caution 9

SECTION 2 - OPERATION DELIVERANCE 10
  EARLINE MOODY, MY WIFE 10
  OTHER PEOPLE 10
  PREAMBLE TO HEALING DELIVERANCE MANUAL 11
    Procedure 11
    Summary 11
  OVERALL: PRAYER - COMMAND - WARFARE 11
    Overall Prayer 11
    Overall Command 12
    Overall Warfare 12
  PRAYERS 12
    Prayer To Establish Basis For Warfare 12
    Prayer Before Deliverance 12
  WITCHCRAFT: PRAYERS - CURSES - COMMANDS 13
    Prayers 13
    Curses 13
    Commands 13
  REVERSAL 14
    Satanic Supernatural Power Reversal 14
    Spiritual Warfare 14
  PERSONAL DELIVERANCE 15

SECTION 3 – DRUGS AND MEDICINES 16
  DRUG ABUSE IN THE WORKPLACE - STARTLING FACTS IN OUR TIMES 17

WHY DO PEOPLE TAKE DRUGS?	18
GENERAL	20
MEDICINE'S BONDAGE TO SATAN (EXCERPTS)	20
THE HIPPOCRATIC OATH (EXCERPTS)	21
MEDICINE AND THE BELIEVER (EXCERPTS)	22
VALIUM AND LIBRIUM (EXCERPTS)	25
A DIRECTORY OF DRUGS	25
Hallucinogens	25
Depressants	27
MINISTRY TO OPPRESSED	27
REFERENCES	28
SECTION 4 - PHYSICIANS AND MEDICINE	29
COMMENTS	29
DEMONIC WOUNDS AND DISEASES	29
Comments	29
Prayer	30
DOCTORS, DEMONS & MEDICINE	30
Medicine's Bondage to Satan	30
The Hippocratic Oath	30
Medicine and the Believer	30
PHYSICIAN	30
MEDICINE	31
BALM	31
OINTMENT	31
REMEDY	31
POULTICE	31
EMULSION	31
DISEASE	31
PAIN RELIEVERS	32
Comments	32
Pain Killers	32
HEALTH CARE	32
REFERENCES	33
SECTION 5 - PSYCHIATRY	34
THE CITIZENS COMMISSION ON HUMAN RIGHTS INTERNATIONAL	34
UNHOLY ASSAULT PSYCHIATRY VERSUS RELIGION	35
REFERENCES	35
SECTION 6 - PRAYERS AND LIST OF DEMONS FOR HEALING	36
GENERAL PRAYER	37
BASIC DELIVERANCE	38
Rejection	38
Bitterness	38
Rebellion	38
BODY CURED AND HEALED BY DELIVERANCE	39
CURSES OF DEUTERONOMY 28	39
LISTS OF DEMONS	39

- Diseases Found in Deuteronomy 28 39
- Diseases Found in the Bible 40
- Princes, Kings & World Rulers 40
- Paralysis 40
- Roots of Infirmity 40
- Ailments 40
- Spiritual Names Of Demons 40
- PRAYER FOR HEALING 41
- SPIRITUAL ROOTS OF DISEASE 42
  - Lists Of Demons 42
    - General Diseases 42
    - Specific Diseases 42
  - Fear, Anxiety and Stress Disorders 42
- BALDNESS - BEARDS - HAIR 43
  - Prayer 43
    - Everybody 43
  - Women 43
  - Men 43
  - Curses 43
  - List Of Demons 43
- DRUGS AND MEDICINES 44
  - List Of Demons 44
- DRUNKENNESS AND GLUTTONY 45
  - Prayer 45
- LIST OF DEMONS 45
- HEALING FOR KIDNEYS 46
  - Prayer 46
  - List Of Demons 46
- DELIVERANCE AND HEALING FOR CANCER AND ARTHRITIS 47
  - Arthritis 47
- CANCER 47
- PERFECTING LOVE 48
  - Prayer 48
  - List Of Demons 48
- ORGANS AND SYSTEMS OF BODY 48
- REFERENCES 49

- SECTION 7 - CHANGE YOUR BRAIN CHANGE YOUR LIFE 50
  - PREFACE 50
  - FIVE OF THE BRAIN SYSTEMS 50
  - PROBLEMS IN THE DEEP LIMBIC SYSTEM 51
    - Deep Limbic Checklist 51
  - PROBLEMS WITH THE BASAL GANGLIA SYSTEM 51
    - Basal Ganglia Checklist 51
  - PROBLEMS WITH THE PREFRONTAL CORTEX 52
    - Prefrontal Cortex Checklist 52
  - PROBLEMS WITH THE CINGULATE SYSTEM 52
    - Cingulate System Checklist 52
  - PROBLEMS - DOMINANT (USUALLY LEFT) TEMPORAL LOBE 52

- PROBLEMS - NONDOMINANT (USUALLY RIGHT) TEMPORAL LOBE 52
- PROBLEMS WITH EITHER OR BOTH TEMPORAL LOBES 53
  - Temporal Lobe Checklist 53
- THE DARK SIDE 53
- BRAIN POLLUTION 53
- THE MISSING LINKS 53
- HELP! 53
  - Relationships 53
  - Work 54
  - Significant Negative Effects 54
- MEDICATIONS 55
- REFERENCE 55

SECTION 8 - SPIRITUAL ROOTS OF DISEASE 56
- DISEASES WITH NO KNOWN MEDICAL CURE 56
- SPIRITUAL BLOCKS TO HEALING 56
- MASTURBATION, PROSTATE CANCER AND PROSTATITIS 57
- FEAR, ANXIETY AND STRESS 57
- THE CONTINUING WORKS OF CHRIST 57
  - Hypothalamus 57
  - Cardiovascular System 58
  - Hypertension 59
  - Stroke And Aneurysm 59
  - Disturbances Of Heart Rhythm 59
  - Muscles And Tension Headaches 59
  - Muscle Contraction Backache 59
  - Rheumatoid Arthritis 59
  - Pulmonary System 59
  - Immune System 59
  - Gastrointestinal System 60
  - Genital Urinary System 60
  - Skin 60
  - Endocrine System 60
- REFERENCES 60

SECTION 9 - GODLY PEOPLE STRICKEN BEFORE THEIR TIME 61
- LIST OF DEMONS 61
- SCRIPTURE 61
- LETTER OF OCTOBER 27, 1991 62
- REPLIES TO LETTER 63
- PRAYERS FOR US 63
- OUR MINISTRY 63
- FUTURE FOR CHRISTIANS 63
- GENERAL COMMENTS 63
- ANSWERS TO QUESTIONS 64
- GOD IN CONTROL 64
- SOVEREIGNTY OF GOD 65
- TRIALS AND TESTINGS 65
- FAITH OF THE SAINTS 66

CHRISTIAN SCOREBOARD	66
PRESENT CHURCH AGE	67
THIS WORLD	67
TEN THOUGHTS FOR YOU	68
CRUCIFIXION OF THE FLESH	68
SERVANTS OF GOD	68
DELIVERANCE WORKERS	69
APOSTLES SUFFERED	69
PRIDE, EGO AND VANITY	70
CONFUSION OF MIND	70
TESTIMONIES OF OTHERS	70
STANDING WITH EACH OTHER	70
HUSBANDS RESPONSIBILITY	70
HUSBAND'S ASKING WIVE'S FORGIVENESS	71
CREDIT TO OTHERS	71
PRAYERS BY GROUP	71
LIST OF DEMONS	72
DISEASES LISTED IN DEUTERONOMY 28:16-68 BY DR. BILL NULL	72
SECTION 10 - DIET & HEALING RECOMMENDATIONS	74
SUMMARY	74
77 SMART DIET & EXERCISE STRATEGIES	74
Eat Smart	74
Exercise Right	75
REFERENCES	75
SECTION 11 - DRUG ADDICTION AMONG CHILDREN	76
PREFACE	76
INTRODUCTION	76
HOW CHILDREN BECOME MENTALLY ILL	77
HOW THE CHILD IS LABELED	77
WHOSE OPINION COUNTS?	77
GETTING PARENTS TO BUY THE DIAGNOSIS	77
HOW TO PROTECT YOUR CHILD	77
LIST OF DRUGS, SIGNS, SYMPTOMS, REACTIONS AND EFFECTS	78
RECOMMENDED READING LIST	79
The Citizens Commission On Human Rights	79
REFERENCES	79
SECTION 12 - CHILDREN'S DELIVERANCE	80
ABUSED CHILD - CHILD ABUSE - RITUAL ABUSE	80
Warning Signs Of Sexual Abuse In Children	80
Symptoms - Observable Behavior	80
Incest Or Child Abuse	81
Symptoms	81
Ritual Abuse	81
Preface	81
Characteristics	81
DEMONIC CHILD ENTERTAINMENT	82

- Thirteen Doctrines Of The New Age 82
- Twenty Warning Signs Of Satanism 83
- Seven Steps To Overcoming Occultism And Satanic Involvement 84
- CHILDREN DRUG ADDICTS 84
  - List Of Drugs, Signs, Symptoms, Reactions And Effects 84

SECTION 13 – CURING AND HEALING THE BODY BY DELIVERANCE 86
- LIST OF SCRIPTURE 86
- STUDY OF CURE - CURED - CURES 87
  - Action By God Or Physicians 87
  - Old Testament (Medicine And Healing) 87
  - New Testament (Relieving And Making Whole) 87
  - Conclusion 87
- EXCERPTS FROM THE BIBLE 88
- POSSIBLE ROOTS OF INFIRMITY (EXCERPTS) 88
- ALTERNATIVE HEALTH PRACTICES 89
  - Healing Through Deliverance 89
  - The Hidden Agenda 89
- ACUPUNCTURE 90
- SICKNESS AND DEMONIC SYMPTOMS 91
  - Epilepsy 91
  - Schizophrenia 91
  - Coprolalia 92
- MUTILATION 92
- SPIRIT OF PARALYSIS (EXCERPTS) 92
- WITCHCRAFT AND SORCERY: PHARMACY - MEDICATION - POISON 93
- BIBLICAL CURSES OF SICKNESSSES AND PLAGUES 93
- REFERENCES 93

SECTION 14 - CANCER AND ARTHRITIS DELIVERANCE 95
- LIST OF SCRIPTURE 95
- ANALYSIS OF MATTHEW 5:44 96
- ANALYSIS OF MATT. 18:21-35 96
  - Law Of Forgiveness 96
  - Kingdom Of Heaven Is Likened To 96
  - Value Of Money 96
  - Value Of Your Salvation 96
- UNFORGIVENESS 96
  - Spiritual Bondage 96
  - Consequence Of Unforgiveness 97
  - Pattern For Being Delivered And Healed 97
- FORGIVENESS 97
- TESTIMONIES 98
  - Earline's Testimony About Indian Curses 98
  - Earline's Testimony About Heart Condition 98
  - Earline's Comments 98
  - Gene's Comments 99
  - Earline's Comments 99
  - Gene's Comments 99

- Earline's Comments 99
- Gene's Comments 99
- Earline's Testimony About Eating 100
- Gene's Comments 101
- Our Testimony About Marie's Broken Shoulder 101
- GENERAL OPERATING PROCEDURES 103
- REFERENCES 104

SECTION 15 - HEALING FOR KIDNEYS AND OTHER DISEASES 105
- FATHER'S BLESSING 105
- SCRIPTURE FOR REINS 106
- DEFINITION OF REINS 106
- DEFINITION OF KIDNEY 106
- DEFINITION OF LOINS 106
- EFFECT ON THE BODY 107
- PREFACE 107
- SPIRITUAL PRINCIPLES 107
- SPIRIT - SOUL - BODY 107
- SIN'S EFFECTS 108
- SPIRITUAL WARFARE 108
- KIDNEY DISEASE 108
- DIABETES 108
- HIGH BLOOD PRESSURE 109
- PLEASANT VALLEY CHURCH 109
- SPIRITUAL ROOTS OF DISEASE 109
- WELLSPRING MINISTRIES OF ALASKA 109
- OTHER DISEASES 109
- PASTOR RON TIFFIN 111
- VICTORIA WEBB 111
  - Conversation 111
  - Positive Actions 112
  - Negative Actions 112
  - Effect Of Others 112
  - Names Of Demons 112
- MEDICAL DICTIONARY 112
- NEPHROLOGY FAMILIES OF DISEASES 112
- WORK BOOKS 113
- REFERENCES 113

SECTION 16 - TESTIMONY - JESUS SET MARIE'S BROKEN ARM 114

SECTION 17 - FAMILY TESTIMONIES 116
- BYRON'S DEATH 117
  - From Death Into Real Life 117
  - Gene's Testimony About Byron's Death 120
  - Earline's Testimony About Byron's Death 121
  - Earline's Testimony About Grief Over Byron's Death 125
- EARLINE'S DEATH 126
  - Gene's Testimony About Earline's Homecoming 126

- Job's Test 126
- Hospital Experience 126
- The Perfect Number Seven 127
- The Future 127
- Gene's Memorial For Earline 127
  - Persecution 127
  - Testimony About How GOD Taught Us Deliverance 127
  - Declaration 129
- OUR DELIVERANCE TESTIMONY 129
  - General 129
  - Pigs In The Parlor 130
  - Faith Tabernacle 130
  - Can A Christian Have A Demon? 130
  - All Christians 130
  - Our Family 130
  - Our Ministry 130
- GENE'S TESTIMONY 130
  - Gene's Testimony About Ahab Characteristics 130
- EARLINE'S TESTIMONY 131
  - Earline's Main Testimony About Deliverance 131
  - Earline's Testimony About Rejection 134
  - Earline's Testimony About Ancestral Background 136
  - Earline's Testimony About Heart Condition 136
  - Earline's Testimony About The Curse Of The Bastard 138
  - Earline's Testimony About Eating 139
  - Earline's Testimony About Maintaining Deliverance 140
  - Earline's Testimony About Schizophrenia Deliverance 144
  - Earline's Testimony About Deliverance From Indian Curses 145
- MARIE'S TESTIMONY 145
  - Earline's Testimony About Marie's Salvation 145
  - Our Testimony About Jesus Setting Marie's Broken Shoulder 146
  - Marie's Testimony About Experience With Demonic Objects 148
- OUR TESTIMONY ABOUT PSYCHIC PRAYERS 148

SECTION 18 - BALDNESS - BEARDS - HAIR 150
- SCRIPTURE 150
  - Baldness 150
  - Beards 151
  - Hair 151
  - Hoary Head 151
- PREFACE 151
- FREEDOM OF CHOICE 151
- JESUS CHRIST 152
- REJECTION 152
- BITTERNESS 152
- REBELLION 152
- INHERITED CURSES 152
- DISEASES 152
- PRIDE, EGO AND VANITY 152

    FEARS AND INSECURITIES 153
    WHIPSAW DEMONS 153
    BEARDS AND BALDNESS 153
    TRYING TO LOOK YOUNG 153
    CHRISTIAN FANTASY 153
    FALSENESS 154
    FEMININE PREACHERS 154
    WOMEN 154
    ASK YOURSELVES SOME QUESTIONS 156
    PERSONAL PREFERENCE 156

SECTION 19 - DRUNKENNESS AND GLUTTONY 157
    LIST OF SCRIPTURES 157
    KEY SCRIPTURES 158
    GENERAL 158
    AMERICANS MUST CHANGE THEIR EATING HABITS! 158
    EARLINE'S TESTIMONY ABOUT EATING 160
    GENE'S COMMENTS 161
    CONCLUSION 161

SECTION 1 - PREAMBLE TO HEALING DELIVERANCE MANUAL

CONTENTS
1. **PREAMBLE**
   1. Normal Numbers
   2. Alternatives For A Changing World
2. **DANGER**
3. **CHRONIC ILLNESS AND DISEASE**
   1. Preface
   2. Skyrocketing
   3. Alarming Facts
   4. Alarming Statistics
   5. Astronomical Rates
4. **PROCEDURE**
5. **SUMMARY**
6. **REFERENCES**
   1. Recommended References
   2. Health Books That Can Be Used To Minister To Others
   3. All Health Books By The Following Authors
   4. Other Health Books Which May Be Of Interest
   5. Caution

PREAMBLE

This is the preamble to the following lessons in the **Healing Deliverance Manual**. It is meant to express my opinion without having to repeat it in every lesson.

Medical books separate disease and sickness into thirty-nine categories. It is not a coincidence that the number of stripes on Jesus' back was thirty-nine. It's THE BLOOD from the stripes that heals.

You have to take care of yourself. You are like a three-legged stool: spirit, soul and body. If you don't take care of anyone of these, the stool will fall down. You have to educate yourself and then apply what you have learned. You can not expect GOD to do it for you.

Your physical health is a function of nutrition, parasites and toxins - what goes into your body. We live in a very polluted world. For instance, cancer may be physical (poor nutrition, attacked by parasites or loaded with chemicals) or spiritual (demonic).

Normal Numbers

The average or normal person over the age of 65 in this country now uses 7 different medications per day - 4 prescribed and 3 over the counter. (One-third of these people will experience some adverse medication event that requires a hospital visit. 10 to 15% of all emergency room visits are related to medication reactions in seniors.)

For reasons I've never understood, most doctors don't seem to have a problem prescribing multiple medications. when questioned, they typically will say the drugs they recommend are safe and have minimal, if any, side effects. Keep in mind, however that there has never been a controlled study on a human being involving more than 3 drugs circulating in the body at the same time. No one knows, or can accurately predict, what's going to happen when you take multiple drugs at the same time. The number of potential side effects becomes impossible to calculate.

Two-thirds of the U.S. population is either overweight or obese right now. An estimated 42% of the entire population will be obese by 2030. (In 2010, 35.9% of adults were obese and another 33.3% were overweight. And 6.6% of the population was severely obese, meaning they were 100 pounds or more overweight.)

Over 8% of the population has diabetes, and another 25% has pre-diabetes. that's roughly one out of every 3 adults that either has diabetes or pre-diabetes. Half of Americans ages 65 and older have pre-diabetes. From 1935 to 1966, the prevalence of diagnosed type 2 diabetes in this country climbed nearly 765%. The trend accelerated tremendously in about 1960, when corn syrup was added to the food supply.

One out of 3 adults has high blood pressure. Another 1/3 of the population has pre-hypertension - blood pressure numbers that are higher than normal but not yet in the high blood pressure range. So, 2/3 of the entire population has either high blood pressure or pre-hypertension.

Over 1/3 of Americans in their mid-50's and older have chronic pain in their neck or back, and almost that many have chronic knee or leg pain.

Over 1/3, or in excess of 90 million people in the Unite States, have digestive disorders.

An estimated 26.2% of Americans ages 18 and older (one out of every 4 adults) suffer from a diagnosable mental health disorder. Almost 10% of the population reportedly suffers from depression.

Approximately 48% of adults report suffering from insomnia each year. And for 25% of the population, it is a chronic problem.

More than 125 million people (over 1/3 of the entire population have at least one chronic condition like diabetes, cancer, glaucoma, or heart disease, and half as many more have more than one chronic disease.

Alternatives For A Changing World

Medical technology is focused on treating problems, not on preventing them. Although the pharmaceutical business is corrupt, it seems to have full support up to the highest levels of our government. Our own government agencies that were formed to help protect the public's interest and be the watchdogs over the drug companies have literally sold out to the pharmaceutical industry. Our available food supply becomes more contaminated and modified each and every year.

DANGER

D.E.A.T.H. - Deteriorative Environmentally Accelerating Threats To Health. The world we live in is killing us. The air we breathe, the food we eat, the water we drink and the clothes we wear contribute to the vast array of toxic exposure:

1. Car exhaust fumes, chemtrails, carcinogenic carpet foam, synthetic carpeting and overstuffed furniture, plywood, cleaning agents, plastics, artificial light, electrical current, radiation, weakened magnetic field, toxic chemicals, environmental pollutants.

2. Parasites, antibiotic-resistant bacteria, overburden of bacteria, genetically-modified viruses, viruses, fungus.

3. Genetically engineered food, growth hormones, food coloring and additives, preservatives.

4. Pesticides, herbicides, insecticides.

5. Pharmaceuticals and drugs: legal and illegal.

6. Most medical studies are wrong: bought and paid for or so slanted that it is meaningless. Brought about by special interests, money, fame, and power is enormous in the research world. There is too much money, greed, power, fame, special interest and notoriety to keep medical science honest. The medical golden rule - do not take any new drug until it has been in use for at least seven years.

CHRONIC ILLNESS AND DISEASE
Preface

The pain of watching a family member lose strength, hope, and health is almost more than one can handle, when deep down we believe that there must be answers out there. We put so much hope into the drugs of modern medicine, but how often do they go beyond management of symptoms, and actually restore health?

The truth is, for most diseases and chronic illnesses, modern medicine can do little beyond symptom management for those who suffer. Drugs may suppress the symptoms but do little to solve the cause of the problem.

Researchers confirm that in the last two decades the strength of the average person's immune system has decreased by 20-25% and continues to decline at 3-5% per year. The reason is two fold. **The first reason is stress on our bodies caused by the toxins in our environment.** Experts tell us that there are now more toxins inside the average home than there are outside. **The second reason is that our modern diet lacks vital nutrients required for optimal health.** Our over-worked soils are depleted of essential nutrients. We harvest our crops before they ripen naturally (green harvesting), process our foods, and make poor choices in our diet selection. Our environment is more toxic than ever and our bodies are ill-equipped for health and healing.

Healthcare professionals tell us that all we need for optimal health are vitamins and minerals, proteins, fats and oils. If these elements were the **complete answer**, then why are the incidents of cancers, diabetes, heart disease, allergies, asthma, fibromyalgia, arthritis, chronic fatigue syndrome, Attention Deficit Disorder, and many other diseases increasing at an alarming rate? Is there a common denominator? Could something be missing; exposure to stress, toxins, pharmaceutical drugs and poor nutrition?

Skyrocketing

Chronic illness and disease are skyrocketing. It's no wonder when an estimated seven billion pounds of toxins and chemical agents are added to the water we drink, the food we eat and the air we breathe each year. The modern diet is full of junk food, processed foods and high levels of preservatives and additives. For many, stress is at an all time high and our bodies are beginning to break down!

Alarming Facts

1 out of 2 people will die of a heart attack. 1 out of 3 people will **get cancer. 1 out of 2 people will get an autoimmune disease. 3 out of 4 people will get an degenerative disease.**

Heart disease is the #1 killer of women. Two-thirds of women who have heart attacks never fully recover. When you have a heart attack, your risk of having another one increases. The top six health risks for women: heart disease, cancer, stroke, chronic obstructive pulmonary disease, Alzheimer's Disease and then diabetes.

It is clear that the feeling ill, take a pill approach is not working! The typical medical response for chronic illness and disease is to use pharmaceuticals for treatment. Families around the world are getting fed up. People are sick and tired of being sick and tired.

Families are beginning to ask questions like, **Why are our family members getting sick in the first place?** How can we protect our family from disease? If a family member is diagnosed with a disease, how can the cause of the problem be addressed and not the symptoms?

Since drugs have lots of side effects, what are the safe alternatives to the traditional pharmaceutical approach to restore health in the body? Does the traditional allopathic healthcare system have the answer for chronic illness and disease? Not likely. **In fact, the healthcare system harms and kills millions of people a year.**

Alarming Statistics

1. More than 196,000 people die and 2.2 million are injured each year by adverse reactions to prescription drugs. The use of prescription drugs is the third leading cause of death in the USA.
2. The annual death toll from hospitalization and out patient care exceeds 424,000 per year.
3. Retail prescription drug sales are rising at well over 18% from previous years.
4. The highest increase of drug consumption is in the age group of children two to five years old.

We have become an over-medicated society. This is bad news for us, but great news for the pharmaceutical companies. It seems most pharmaceutical companies are aggressively looking to increase profits by creating new long-term treatments - not looking for cures.

In 2002, the combined profits of the ten drug companies in the Fortune 500 were 35.9 billion. That's more than the profits for all the other 490 businesses put together.

You can no longer put the responsibility of your health in the hands of your doctors (and their pharmaceutical partners), insurance companies or the government. You must be proactive and take responsibility for your own health and the health of your family. You must not be complacent.

Don't be mistaken that good health is present when there is an absence of pain or symptoms. Symptoms are the last and final state of a breakdown that has been in process for years or even decades. Just because you don't fell bad, doesn't mean that you are disease-free. Cancer for example, takes between five to thirty years to develop. You won't even be aware that it is spreading. **By the time it is diagnosed, it will have already run 90-95% of its course and you are left fighting for your life.**

Astronomical Rates

In the past twenty years alone, diabetes has risen by 500% and allergies by 800%. Heart disease, cancer and other ailments also have risen by astronomical rates.

PROCEDURE

I believe that we should do the following when we need healing or deliverance from diseases:

1. **First,** we should seek GOD for deliverance and healing. This means applying the principles of casting out demons and anointing with oil for healing.
2. **Second,** we should fast and pray to the LORD for our deliverance and healing. We should allow time for GOD to answer us. This may not be a short period of time.
3. **Third,** if GOD does not heal or deliver us from the infirmity, seek the medical profession for curative medicines or even operations.
4. **Fourth,** have someone take us through deliverance (or do self deliverance) for any spiritual effects of taking pharmaceuticals or of the cutting of the flesh. Break and return evil curses that may have been put upon you.

The process above only apples to Christians. **If you are not a Christian, then you need to get saved by JESUS CHRIST.** If you choose not to get saved, then your only choice is to use the medical profession.

I have seen GOD heal and deliver many people. I have seen Christians who have been healed and/or delivered of some ailments, and who also have used doctors for other ailments. It depends on each circumstance. If you have to use doctors, do not think you are a second-class Christian.

The **Healing Deliverance Manual** is oriented to being healed through the casting out of demons primarily and anointing with oil to pray the prayer of faith secondarily. You may be healed through deliverance, or the prayer of faith, or some combination of both. GOD told me to first take someone through deliverance and secondly pray for them to be healed. **And as ye go, preach, saying, the kingdom of heaven is at hand. Heal the sick,**

cleanse the lepers, raise the dead, cast out devils: freely ye have received, freely give. (Matt. 10:7-8). This is my motto.

I can not tell you not to use the medical profession. Nor can I tell you to ignore GOD and THE HOLY BIBLE. You have a free will given by GOD to make your choice of how you will live your life. Seek THE HOLY SPIRIT as to what you should do.

GOD does not condemn us; Satan does. GOD convicts us. I do not want to bring you into bondage of condemnation, fear, guilt, intimidation, or any other disturbing emotion for using the medical profession. For many years my family walked in divine health but we have had to use the medical profession.

I do believe that the medicine should be curative and bring healing to your body. This means obtaining a physician that provides a curative medicine that makes you well. Proper medication is part of the healing process.

In addition to the lessons in the **Healing Deliverance Manual**, I would recommend studying healing in THE BIBLE. A good list of healing scriptures is found in the lesson, **Body Cured And Healed By Deliverance**. Many times GOD heals through the anointing with oil, and praying the prayer of faith. Study the Scriptures to see how healing is accomplished.

The best discussion of some spiritual aspects of using the medical profession are explained in **Insights Into Pharmakeia And Sorcery** by Henry W. Wright, Pleasant Valley Publications, Thomaston, Georgia. I also highly recommend his other books. He takes the approach of healing primarily and deliverance secondarily. He has discovered many spiritual roots of disease (sins).

A good example is cancer. I have cast out spirits of cancer and knew they were in the person because they manifested as their names were called out. **I can not say that all cancer is a spirit (demon).** But, it is worthwhile to try the spirits in deliverance to see if they are within a person who has cancer, or any other disease, and then pray for healing. We are constantly learning and will never have full knowledge until we get to Heaven.

We can not coerce or force GOD to heal us. We must humble ourselves before GOD. However, we do have the power to drive out demons. First, the legal right before GOD must be taken away before the demon can be driven out. This includes forgiveness, repentance and renunciation as is appropriate for the sin.

JESUS CHRIST choose Luke to be an apostle, one of the twelve disciples. He was a physician and GOD did not reject him because of his profession.

There are many Christians who do not believe that GOD will heal them in this life. Their only choice is to use the medical profession.

SUMMARY

If you need healing, become a Christian, go through deliverance, pray for healing, and wait on GOD. If necessary, then go to the medical profession and finally go through deliverance.

REFERENCES
Recommended References

I recommend the following references to help you take care of your health and to minister to others:

Prescription for Nutritional Healing by Phyllis A. Balch and James F. Balch, Avery
Healthy Healing by Linday Rector Page, Healthy Healing Publications
The Cure For All Diseases, **The Cure For All Cancers**, **The Cure For All Advanced Cancers** and **The Prevention Of All Cancers** by Hulda Regehr Clark, New Century Press
Apple Cider Vinegar - Miracle Health System, **Bragg Healthy Lifestyle**, **Bragg's Vegetarian Health Recipes**, **Miracle of Fasting**, **Healthy Heart & Cardiovascular System**, **Bragg Back Fitness Program for Pain-Free Strong Back**, **Water-The Shocking Truth**, **Super Power Breathing**, **Build Powerful Nerve Force**, and **Build Strong Healthy Feet** by Paul C. and Patricia Bragg, Health Science
Linda Page's Healthy Healing, and **Herbal Pharmacist**, Healthy Healing

Detoxify Or Die, **The Cholesterol Hoax**, **The High Blood Pressure Hoax**, **No More Heartburn**, **You Are What You Ate**, **Wellness Against All Odds**, **Macro Mellow**, **The Cure Is In The Kitchen** by Sherry A. Rogers, Prestige Publishing

Overcoming Arthritis, **The Guide To Healthy Eating**, **The Miracle Of Natural Hormones**, **Drugs That Don't Work And Natural Therapies That Do!** and **Salt Your Way To Health** by David Brownstein, Medical Alternatives Press

Health and Nutrition Secrets, Health Press
Eat Right 4 Your Type, C.P. Putnam's Sons
Colloidal Silver, Silver Protects
Sugars That Heal, Ballantine Books
Death By Diet, and **The Calcium Factor**, Triad Marketing
The pH Miracle, Warner Books
The Hidden Agenda, Thomas Nelson
Change Your Brain Change Your Life, Three Rivers Press
Why Christians Get Sick, Destiny Image Publishers
Complete Home Medical Guide, Consumers Union
Home Remedies, Thrash Publication
Dr. Koop's Self-Care Advisor, The Health Publishing Group
Doctor and the Word, Creation House
The Woodland Health Series Booklets, Woodland Publishing
AICR Publications Catalog, American Institute for Cancer Research
Moses Wasn't Fat, Axion Publishers

Health Books That Can Be Used To Minister To Others
Complete Drug Reference, United States Pharmacopeia
PDR Medical Dictionary, and **PDR for Herbal Medicines**, Medical Economics Company
Pathophysiology - The Biologic Basis for Disease in Adults and Children, Mosby
Taber's Cyclopedic Medical Dictionary, F.A. Davis

All Health Books By The Following Authors
Mary Ruth Swope, Swope Enterprises, Lone Star, Texas
Henry W. Wright, Pleasant Valley Publications, Thomaston, Georgia
Art Mathias, Wellspring Ministries of Alaska, Anchorage
Citizens Commission on Human Rights, Los Angeles, California
Busiest Bee Publications, Scottsdale, Arizona
Consumers Union, Mount Vernon, New York
David Williams, Mountain Home Publishing, Ingram, Texas
Good Health Guides, Keats Publishing, New Canaan, Connecticut
Don Colbert, Siloam Press
National Safety Council, Itasca, IL
Second Opinion Publishing, Dunwoody, Georgia
Linday Rector Page, Healthy Healing Publications
Sherry A. Rogers, Prestige Publishing
David Brownstein, Medical Alternatives Press
Phyllis A. Balch and James F. Balch, Avery

Other Health Books Which May Be Of Interest
The Honest Herbal, and **Herbs of Choice**, Pharmaceutical Products Press
The People's Pharmacy, St. Martin's Paperbacks
Herbally Yours, Sound Nutrition
Fit For Life, Warner Books
Forty Something Forever, Health Savers Press
Understanding Fats & Oils, Progressive Health Publishing
DMSO Nature's Healer, **Enzyme Nutrition**, and **Jumping For Health**, Avery Publishing Group
The Miracle Nutrient Coenzyme Q10, Bantam Books
Food Enzymes, Hohm Press
Psychology Made Simple, Made Simple Books
The Sweet Miracle Of Xylitol, Basic Health
Alive And Well, Price-Pottenger Nutrition Foundation
Heal With Amino Acids And Nutrients, Pain And Stress Publications
Modern Foods - The Sabotage Of Earth's Food Supply, Casper & Stone
Nutrition Against Disease, Price-Pottenger Nutrition Foundation
Natural Mercury Detoxification, Metabolic Balance Press
The Maker's Diet, Siloam
Transdermal Magnesium Therapy, Phaelos Books
Syndrome - The Silent Killer, Simon & Schuster
Protein Power, Bantam Books

Low Fat Lies - High-Fat Frauds, LifeLine Press
The Slow Burn Fitness Revolution, Broadway Books

Caution
Check what you read by The Holy Bible, leadership of The Holy Spirit, and your intelligence and common sense. Everyone does not walk in the same knowledge of God. Separate the wheat from the chaff. There are good things in every book but every book is not perfect according to God's laws.

SECTION 2 - OPERATION DELIVERANCE

CONTENTS
1. EARLINE MOODY, MY WIFE
2. OTHER PEOPLE
3. PREAMBLE TO HEALING DELIVERANCE MANUAL
    1. Procedure
    2. Summary
4. OVERALL: PRAYER - COMMAND - WARFARE
    1. Overall Prayer
    2. Overall Command
    3. Overall Warfare
5. PRAYERS
    1. Prayer To Establish Basis For Warfare
    2. Prayer Before Deliverance
6. WITCHCRAFT: PRAYERS - CURSES - COMMANDS
    1. Prayers
    2. Curses
    3. Commands
7. REVERSAL
    1. Satanic Supernatural Power Reversal
    2. Spiritual Warfare
8. PERSONAL DELIVERANCE

EARLINE MOODY, MY WIFE

This is the testimony about what happened to my wife when she cut the tip end off her finger. She lost her joy in THE LORD. Pastor Win Worley was in my home after it happened and took Earline through deliverance.

The doctor sewed her finger into her palm to cut out a new tip. When I found out that spirits can come into a person when they have an operation, I prayed continuously when Earline was in the operation room to cut her finger out of her palm. When we got her home, I discovered that my prayers didn't work and I had to take her through deliverance again.

OTHER PEOPLE

I have ministered to other people over a period of about twenty years that have had operations. The ministry was for the operation and for the drugs taken. When you are under anesthesia, your spiritual armor is not intact and spirits can attack the body. It is similar to a person getting drunk, falling down on the floor and spirits coming into the body.

Spirits can come in with the drugs that are taken especially when the person becomes addicted to them. They answer to the names of the drugs. A demon told Pastor Win Worley that the demons love medicines.

Everyone needs deliverance that has had an operation under the influence of anesthesia.

Why minister in witchcraft? Many Christians are attacked by witchcraft. It is good to cover this area just in case that is the situation.

PREAMBLE TO HEALING DELIVERANCE MANUAL
Procedure
I believe that we should do the following when we need healing or deliverance from diseases:
First, we should seek GOD for deliverance and healing. This means applying the principles of casting out demons and anointing with oil for healing.
Second, we should fast and pray to the LORD for our deliverance and healing. We should allow time for GOD to answer us. This may not be a short period of time.
Third, if GOD does not heal or deliver us from the infirmity, seek the medical profession for curative medicines or even operations.
Fourth, have someone take us through deliverance (or do self deliverance) for any spiritual effects of taking pharmaceuticals or of the cutting of the flesh. Break and return evil curses that may have been put upon you.

The **Healing Deliverance Manual** is oriented to being healed through the casting out of demons primarily and anointing with oil to pray the prayer of faith secondarily. You may be healed through deliverance, or the prayer of faith, or some combination of both. GOD told me to first take someone through deliverance and secondly pray for them to be healed. **And as ye go, preach, saying, the kingdom of heaven is at hand. Heal the sick, cleanse the lepers, raise the dead, cast out devils: freely ye have received, freely give.** (Matt. 10:7-8). This is my motto.

Summary
If you need healing, become a Christian, go through deliverance, pray for healing, and wait on GOD. If necessary, then go to the medical profession and finally go through deliverance.

OVERALL: PRAYER - COMMAND - WARFARE
Overall Prayer
Almighty God, please forgive us for omission - commission, known - unknown, deliberate - inadvertent sins by the blood of Jesus Christ. We forgive our enemies, pray for their salvation, and break curses placed on us. We thank God for power and authority over the enemy: satan and his kingdom. We are strong in the Lord, and the power of his might. We cover us with the blood of Jesus Christ. We make a blood covenant with the father, the son, the holy spirit. We ask God to send our guardian angels, and an army of angels for warfare. Where God uses all and shall in the bible, we agree and declare in our lives. We use overall prayer as a preface for other prayers. We pray the holy bible, and ask in the name of Jesus Christ: Lord - master - savior. Amen! So be it!

Overall Command
<u>We wrestle-bind-loose-command the kingdom of evil, the power of the enemy, principalities, powers, rulers of darkness of this world, spiritual wickedness in high places.</u>

We use the power of God given to believers. We take authority over the kingdom of evil. We bind, subdue satan's empire. We enter into spiritual warfare, assault the kingdom of darkness. We bind the forces of evil; destroy the kingdom of evil. We send armies of warring angels to attack. We use every verse in the holy bible that wars against the demonic forces. We use overall command as a preface for other commands.

Overall Warfare
<u>CONCERNING THE WORK OF MY HANDS COMMAND YE ME. WE EXERCISE AUTHORITY OVER THE WORK OF GOD'S HANDS. WE BIND AND LOOSE ON EARTH WHAT IS BOUND AND LOOSED IN HEAVEN.</u>

We command the devil's forces to destroy each other. By the blood of Jesus Christ, we take dominion over satan. We put on the whole armour of God. We close doorways to demons. We come against the kingdom of evil. We use the word of God, written and spoken, against the forces of evil. We are the army of the Lord. We exercise dominion over nations and kingdoms. We use our tactics and weapons of war against the enemy. We return curses and weapons formed against us. We use overall warfare as a preface for other warfare.

PRAYERS
Prayer To Establish Basis For Warfare
I forgive anyone that has had spiritual, secular, carnal authority over me including mental, physical, financial. I forgive ancestors and anyone that has hurt, cursed, controlled me. I break curses, control, soul ties brought upon me by them. I ask that God bless, forgive them, save their souls. I set myself free from those who would hurt me.

Forgive me Lord for my many sins. I forgive myself for sinning against my body. I break curses, soul ties that I have brought upon myself. In Jesus name I pray.

Prayer Before Deliverance
We ask God to send the holy spirit, the seven-fold spirit of God, warrior angels, ministering angels, twelve legions of angels. We ask the warrior angels to come with their flaming, sharp two-edged swords capable of dividing spirit and soul.

We ask God to surround us, cut off communications between the demons outside and the demons inside, remove loose demons around us.

We bind fallen angels and demons; loose ourselves from them. We call for spiritual warfare to set the captives free. We bind forces of evil, loose forces of good that we have the power and authority to do so. In Jesus name I pray.

WITCHCRAFT: PRAYERS - CURSES - COMMANDS
Prayers

WE PROCLAIM, DECLARE, AGREE WITH THE HOLY WORD OF GOD. WE CLAIM THE WORLD FOR THE LORD.

We confess contact with and close doors to satan through new age, occultism, witchcraft, satanism. We forgive our ancestors and others cursing us by practicing these things. Please forgive us for practicing these things cursing ourselves. We renounce satan and his kingdom.

We have sought supernatural experience apart from God. We forgive enemies, false prophets, diviners, witches; individuals working with evil spirits; covens of witches, warlocks, wizards; persons in witchcraft, sorcery; casting spells, potions, enchantments, curses; psychic prayers, witchcraft control, those who have cursed us.

We renounce satan and his kingdom of evil. We hate satan, demons, evil works. We come against water spirits and witchcraft attacks in dreams. In the name of Jesus Christ: Lord - master - savior, we pray and take authority over the forces of evil.

Curses

Jesus Christ became a curse on the cross and blotted out the handwriting of ordinances against us. We break curses, spells, hexes, other evil sent upon us by enemies who seek to steal, kill, destroy: mentally, physically, spiritually, financially.

We renounce and destroy occult literature, going to fortune tellers, reading horoscopes, believing in reincarnation, psychic and occult contact. We break ancestral curses, legal holds, grounds back to Adam and Eve. We break control, soul ties, curses.

We break curses of witchcraft, magic, ouija boards, occult games; fortune telling, palm reading, tea leaf reading, crystal balls, tarot cards; astrology, birth signs, horoscopes; reincarnation; metaphysics, spiritualism; hypnosis; rock music; transcendental meditation, eastern religions; idol worship; yoga, martial arts; water witching, dowsing; levitation, table tipping, body lifting; psychometry (divining through objects); automatic writing; soul travel, demonic skills; denying the blood and the deity of the Lord Jesus Christ.

Commands

We bind and order demons to return to senders escorted by angels to destroy seats of witchcraft. The demons are commanded to confuse, and sow terror and panic in the hearts of witches, warlocks, wizards. We have power over the demons through the name of Jesus Christ of Nazareth. We command the demons to attack their works, destroy each other, shake the kingdom of evil. We command the demons, their families and works to come out.

We use the sword of the Lord to sever demonic ties (between spirits and souls, other ties), ley lines (lines of energy, telepathic communication), silver cords (astral projection, soul travel, bilocation) of anyone who would travel into our presence through communications, crystal balls or by their souls and spirits. We break demonic balls, cords, bowls, pitchers, wheels used against us.

We bind and cast down satan, angels, demons, strongmen, strongholds over new age, occultism, witchcraft, satanism, demonic arts: principalities, powers, rulers of darkness of this world, spiritual wickedness in high places; might, kingdoms, thrones, dominions, nobles, princes, kings; ascended masters, spirit guides; mind control, mind occult, mind binding; witchcraft, sorcery, divination, necromancy; eastern mysticism, reincarnation, transcendental meditation, soul travel; martial arts, yoga; visualization, demonic inner healing; familiars; crystal helpers; bodiless spheres of light; universal intelligence.

We bind-restrain, loose-destroy demonic practices: you are God, I am God, denying existence of personal God, insisting universe itself is God, new age, occultism, witchcraft, satanism, apostate Christianity, one world: government - religion - finances, obtaining: fame - power - money:

Spiritual healing, psychics, clairvoyants, mediums, channelers; sects, cults; religious and occult philosophies; pantheism, animism, freemasonry, theosophy, illuminati, Islam, Taoism, Buddhism, Sufism, Hinduism, Babylonian pagan religions; palm reading, tarot card reading, past life therapy, spiritual counseling; evolution as Gods, Goddesses; swamis, gurus, yogis, lamas, demonic teachers;

Astrologers, mystic path, mysticism, ascetic life-style; yoga, meditation; mother earth gaia, shamanism; kundalini energy; universal oneness; worship of Lucifer, occult inner circle;

Occult knowledge; esoteric truth; ancient mysteries; the Christ; Luciferian age of Aquarius; the plan; the great work of ages; world servers; Masonic religion of evolution; divine aspects of man; dark magic arts.

REVERSAL
SATANIC SUPERNATURAL POWER REVERSAL
WE REVERSE SATANIC SUPERNATURAL POWER AGAINST CHRISTIANS FROM: DEMONIC PRAYERS, BLASPHEMY (CONTEMPT), EXECRATION AND IMPRECATIONS (CURSING), INVOCATIONS (CONJURING), PROFANITY (LANGUAGE), RETRIBUTIONS (PUNISHMENT). WE REVERSE HARM, AFFLICTION, INJURY, EVIL, MISFORTUNE TO THOSE WHO SENT THEM.

SPIRITUAL WARFARE
WE BREAK AND RETURN CURSES. WE COMMAND DEMONS THAT HAVE BEEN SENT TO ATTACK US TO ATTACK THE SENDERS. WE ASK THE ANGELS TO RETURN WITCHCRAFT SENT TO ATTACK US AND DESTROY WITCHCRAFT. EVERY EVIL THING THAT THEY WANT TO BE DONE TO US, WE COMMAND THAT IT BE DONE TO THEM.

PERSONAL DELIVERANCE

1. Open in prayer.
2. Identify names of hospital, doctor, anesthesiologist.
3. Consider other personnel: nurses, attendants, pharmacists as a group.
4. Forgive each one for anything they did that would have cursed you.
5. Break the curses.
6. Break soul ties.
7. Ask GOD to forgive you for anything you did that would have brought on the need for an operation.
8. Forgive anyone else for anything they did that would have brought on the need for an operation.
9. Identify the names of medicines taken after the operation especially if they have become addictive.
10. What organs were removed?
11. Command the spirits to come out that came in through curses, soul ties, medicines, cutting of the flesh, scar tissues and the operation.
12. Command the spirits to come out that reside in the cavities where the organs were removed.
13. Anoint with oil and pray for healing for the operation and where the spirits have left in the body.

SECTION 3 – DRUGS AND MEDICINES

CONTENTS
1. **LIST OF SCRIPTURE**
2. **DRUG ABUSE IN THE WORKPLACE - FACTS IN OUR TIMES**
3. **WHY DO PEOPLE TAKE DRUGS?**
4. **GENERAL**
5. **MEDICINE'S BONDAGE TO SATAN (EXCERPTS)**
6. **THE HIPPOCRATIC OATH (EXCERPTS)**
7. **MEDICINE AND THE BELIEVER (EXCERPTS)**
8. **VALIUM AND LIBRIUM (EXCERPTS)**
9. **A DIRECTORY OF DRUGS**
    1. Hallucinogens
    2. Narcotics
    3. Stimulants
    4. Depressants
10. **MINISTRY TO OPPRESSED**
11. **REFERENCES**

LIST OF SCRIPTURE

Ex. 7:10-12	Aaron's rod swallowed their rods.
22:18	Kill the witches.
Lev. 19:26-31	God forbids these practices.
20:6	Rejected by God
20:27	Punished by death
Deut. 18:9-12	Abominations
I Sam. 15:23	Rebellion and stubbornness
28:3	Familiar Spirits
II Kings 21:5-6	Wickedness
II Chron. 33:6	Evil
Psalm 73:9	Evil tongue
Isa. 2:6	Soothsayers
5:13-14	Alienate believer from God
8:19	Familiar Spirits
Jer. 17:5	**Oath brings a curse from God.**
27:9-10	Prophesy lies
Zech. 10:2	God's presence
Hosea 4:6	**Ignorance of Word of God**
Mal. 3:5	Fear not God.
Matt. 5:14-16	Help others
5:34-37	Swearing or taking an oath
Acts 8:9	**Sorcery**
16:16-18	Soothsaying
19:19	Curious arts
Rom. 6:16	Slaves

I Cor. 6:19	Sacred Temple
10:31	Glorify God
II Cor. 4:4	Satan is God of this world.
I Tim. 4:1-3	Depart from faith
II Tim. 1:7	Sound mind
3:8	Corrupt minds
Rev. 9:11	**Apollyon**
9:21; 18:23;	Sorcery
21:8; 22:15	Sorcery

DRUG ABUSE IN THE WORKPLACE - STARTLING FACTS IN OUR TIMES

There is growing concern among America's CEO's over the toll that our national drug problem is taking on their organizations and communities. A recent **Allstate/Fortune** magazine survey underscores how troubled corporate America is about this issue. The drug problem ranked second to the federal deficit in responses to the question: **What is the largest problem facing the U.S. today?**

1. The drug generation has entered the work force. Young adults tend to bring their drug habits with them. A 1986 survey showed that five years after graduating from high school, half of those who used marijuana daily in high school continue to do so.
2. One in four employed twenty to forty year old adults reported using an illicit drug in 1986; one in five reported at least one use in the past month.
3. As many as one in five American workers may have alcohol and drug problems. Ten percent of the labor force (11.5 million people) have a drinking problem.
4. A majority of employers responding to a recent survey said that between 6% and 15% of their employees have an alcohol or drug problem.
5. Approximately half a billion workdays are lost each year because of alcoholism alone, a 2% loss in productivity.
6. The federal government estimates that alcohol and drug abuse cost the economy $177 billion a year, including $99 billion attributed to lost productivity. Two-thirds of the cost is attributed to alcohol.
7. A University of Michigan study shows that lost profits as a result of abuse amount to $10 billion in the construction industry alone.
8. Nine of ten utilities, eight to ten transportation operations and over half of all sports associations and government agencies have implemented some kind of drug testing program.
9. Over half (57%) of all high school seniors had tried an illicit drug; and over a third had tried an illicit drug other than marijuana.
10. Among college students one to four years beyond high school, one in three used marijuana in the last year. Nine of ten used alcohol, and more than one in ten used cocaine.
11. Abuse of prescription drugs is a widespread problem, especially among adult women. The non-medical use of tranquilizers doubled between 1982 and 1985.
12. Absenteeism, medical expenses and lost productivity as a result of abuse are costing employers an average of 3% of their total payroll - roughly half the typical company's payments for an employee's Social Security coverage.

13. At least seven companies in the study said they calculated the cost of alcohol and drug abuse at more than $50 million each.
14. **How bad is the situation years after this study?**

WHY DO PEOPLE TAKE DRUGS?

I am always interested in the reasons why we do the things we do. The Bible tells us in Gal. 6:7-8, **Do not be deceived and deluded and misled; God will not allow Himself to be sneered at - scorned, disdained or mocked (by mere pretensions or professions, or His precepts being set aside).** He inevitably deludes himself who attempts to delude God. For whatsoever a man sows, that and that only is what he will reap. **For he who sows to his own flesh (lower nature, sensuality) will from the flesh reap decay and ruin and destruction; but he who sows to the Spirit will from the Spirit reap eternal life.** If you are in trouble, the Bible tells you that you are reaping what you have sown. The Bible also tells us that God has made a way for us to recover all (some times even better that it was before). We have to apply ourselves to diligently following the instruction given in the manual (Bible).

As I have pondered, prayed and studied the problem of drugs and their destructive power, I have become convinced that the overriding problem behind the use of destructive drugs is rejection. Many children today are not allowed to bond with their parents, therefore they never feel truly accepted or at oneness with the people they are naturally supposed to bond with. One of the causes of this is early baby days spent in nursery or day care situations where the care giver changes rapidly. It is very unsettling to try to settle alignment and affections on someone and have them leave you to quickly. Because of this, we have a whole generation of young people trying to fix something but they do not know what it is that needs fixing so how can they fix it? Another reason is being brought up in an unhappy, uncaring home. God has told parents to rear children (tenderly) in discipline, wise counsel and admonition of the Lord (Eph. 6:1-4 and II Tim. 3:1-3). One reason for so much divorce is this inability to relate intimately with others. The abuse of drugs is an attempt to satisfy rejection.

Looking up rejection in the Bible, I have found that God has not rejected a single person who has not persisted in rejecting God. See I Sam. 8:7; I Sam. 10:19; 15:23, 26; 16:1; II Kings 17:15, 29; Isa. 53:2; Jer. 6:19, 7:29-30, etc. All of these scriptures reassure us that if we heed God's call to us, He will not reject us.

When people come into the world we say, **What a cute, little innocent baby.** As far as sins they have committed, they are innocent. But some other gifts besides life that we have given them frequently puts them in bondage before birth. Because of the sins of their ancestors, they may be in bondage due to curses lasting many generations. These curses allow demon spirits to follow them, coerce them, and try to trick them into sins that will allow demons to control them in that demon's particular area.

We have not found a single person who has escaped the problem of rejection. Even if we are not rejected, rejection works very well when demons can convince us that we are rejected. Rejection is one of the best ideas the Devil ever had and it works so well he uses it against all people. Even Jesus did not escape rejection. **He was despised and rejected and forsaken by man,....He was despised, and we did not appreciate His worth or have any esteem for Him** (Isa. 53:3). Jesus was totally rejected of men. The Devil did not stop using rejection on Jesus even when He was on the cross. Jesus' response was, **Father, forgive them for they don't know what they do.**

The Devil used rejection on Eve when he told her she would be like God. Was not that question in response to what Eve was probably thinking? If she had not been thinking this she would not have taken the bait.

What does rejection do to you? It makes you open to all kinds of seduction because you do not feel complete nor settled. It may be a respectable seduction like food, work, play, prestige, money or non-respectable like street drugs, abnormal sexual activities, murder, abortion, witchcraft, etc. The person is always trying to find something to fix that spot so they will feel all right.

Rejection is behind over doing, lying, greed, denying a problem exists or our ability to control it, deception, etc. The work of the Holy Spirit within us is to bring us into proper self-control, peace and joy (Gal. 5:22-26).

We have a very large portion of young people today into all kinds of self-destructive practices. They can be seen congregating in many areas across the country. They are usually rejected children from rejected parents. As rejection passes down the generations, it picks up momentum in each succeeding generation unless someone applies the Biblical process to destroy its effects in a family.

One of the main reasons we go to doctors so much is to try to fix that spot of rejection. Before I received deliverance from rejection, I used to go to doctors who seldom could find anything wrong with me. I thought some drug would fix **it**. I was trying to get something done about the spot that was not satisfied.

Do you know that the rejection demons that have been cast out of you are always around looking for a chance to trap you and get back in. Here's an example of rejection at work: I went to the doctor to have him check to see if I had cracked any ribs. I had a minor wreck with my car and I hit my chest on the seat belt. I was feeling great when I went in but tested with high blood pressure. I was given a medicine for high blood pressure. I took one tablet and shortly began to see a kaleidoscope before my left eye. Since the pressure was not down enough, I was given another pill to try. I am discussing with Gene whether to take it or not. In the mist of this conversation Gene tells me I have always been stubborn. I decide to take the pill and be a nice obedient patient. By the end of three weeks I have depression, diarrhea if I eat, stomach pains if I didn't eat, bad headaches, dizziness, etc. When I returned in two weeks, I was indeed very ill. I also noticed that I had the symptoms of all the things he had said the blood test suggested I might have. I am beginning to wonder if drugs to cause emotional problems and symptoms are not added to curative drugs. Since I have been off the drug for three weeks, I no longer feel any symptoms that were suggested to me.

I feel that often times the side effects of medicines are demon spirits. As you can see, I had played with one demon, Rejection, and had several of his friends come along with him.

When rejected people have not recognized that they are dealing with rejection, they will look all over, into and try a lot of things to help themselves. Their demons are so happy. The demons will help each other get into you. Of course they cannot just jump in; they have to have you give them the right to come in. Demons are just like us in that they are a spirit with a soul (mind, will and emotions) but they have no body. A body is what you have that they want. Many of the bad emotions we have are theirs. We must learn to separate our emotions and thoughts from theirs. Demons are never going to tell you that they are talking. They talk just like the body belongs to them. Ask the Lord to show you how they have worked you all this time. In James Chapter 1, God promises to give wisdom to all who ask.

Why would a person of normal intelligence do things that will destroy themselves? The Bible tells us that no man ever hated his own body (Eph. 5:29). If one desires to destroy himself, it must be someone using his mind and not him. Why do some people get on harmful drugs, become grossly over weight, work themselves to death or live in terrible fears? Often these things have roots in rejection.

GENERAL

1. Only the **cleansed priest** could go into the Holy of Holies. If he was not right with God he was killed and pulled out by a rope.
2. **Drugs** - To prescribe or administer drug mixtures.
3. **Pharmacist** (Greek - Pharmakia) To practice witchcraft or use medicine; also poison or medicine.
4. **Pharmacological** (Gr. Pharmakia) - Drugs, mania, madness, inordinately addicted to using drugs.
5. **Witchcraft** - One type is charmer or enchanter who uses amulets, potions or drugs to cast spells and control others for personal gain. This is the power or practices of witches, sorcery, black magic or irresistible fascination with Satan and his demons.
6. **Idolatry** (worship of evil spirits) - enchantment (sorcery), occultism, magic, witchery, witchcraft, charm, bewitched and medicine man; all these use drugs (poisons) **to cause illness or influence others** against their will.
7. God says this about witchcraft, enchanters and others who use these methods to change or **control other people** - see Old Testament verses.
8. Your **mind is unsound** when under the influence of drugs or alcohol. Satan becomes a part of your mind at those times, not God.

MEDICINE'S BONDAGE TO SATAN (EXCERPTS)

1. **Medicine** and **physician** in the Scriptures mean **to cure, heal or recover completely**. Satan has managed to reverse these meanings.
2. Matthew 5:34-37 forbids swearing or taking an oath to false Gods. **It is interesting to see the oath Satan has most doctors taking.** Although it sounds good it brings a curse from the Father Himself (Jer. 17:5).

3. **The first part of the Hippocratic Oath is a covenant or solemn agreement concerning the relationship of apprentice to teacher and the obligations of the pupil.** The second part is the ethical code which reflects Pythagorean ethics.

THE HIPPOCRATIC OATH (EXCERPTS)

"I swear by **Apollo** the physician and **Aesculapius** and **Health** and **All-heal, and the Gods and Goddesses** that according to my ability and judgement I will keep this oath and this stipulation to reckon him who taught me this art equally dear to me as my parents; to share my substance with him and relieve his necessities if required; to look upon his offspring in the same footing as my own brothers and to teach them this art if they shall wish to learn it without fee or stipulation; and that by precept, lecture, and every other mode of instruction **I will impart a knowledge of the art to my own sons and those of my teachers and to disciples bound by a stipulation and oath according to the law of medicine but to none others.**

I will follow that system of regimen which, according to my ability and judgement I consider for the benefit of my patients, and abstain from whatever is deleterious and mischievous. I will give no deadly medicine to anyone if asked nor suggest any such counsel, and in like manner **I will not give to a woman a peccary to produce abortion.** With purity and with holiness I will pass my life and practice my art.

I will not cut persons laboring under the stone but will leave this to be done by men who are practitioners of this work. Into whatever houses I enter, I will go into them for the benefit of the sick and will abstain from every voluntary act of mischief and corruption, and further, **from the seduction of females or males, of freemen and slaves.**

Whatever, in connection with my professional practice, or not in connection with it, I see or hear, in the life of men, which ought not be spoken of abroad, I will not divulge as reckoning that all such should be kept secret.

While I continue to keep this oath unviolated, may it be granted to me to enjoy life and the practice of the art, respected by all men, in all times, **but should I trespass and violate this oath, may the reverse be my lot.**"

The word Apollyon comes from the same root as **Apollo** (Revelation 9:11). He is the God of destruction, medicine, archery, prophecy, music, poetry and represents the highest type of masculine beauty.

Aesculapius is the God of medicine, the son of Apollo by a demon nymph. **All Gods and Goddesses**: the **caduceus** is the staff of Mercury (twined by two serpents) God of commerce, messenger of the Gods, cleverness, lying, thievery, eloquence, travel, etc.

Satan plans the sickness, then programs the symptoms which are treated by sincere and duty-bound doctors. **Because of this a believer should move to break any evil soul ties with satanic medication and pray much about use of such things.**

For a real eye-opener, go to the public library and ask to see the **Physicians Desk Reference (PDR)**. It lists all the prescription drugs and their possible side effects. Sometimes the side effects produced by the chemicals are similar to the symptoms being treated.

MEDICINE AND THE BELIEVER (EXCERPTS)

The word medicine is used twice in the Old Testament (Prov. 17:22; Jer. 30:13). **Medicine** also occurs two other times (Ezk. 47:12; Jer. 46:11). The root words are Gehah (a cure); Gahah (to remove or heal); Teruwthah (a remedy) and Rephuah (heal). In each case the words mean to effect a complete cure or restoration to the one treated - to heal or restore completely.

The word physician is used five times in the Bible. In the Old Testament the Hebrew root word is Rapha or Raphan meaning to stitch, restore, make whole and heal thoroughly. The Greek root word in the New Testament means to cure or make whole.

Satan, as the God of this world, has introduced into the realm of medicine a group of chemicals and drugs spelled relief, relievers, tranquilizers, uppers, downers, etc. These are both prescribed and are on the shelf with the assumption they are safe to use or they would not be available. **Such drugs and chemicals in the Bible are associated with sorcery (Greek: Pharmakia) - medication: Pharmacy: means magic, witchcraft, a drug, spell-giving potion, a druggist, pharmacist, magician, sorcerer, poisoner. In other words, the uses of chemicals by sorcerers in the Bible was to make it easy for the user to be invaded by evil spirits.** Scriptures on sorcery: Acts 8:9; Rev. 9:21; 21:8; 22:15; 18:23.

In the light of these facts the question arises: What chemicals or drugs can a Christian take without affecting his spiritual sensitivity and desire to serve the Lord?

Scripture declares that real medicines heal or cure. Our problem arose when Satan caused worldly scientists, researchers and the medical profession to endorse **reliever drugs** which have no curative value but only serve to deepen the plight of the victim. So often a **righteous** church member may condemn alcohol as a **reliever** yet in her purse she carries Valium or Librium as a reliever for herself. (Have a pill dumping!)

Behind the scenes Satan's demons manipulate and interfere to bring about aches, pains, agony, diseases, etc. which afflict the minds, wills and emotions of their victims. **Reliever drugs only mask the symptoms but do not cure them.** Many of the modern pain relievers are so powerful they are capable of veiling the mind or setting up barriers between the Holy Spirit and the person's will or desire to seek the Father. This produces tension, worry and anxiety, necessitating an even stronger mind separator, i.e., tranquilizers. These can separate a person's mind from reality and (when prescribed by a reputable doctor, psychologist, or specialist) can further alienate the uninformed believer from God (Isaiah 5:13-14).

Viewed this way, many strong pain killers, tranquilizers and mind altering drugs constitute instant witchcraft, regardless of who prescribes or advises taking them. In a sense a believer taking some of these drugs while crying out to God for healing would be like a man begging the fireman to extinguish a fire while he continues to pour gasoline on it!

A mind-boggling drug produces two complications for a believer. First it may well constitute sorcery or witchcraft - seeking help from man, the flesh and the demonic. In that instance he would come under a curse from God because of involvement with the occult. It could also paralyze built-in defenses against the demonic opening the way for entrance of evil spirits just as in hypnosis, transcendental meditation and yoga.

Is all medicine bad? No, curative and healing arts which do not alter the mind or attitude toward God are what the Scripture calls medicine. But mind altering drugs are definitely in the caution area for believers.

Believers have an obligation to ask their physician or other knowledgeable person just what the function and action is for any so-called medication which is prescribed. They then have a choice and can pray to determine whether or not they should use any substance. The Bible definition of **physician** is one who restores (by stitching) or makes whole.

When considering the drug world it becomes obvious that we have been snared in a clever trap of Satan. Many mental institutions routinely give most inmates tranquilizers daily. Even in some schools, hyperactive children are given a pill a day to make them more controllable. Rather than following scriptural admonitions to do the work of Christ by delivering the bound person from spirits of nervousness, confusion, mind control, etc., chemical controllers are administered. Only obeying the full gospel will bring curative, rather than covering, action.

Because Satan is the God of this world (II Cor. 4:4), his philosophy and definitions, almost universally are accepted, even by the Christian community. Truly his **tongue** walks through the earth (Psalm 73:9). His control of the mental institutions, hospitals and their policies and procedures is often covert and cleverly hidden. This due to the widespread ignorance of God's people of the warnings and instructions of the Word of God (Hosea 4:6). When inmates are treated with daily dosages of mind-boggling pills they are further separated from reality and mental awareness and any real help.

If a believer is attempting to become more sensitive to the Father's guidance, he must realize that even the mildest pain killers (aspirin) or tranquilizers (promethazine) desensitizes the mind somewhat so as to dull sensitivity to the leadership of the Holy Spirit. In other words, the chemical changes can definitely affect areas of spiritual communication. This will be to a greater or lesser extent, depending on the strength and effects of the chemical substances, coupled with the vulnerability and susceptibility of the individual patient.

When God is dealing with a person by permitting buffeting of some nature, drugs may be employed to mask symptoms, thus delaying the showdown called for by the Lord. We routinely advise persons to leave off all drugs for at least a day before coming for prayer. Strong drugs surround and protect the demons, making it much more difficult to cause them to manifest or come out.

It must be emphasized here that, although we are quite sure of the demonic roots of many of these afflictions, we are still searching for the keys to dislodge all the intruders. The progress made thus far is indeed encouraging, but we are always learning more.

A recent pharmaceutical survey of practicing physicians shows the number one prescribed drug to be Valium for the four previous years (millions of doses). This demonstrates that nerves, tension, anxiety, worry and related problems are connected with the majority of cases they see.

Also many doctors apparently have found that rather than to attempt to probe and reprogram the real cause of worry, anxiety and nervousness it is far easier to disconnect patients from reality. With Valium or some similar drug, the mind is floated to a new level of unreality and kept there by a regulated dosage. This makes it more unlikely that the person will ever really seek and find help from the Lord.

The following is a partial list of drugs in the **Physician's Desk Reference**:

Tranquilizers	**Antidepressants**	**Sedatives**
Ativan	Adapin	Alurate
Serax	Aventyl HCl	Amytal
Verstran	Deprol	Belap
Haldol	Elavil	Bentyl
Inapsine	Engep	Buticaps
Innovar	Etrafon	Butisol
Libritabs	Imavate	Cantil
Menrium	Janimine	Carbrital
A-poxide	Marplan	Dialog
Librium	Nardil	Donphen
Lavium	Norpramin	Emesert
Atarax	Pamelor	Eskabarb
Vistaril	Parnate	Levsin/Pheno-
Eskalith	Petrofrane	barbital
Lithane	Presamine	Matropinal
Lithium	Sinequan	Mebaral
Lithonate	Togranil	Nembutal
Deprol	Triavil	Pamine
Equanil	Vivactil	Plexonal
Meprospan		Repan
Millpath		Seconal

Milprem		Sedapap
Miltown		Solfoton
Miltrate		Aquachloral
Pathibamate		Beta-Chlor
Lidone		Dalmane
Tranquilizers		Sedative
Continued		Continued
Compazine	**Hypnotics**	Equanil
Etrafon	Aquachloral	Levoprome
Mellaril	Carbrital	Noctec
Permitil	Dalmane	Noludar
Prolixin	Doriden	Parest
Quide	Matropinal	Phenergan
Serentil	Nebutal	Quaalude
Stelazine	Noctec	Sopor
Thorazine	Noludar	Tranxene
Tindal	Placdyl	
Triavil	Quaalude	**Pain Killers**
Trilafon	Triclos	Aspirin, Etc.
Vesprin	Valmid	All

VALIUM AND LIBRIUM (EXCERPTS)

Introduced in 1963, by 1975 the Federal Drug Administration announced that Valium had become the most abused drug in the nation. In 1976, 60,000,000 prescriptions were written bringing $300,000,000 to the manufacturers.

Valium is prescribed to relieve tension; muscle aches; control spasticity; aid withdrawal from alcohol; calm presurgery patients and induce labor.

The drug is a crutch, a sister to Librium, which tranquilizes without reducing alertness. There have been no deaths from over-doses but it is highly addictive.

The drug is common among the higher income middle-aged housewives. Daily dosages range from 80-120 mg. of Valium. In forty to sixty days it brings addiction. Sudden withdrawal can cause severe convulsions.

Usually a more gentle withdrawal is cushioned with three weeks of phenobarbital to prevent convulsions. Self treatment results in seizures 30 percent of the time.

A DIRECTORY OF DRUGS
Hallucinogens

Drugs, Slang Name	Description	Medical Use	Risk of Abuse
Marijuana perceptions, (Pot, Grass, Boo) judgement	Flowering resinous top of female hemp plant	None	Altered impaired

Drugs, Slang	Name Description	Medical Use	Risk of Abuse
Peyote (Magic Mushroom, Cactus)	Dried cactus buttons containing mescaline	Some experimental study	Visual hallucinations impaired judgement, possible psychosis
LSD (Acid, Hawk, The Chief)	Synthetic chemical 400 times more powerful than mescaline	Some experimental study	Visual and auditory hallucinations, impaired judgement, possible psychosis
DMT	Synthetic chemical similar to mushroom alkaloid psilocybin	Some experimentation, chemical warfare.	Possible psychotic reaction
STP	Atropine-like synthetic	None	Same effects as LSD, but more intense and lasting 3-4 days

Narcotics

Drugs, Slang	Name Description	Medical Use	Risk of Abuse
Opium	Dried coagulated milk of unripe opium-poppy pod	Treatment of pain, severe diarrhea	Loss of appetite, temporary impotency or sterility. Painful withdrawal symptoms
Morphine (M, Miss Emma)	10-1 reduction of crude opium	Treatment of severe pain	Same as above
Heroin (H, Horse, Junk, Smack)	Converted morphine	None	Same as above

Stimulants

Drugs & Slang	Name Description	Medical Use	Risk of Abuse
Cocaine (Coke, Corrine, Happy Dust, Snow)	Isolated alkaloid of cocoa leaf	Anesthesia of eye and throat	Loss of appetite, weight loss, insomnia irritability,

| Benzedrine hypertension (Bennies-Pep conf- | Synthetic central-nervous system stimulant litis, fatigue, aggressiveness depression | Treatment of obesity, narco-lepsy, encepha- | Nausea, irritability, sion, delirium, |

Depressants

Drugs, Slang Name	Description	Medical Use	Risk of Abuse
Nembutal (Yellow Jackets)	Barbituric acid derivative insomnia symptoms, including vomiting, tremors, convulsions	Sedation, treatment of possible respiratory arrest, addiction with withdrawal	Incoherency, depression,
Seconal (Red Birds)	Same as above	Same as above	Same as above
Luminal (Purple Hearts)	Same as above	Same as above	Same as above
Amytal (Blue Heavens)	Same as above	Same as above	Same as above
Miltown & Equanial	Non-barbiturate sedative	Same as above	Same as above
Doriden	Same as above	Same as above	Same as above
Librium vision,	Tranquilizer anxiety, confusion, possible tension, severe depression alcohol, when combined with neurosis alcohol	Treatment of	Blurring of

MINISTRY TO OPPRESSED

Ask **forgiveness** for taking drugs and medicines, and alcoholic beverages. Break **soul ties** with doctors, psychiatrists, social workers, psychologists, mental institutions, nurses, etc.

Cast out demon families of **Rejection**, **Bitterness** and **Rebellion** (Basic Deliverance) including their familiar spirits. Cast out demons of drugs and medicines, various spirits, groups of drugs, appetites and addictions, hallucinogens, narcotics, stimulants, depressants, tranquilizers, antidepressants, sedatives, pain killers, Valium, Librium, etc. including their side effects.

REFERENCES
Seven books written by Rev. Win Worley, Hegewisch Baptist Church, Highland, Indiana.
Most of the research was done by Dr. J.M. Haggard, (Doctor Veterinarian Medicine).

SECTION 4 - PHYSICIANS AND MEDICINE

CONTENTS
1. COMMENTS
2. DEMONIC WOUNDS AND DISEASES
    1. Comments
    2. Prayer
3. DOCTORS, DEMONS & MEDICINE
    1. Medicine's Bondage to Satan
    2. The Hippocratic Oath
    3. Medicine and the Believer
4. PHYSICIAN
5. MEDICINE
6. BALM
7. OINTMENT
8. REMEDY
9. POULTICE
10. EMULSION
11. DISEASE
12. PAIN RELIEVERS
    1. Comments
    2. Pain Killers
13. HEALTH CARE
14. REFERENCES

COMMENTS

There are two elements to the use of physicians and medicine. **A Christian can use them when the result is curing, healing and recovering.**

A Christian should not use them when they cross the line into magic, sorcery, witchcraft and spells with their related practices.

Related lessons are **BODY CURED AND HEALED BY DELIVERANCE** and **DRUGS AND MEDICINES**. Also see the **PREAMBLE TO THE HEALING DELIVERANCE MANUAL**.

DEMONIC WOUNDS AND DISEASES
Comments

Some wounds and diseases are purely physical, and some are caused by demons. The alteration in our physical bodies caused by sin makes us vulnerable to an array of physical illnesses. What happens in our spiritual bodies affects our physical bodies. When no cause can be found medically; it is usually demonic.

Prayer

We repent for our sins, forgive others for hurting us and renounce anything we are addicted to. We anoint with oil, command the demonic diseases to leave us and pray the prayer of faith for healing in THE NAME OF JESUS CHRIST.

DOCTORS, DEMONS & MEDICINE
Medicine's Bondage to Satan

Medicine and **physician** in the Scriptures means **to cure, heal or recover completely**.

The Hippocratic Oath

Matthew 5:34-37 forbids swearing or taking an oath to false Gods. The Hippocratic Oath - I swear by **Apollo** the physician and **Aesculapius** and **all the Gods and Goddesses**, that according to my ability and judgement I will keep this oath ---. **Apollo** is the God of medicine, etc. **Aesculapius** is the God of medicine, the son of **Apollo** by a demon nymph. **All Gods and Goddesses**; the **caduceus** is the staff of **Mercury** (twined by two serpents) God of commerce, etc.

Because of this a believer should move to break any evil soul ties with satanic medication and pray much about the use of such things. A person may become addicted to a medicine and receive a spirit by that name.

Medicine and the Believer

Medicine: a cure, to remove or heal, a remedy, heal. **The words mean a complete cure or restoration, to heal completely.**

Physician: to stitch (operation), restore; means to cure or make whole. The Bible definition of **physician** is one who restores **(by stitching)** or makes whole.

What chemical or drugs can a Christian take without affecting his spiritual sensitivity and desire to serve the Lord? Scripture declares that real medicines heal or cure.

Is all medicine bad? No, for there are curative and healing arts which do not alter the mind or attitudes toward God. These are what the Scripture calls medicine.

Very few follow scriptural admonitions to do the work of Jesus in deliverance, but chemical controllers are administered instead. **Obedience to the full gospel** will bring curative, rather than a covering action.

PHYSICIAN

Physician: Jer 8:22, Mt 9:12, Mk 2:17, Lk 4:23 & 5:31, Col 4:14.

Physicians: Gen 50:2, 2 Chr 16:12, Job 13:4, Mk 5:26, Lk 8:43.

Strong's: to cure, heal, make whole, to mend by stitching, cure, cause to heal, repair, **thoroughly make whole**, to slacken, abate, cease, consume.

MEDICINE

Medicine: Prov 17:22, Eze 47:12.

Medicines: Jer 30:13 & 46:11.

Strong's: a medicament, heal, a remedy. Also see physician.

BALM

Balm: Gen 37:25 & 43:11, Jer 8:22 & 46:11 & 51:8, Eze 27:17.

Strong's: a medicinal balsam.

OINTMENT

Ointment: Ex 30:25, 2 Kin 20:13, 1 Chr 9:30, Job 41:31, Ps. 133:2, Prov 27:9 & 16, Eccl 7:1 & 9:8 & 10:1, Song 1:3, Is 1:6 & 39:2 & 57:9, Mt 26:7 & 9 & 12, Mk 14:3 & 4, Lk 7:37 & 38 & 7:46, Jn 11:2 & 12:3 & 5.

Ointments: Song 1:3 & 4:10, Amos 6:6, Lk 23:56, Rev. 18:13.

Strong's: to rub with oil, to anoint, aromatic, confection, oily, fat, from the olive, perfumed, richness, fruitful, ungent, compound, myrrh, alabaster box of ointment.

REMEDY

Remedy: 2 Chr 36:16, Prov 6:15 & 29:1.

Strong's: curative, medicine, **deliverance**, cure, healing.

POULTICE

Poultice: 2 Kin 20:7 **And Isaiah said, Take <u>a lump of figs</u>. And they took and laid it on the boil, and he recovered.**

EMULSION

Emulsion: Lk 10:34 **And they went to him, and bound up his wounds, <u>pouring in oil and wine</u>, and set him on his own beast, and brought him to an inn, and took care of him.**

DISEASE

See Disease, Diseased and Diseases in Stong's. There are a good number of verses.

Strong's: afflicted; grief, disease, infirmity, pain, malady, anxiety, calamity, sickness, **evil favored**, debility, impotent, without strength, disability, feebleness, frailty, weakness.

Various Kinds Of: abortion, ague, atrophy, blain, blemish, blindness, boil, congestion, consumption, deafness, demons, dropsy, dysentery, dyspepsia, epilepsy, fever, gonorrhea, gout, hemorrhage, hemorrhoids, insanity, itch, lameness, leprosy, murrain, paralysis, pestilence, scab, scall, scurvy, spermatorrhea, stammering, sun stroke, turmor, worm. **See Deuteronmy Chapter 28.**

PAIN RELIEVERS
Comments

When God deals with a person by permitting some type of buffeting, drugs may mask symptoms, thus delaying the showdown called for by the Lord. **When a person has a problem, the easy way in the short term is to seek the medical profession rather than God for the long term solution.**

Particularly dangerous are the mind altering drugs. Certainly, mind altering drugs are in the caution area for believers. These have no curative value but may serve to deepen the plight of the victim. **They treat the symptoms rather than the cause; the person is never healed.**

Many modern pain relievers are so powerful that they are quite capable of veiling the mind. This can set up barriers between the Holy Spirit and the person's will or desire to seek the Lord. **They may be used to control mental patients and inmates.**

Pain Killers

When is it alright to use pain killers? If it is alright to use physicians to operate, then it is necessary to use anesthesia which is a type of pain killer, and to use pain killers after surgery to assist in recovery.

What about a person with a terminal illness who is in pain and is dying? We can not deny the comfort to resist the severe pain.

It depends on the person's situation and the purpose of the pain killers. If the Christian believes that God can heal on earth, then that person should seek God first before using the medical profession.

HEALTH CARE

What country spends more money and more percentage of GDP on health care than any other country in the world? Despite that, this country has the highest rates of heart disease, diabetes, autism, cancer, and all other major diseases. That same country has infant mortality rates and longevity rates worse than third-world countries. And that country's health care system ignores the causes of all this-and abysmal diet of "foods" nearly devoid of nutrition, a diet poisoned with chemicals and additives, and more toxic drugs and vaccines than most all other countries combined. What country? Ours!

We are at or near the bottom in most key areas of health: infant mortality, low birth weights, injuries and homicides, teenage pregnancies, sexually transmitted diseases, prevalence of HIV and AIDS, drug-related deaths, obesity, diabetes, heart disease, chronic lung disease and disability. Our life expectancy is lower and nearly two-thirds of that discrepancy can be contributed to deaths before the age of 50. On average, infants, children, and adolescents in the US die younger and have greater rates of illness and injury that youth in other countries.

REFERENCES

1. **DOCTORS, DEMONS & MEDICINE** by Win Worley, Hegewisch Baptist Church, Highland, IN
2. **THE NEW STRONG'S EXHAUSTIVE CONCORDANCE OF THE BIBLE** by James Strong, Thomas Nelson Publishers
2. **NAVE'S TOPICAL BIBLE** by Orville Nave, Macdonald Publishing Company
3. **THE NEW TREASURY OF SCRIPTURE KNOWLEDGE** by Jerome Smith, Thomas Nelson Publishers

SECTION 5 - PSYCHIATRY

CONTENTS
1. THE CITIZENS COMMISSION ON HUMAN RIGHTS INTERNATIONAL
2. UNHOLY ASSAULT PSYCHIATRY VERSUS RELIGION
2. REFERENCES

THE CITIZENS COMMISSION ON HUMAN RIGHTS INTERNATIONAL

1. Psychiatry monopolizes international mental health and demands trillions of dollars from governments each year for its services.
2. Insurance in the United States alone pays out $69 billion in mental health costs annually.
3. Psychiatric service costs exceed those of general medical services by almost 200%
4. International psychiatric drug sales total in the range of $76 billion per year. And what are governments and societies getting in return?
5. By their own admission, psychiatrists do no know how to cure a single mental problem.
6. They do not know how their treatments affect patients.
7. According to one study, psychiatric treatment scored a 99% failure rate in patient recovery.
8. In the last 40 years, nearly twice as many Americans have died in government psychiatric hospitals as American soldiers killed in battle in all wars the United States has fought since 1776.
9. More that 20 million children worldwide are on prescribed psychiatric drugs known to cause violence, psychosis, hallucinations, suicide, homicide, strokes, diabetes, heart attacks and death for alleged disorders that have never been scientifically proven to exist.
10. Antidepressant "wonder drugs" are so widely prescribed that more than 150 million people worldwide have taken Selective Serotonin Reuptake Inhibitor (SSRI) antidepressants. These drugs are under fire by drug regulatory agencies, not only for their potential to create violence and suicidal impulses, but because drug trials have found they perform no better than placebos (sugar pills).
11. The number of American seniors aged 65 who receive electroshock is more than three and a half times that of those aged 64. Why? Government health insurance for senior citizens becomes available at 65.
12. In 2005, the United States Food and Drug Administration (FDA) reported grievous damage from electroshock-patients sustaining severe burns, pregnant women suffering miscarriages and even death.
13. Yet while almost half of the elderly who receive ECT die within two years, psychiatrists continue to electroshock millions of people throughout the world, killing as many as 10,000 people. More than two-thirds of ECT victims are women.

UNHOLY ASSAULT PSYCHIATRY VERSUS RELIGION

Psychologists were inspired by Pavlov in their denial of the existence of the soul and denigration of man and religion. The concept of good and bad behavior, right and wrong conduct and personal responsibility have taken such a beating that people have few or no guidelines for checking, judging or directing their behavior. The war on religion waged by the materialistic practices of psychiatry and psychology charted the course of a religious and moral decline the world over. The soul was a waste of energy and that man was simply another animal. Religious ideas and feelings belonged before the tribunal of psychology. The idea of the spirit was scientifically relegated to primitive races. Psychological studies targeting religious orders had corrupted them. Religious people have been betrayed by Sensitivity Training and other psychological counseling techniques which grew from atheist roots.

The time when psychiatrists considered that they could cure the mentally ill is gone. In the future, the mentally ill have to learn to live with their illness. The high rate of criminal convictions for mental health professionals disproves any claimed expertise in understanding the human psyche. A review of more than 800 convictions of psychiatrists, psychologists and psychotherapists reveals convictions were for fraud, theft and embezzlements; sex crimes and manslaughter and murder. To adopt psychiatry's biological model, one has to believe in a materialistic non-spiritual world. The medical model claims there is no mental activity that is due to the spiritual dimension. All activity, even one's religious beliefs or the belief in GOD, are nothing more than the workings of the brain.

In short, the nature of the hallucinations of JESUS, as they are described in the orthodox Gospels, permits us to conclude that the founder of the Christian religion was afflicted with religious paranoia. Everything that we know about him conforms so perfectly to the clinical picture of paranoia that it is hardly conceivable that people can even question the accuracy the diagnosis. The failure of JESUS to develop ideas of injury and persecution rules out the possibility of a paranoid psychosis. This is not necessarily true; some paranoids manifest ideas of grandeur almost entirely. JESUS CHRIST might simply have returned to his carpentry following the use of modern psychiatric treatments.

REFERENCES

The Citizens Commission On Human Rights International, Los Angeles, CA:
Psychiatry: An Industry Of Death Documentary Supplement
Psychiatry's Multibillion-Dollar Fraud
Psychiatry's Betrayal
Psychiatric Rape
Psychiatry Education's Ruin
Psychiatry A Human Rights Abuse And Global Failure
Psychiatry Destroys Minds
Psychiatry Destroying Religion
Psychiatry Victimizing The Elderly
Psychiatry Manipulating Creativity

Psychiatry Eradicating Justice
Psychiatry Shattering Your World With Drugs
Psychiatry Committing Fraud
Psychiatry Destroying Morals
Unholy Assault - Psychiatry Versus Religion
The Real Crisis In Mental Health

SECTION 6 - PRAYERS AND LIST OF DEMONS FOR HEALING

CONTENTS
1. GENERAL PRAYER
2. BASIC DELIVERANCE
    1. Rejection
    2. Bitterness
    3. Rebellion
3. BODY CURED AND HEALED BY DELIVERANCE
    1. Curses Of Deuteronomy 28
    2. Lists Of Demons
        1. Diseases Found in Deuteronomy 28
        2. Diseases Found in the Bible
        3. Princes, Kings & World Rulers
        4. Paralysis
        5. Roots of Infirmity
        6. Ailments
        7. Spiritual Names Of Demons
            1. Functional Diseases of Body
            2. Emotional
            3. Body Pain
    3. Prayer For Healing
4. SPIRITUAL ROOTS OF DISEASE
    1. Prayer
    2. Lists Of Demons
        1. General Diseases
        2. Specific Diseases
        3. Fear, Anxiety and Stress Disorders
5. BALDNESS - BEARDS - HAIR
    1. Prayer
        1. Everybody
        2. Women
        3. Men
        4. Curses
    2. LIST OF DEMONS
6. DRUGS AND MEDICINES
    1. List Of Demons
7. DRUNKENNESS AND GLUTTONY
    1. Prayer

   2. List Of Demons
- 8. **HEALING FOR KIDNEYS**
  1. Prayer
  2. List Of Demons
- 9. **DELIVERANCE AND HEALING FOR CANCER AND ARTHRITIS**
  1. Prayer
  2. Arthritis
  3. Cancer
- 10. **PERFECTING LOVE**
  1. Prayer
  2. List Of Demons
- 11. **ORGANS AND SYSTEMS OF BODY**
- 12. **REFERENCES**

GENERAL PRAYER

I forgive my ancestors (upwards), descendants (downwards) and anyone else (outwards) that has cursed or hurt me (those outside of me). I ask you to forgive them for their many sins and mistakes. I remit their sins, sever any demonic ties and set myself free. I ask GOD to bless them with spiritual blessings, bring them into truth and meet their needs out of His Riches in Glory through CHRIST JESUS. I ask that GOD will forgive me (Godwards) for my many sins and I forgive myself (inwards) for sins against my body.

I forgive my ancestors, descendents and anyone else that has cursed me with <u>weakness, sickness, disease, illness, injury or trauma</u>. Please forgive me for sins that would open me up to these attacks and I forgive myself for my mistakes.

<u>LORD JESUS CHRIST, please forgive me for spiritual blocks to healing</u>: unforgiveness, ignorance or lack of knowledge, no relationship with GOD according to knowledge, personal and family sins, not having faith in GOD, the need to see a miracle, looking for signs and wonders, expecting GOD to heal on one's own terms, looking to man rather than GOD, not being honest and transparent, flagrant sin or habitual sin, robbing GOD in tithes and offerings, sin of our parents, looking to symptoms and not to the Healer, letting fear enter your heart, failure to get away in prayer and fasting, improper care of the body, not discerning the Lord's Body, touching GOD's anointed leaders, immoderate eating, pure unbelief, failing to keep our life filled up with GOD, not resisting the enemy, just giving up, looking for repeated healings instead of divine health, rejecting healing in the Atonement as part of the covenant for today, trying to bypass the penalty of the curse, murmuring and complaining, hating and not obeying instruction. I ask this is THE NAME OF JESUS CHRIST, LORD, MASTER AND SAVIOR.

In THE NAME OF JESUS CHRIST I command the spirits to come out of the Unconscious, Subconscious and Conscious Mind. I command families of demons to come out of me and bring their works with them as your name is called.

BASIC DELIVERANCE

It is good to start with BASIC DELIVERANCE because these families of demons are precursors to disease. Rejection, Bitterness and Rebellion are the most important demon families that get us into trouble. See the **DELIVERANCE MANUAL, Mass Deliverance Manual** for Lists of Demons which may be applicable to lessons.

We have learned to repent and forgive in preparation for deliverance. Be honest with yourself and GOD. Cast out demons after you have forgiven and repented. Take time to let THE HOLY SPIRIT lead you since everyone has their particular problems. The lists are for those commonly found associated with these problems. You will discover demons not on the lists. It is good to read scriptures on deliverance during the deliverance sessions.

Rejection

Feelings of being Rejected, Refused, Repudiated, Declined, Denied, Rebuffed, Repelled, Renounced, Discarded, Thrown Away, Excluded, Eliminated and Jettisoned.

Rejection, Fear of Rejection, Self Rejection, Poor in Spirit, Pride - Ego - Vanity, Double Mindedness, Roots of Rejection, Ahab-Jezebel Complex, Destruction of Family Priesthood, Dominance, Homosexuality, Lesbianism, Rebellion, Withdrawal, Overpermissive, Too Harsh, Lying, Guilt, Distrust, Inability to Communicate, Witchcraft Control, Ugliness, Schizophrenia, Anger, Rejection from the Womb, Smoking, Drinking, Dementia Praecox, Instability, Agony, Inability to Give or Receive Love, Insecurity, Inferiority, Fantasy, Unreality, Sexual Perversion, Frustration

Bitterness

Feelings of being Bitterly Cursed, Rebellious, Sharp, Acrid, Embittered, Poisoned, Violent, Provoked, Vexed, Grieved, Sorrowing, Bitter Herb, Calamity, Bile, Venom, Angry, Chafed, Most Bitter and Provoked.

Bitterness: Resentment, Hatred, Unforgiveness, Violence, Temper, Anger, Retaliation, Murder.

Diseases: Cancer, Arthritis and diseases that come in through Bitterness and Unforgiveness.

Rebellion

Feelings of being Disobeyed, Transgressed, Violated, Disregarded, Defied, Infringed, Shirked, Resisted, Mutiny, Rebelled and Revolted.

Rebellion, Self-will, Stubbornness, Disobedience, Anti-submissiveness, Evil Plotting and Planning, Lying, Greed, Hate, Evil Control of Others, Destruction, Unrighteous Judgement, Subversion, Rock Music, Resistance, Christian Rock, Interference, Deceit, Friction, Trickery, Repulse, Betrayal, Defiance, Pride, Aggressiveness, False Love, Scorn, Arrogance, Sorcery, Conniving, Seduction, Confusion, Sullen Masculine Women, Taking

Tranquilizers, Effeminate Men, Taking Drugs, Insecurity, Restless, Frustration, Witchcraft, Depression, Unholy Sex, Doubt.

BODY CURED AND HEALED BY DELIVERANCE
CURSES OF DEUTERONOMY 28

<u>I break the curses of Deuteronomy 28 as follows</u>: cursed in city and field, cursed shall be basket and store, cursed shall be children, crops, cattle, sheep, cursed going in and coming out, cursing, confusion and failure in job and work, destruction, perishing, plague, pestilence, sickness, death, consumption (wasting disease), fever, inflammation (blood poisoning), extreme burning (high fever), madness (encephalitis), wars, crop failure, famine, pestilence, pursue until perish (harassment), Heaven as brass, no rain (hot sun), earth as iron (hard dry ground), land becomes powder and dust, dust shall cover you (dust storms), eye trouble from dust, asthma, emphysema, heart trouble, defeat and terror before enemies, body shall not be buried, wild beast will eat it, botch (skin ulcers and boils), itch, scurvy, pellagra, beriberi, psoriasis, madness, blindness, astonishment of heart (terror, amazement), tumors, hemorrhoids, groping at noonday, poverty, oppression, robbed, no deliverance, wife in adultery, raped, home stolen, wages stolen or lost, ox slain, ass stolen, sheep taken, none to rescue, son and daughters run away from home and taken into bondage for sex, eye and heart fail waiting for their return, enemies will take your wages and property, oppression and destruction (crushed), madness, helpless, hapless, powerless, boils, ulcers (from sole of feet to top of head), impetigo, eczema, foreign rulers and Gods, astonishment, a proverb among nations, laughing stock, ridicule, belittlement, worms will eat grapes, crop and job failure, locust will eat crop, olive tree shall fail, sons and daughters go into captivity, drugs, witchcraft, sex, harlot, foreign oppression, debt, hunger, thirst, nakedness, poverty, destruction, defeat by foreign nation, unmerciful enemy, destruction of cattle and crop, robbery of all possessions, siege of cities, destruction of defenses, conquest of land, cannibalism, famine, distress, complete poverty, wonderful plagues, plagues on children, long chronic illness, destruction of race (genocide), plucked off land (exile), dispersion among the nations (exile), no rest, fearful, terror, blindness, depression, heaviness, fear of death, no assurance, fretting and worry always, constant danger, bondage, slavery, <u>ALL DISEASES OF EGYPT AND, EVERY SICKNESS AND EVERY PLAGUE IN BOOK OF LAW</u>.

LISTS OF DEMONS
Diseases Found in Deuteronomy 28

confusion, destruction, perishing, plague, pestilence, sickness, death, consumption (wasting disease), fever, inflammation (blood poisoning), extreme burning (high fever), madness (encephalitis), pestilence,, eye trouble from dust, asthma, emphysema, heart trouble, botch (skin ulcers and boils), itch, scurvy, pellagra, beriberi, psoriasis, madness, blindness, astonishment of heart (terror, amazement), tumors, hemorrhoids, eye and heart fail waiting for their return, destruction (crushed), madness, boils, ulcers (from top of head to sole of feet), impetigo, eczema, astonishment, destruction, distress, wonderful plagues, plagues on children, long chronic illness, no rest, fearful, terror, blindness, depression, heaviness, fear of death, no assurance, fretting and worry always, constant danger, **ALL DISEASES OF EGYPT AND, EVERY SICKNESS AND EVERY PLAGUE IN BOOK OF LAW.**

Diseases Found in the Bible
Ague, Blains, Boils, Blemish, Blindness, Botch, Broken-Handed, Broken-Footed, Bruises, Canker, Crook-Backed, Dropsy, Dwarf, Emerods, Flat Nose, Flux, Gangrene, Halt, Impotent, Infirmity, Inflammation, Issue, Itch, Lameness, Leprosy, Lunacy, Madness, Maimed, Murrain, Palsy, Pestilence, Scab, Scale, Scurvy, Sores, Wen, Withered, Worms, Wounds

Princes, Kings & World Rulers
Accident, Accident Prone, Bone Breaker, Back Breaker, Traumatic Shock

Paralysis
Crippling, Deformity, Atrophy, Depression, Discouragement, Hopelessness, Despair, Suicide, Death, Affliction, Spinal Cord Scar Tissue

Roots of Infirmity
Shame and Embarrassment, Rebellion & Idolatry, Grief, Troubled Will in Conflict, Resentment & Envy, Disobedience, Curse of Jezebel, Vanity & Pride, Curse of the Law, Acupuncture & Acupressure, Witchcraft & Occult, Envy & Jealousness, Hypnotism & Demonism, Taoism & Pantheism, Reincarnation, Astrology, Psychic Healing, Spiritualistic Healing, Hate, Metaphysical Healing, Occult Healing

Ailments
Tooth Decay, Christian Science Healing, Traumatic Shock, Leukemia, Cancer of Bone, Traumatic Death, Tuberculous of Bone, Acne, Carbuncles, Skin Cancer, Menstrual Cramps, Diarrhea, Colitis, Cancer of Bowels, Eye Trouble, Bowel Upset, Cancer, Hernia, **Kidney Stones, Kidney Failure, Kidney Infection, Kidney Panic**, Heart Disturbances, Melancholy (sadness), Scalp Ailments, Falling Hair, Restlessness, Inability to Sleep, Aimlessness, Futility, Pestilence, Consumption (T.B.), Fever, Inflammation, Botch (boils), Madness, Emerods (Hemorrhoids), Blindness, Encephalitis, Schizophrenia, De la Touretts Syndrome, Polio, Huntington's Cholera, Muscular Sclerosis, Stroke, Scab (measles, small pox), Spinal Meningitis, St. Vita's Dance, Blasting (prevents growth), Scoliosis, Brutishness (unteachable ignorance), Female Cancer (uncontrollable body odor), Heart Attack (astonishment of heart), Venereal Disease (inflammation of a fungus infection in sex organs)

Spiritual Names Of Demons
Functional Diseases of Body: Meriham (controller - females allergies), Tiepea (mouth, gums), Woteige (gluttony, body illness, ruler of Octopus), Felus (gluttony), Arcolias (fatness, sins of Sodom and Gomorrah), Lukolias (pain of sternum), Blargy (infection of colon and colon cancer), Bozo (stomach infection), Boice (pancreas), Carpa (stomach nerves), Denemis (Gall Bladder), Hiawatha - Indian (glandular malfunctions and body fluids, swelling), Moxie (chest pains), Monroe (breast cancer under ruler Cerulias - controller), Prince Damulias (right breast), Ruler Arculias (left breast), Taile (lymph glands of breast), Verico (mushroom growth type breast cancer), Colbeck (bone marrow), Upeedes (ear, deafness), Optias (puts parasites and organisms into body), Targa (broken

rhythm into heart), Yondacola (blood cancer), Citicizan (convulsions and epilepsy), Rezpan (pituitary glands), Goratus (pituitary glands - violent), Woepe (heart blockage), Csarbolias (foot pain), Pontolias (right foot), Pintolias (left foot), Nickulias (pain in neck), Eraualias (ear infections)

Emotional: Belfagar (vanity), Contressie (flippancy of emotions), Collodus (stoicism - no feeling), Repanel (controller), Ashtroth (accusation, criticism), Petragrammation (selfishness), Philanfesus (sloth), Felix (self pity, fear of disapproval), Varrier (controller - disobedience against obedience), Vermo (guilt), Eland (resentment, sorrow), Remus and Remur (cause sleep in spiritual environment), Soonelton (rebellion), Vormo (excessive tiredness), Phonique (play acting, dramatic, choreography), Voltare (game playing, taunting), Boletta (game playing, taunting), Whocarto (over concern of what others think) Puno (blood pressure), Triano (blood pressure), Targa (rapid heartbeat), Woepe (heart blockage), Optias (puts cancer cells into human anatomy)

Body Pain: Condor (controller prince), Artrize (shaking of the body), Colbeck (bone and marrow), Sutias (back pain), Shiton (back pain in spine, serpent - Jean Dixon's snake), Larkopious (knee), Rockalious (knee), Lukolidus (sternum), Damelious (body pain), Sarkolious (pain, energy force from outer space), Romulious, Nickolious (pain from outer space), Arkilious (radiational force), Taepe (copy demon - copy other characteristics), Pycone (back of neck), Osmodaus (back of neck), Porox (blocks human will), Carbare (ruler of spiritual blockage), Ruschon (fights against JESUS CHRIST), Morondo (blocks reading of Word), Meganosis (blocks all knowledge), Armenious (false doctrine)

PRAYER FOR HEALING

In THE NAME OF JESUS CHRIST, we thank you for the healing of our bodies as the above spirits were cast out (Healing Through Deliverance). We ask that the systems of our body be healed (Healing Through The Prayer Of Faith):

circulatory (cardiovascular, conduction, impulse conducting, portal, vascular)
digestive (gastrointestinal, alimentary)
endocrine
HEMATOLOGIC (hematopoietic)
immune
internal organs (chromaffin, cytochrome, hypophyseoportal, microsomal ethanol oxidizing, reticuloendothelial)
lymphatic (lymphoreticular)
muscular (estrapyramical motor)
nervous (neurologic, autonomic, central, parasympathetic, peripheral, sympoathetic, vasomotor, vegetative, visceral efferent)
renal
reproductive (genital)
respiratory (pulmonary)
skeletal (haversian, osseous)
skin (integumentary)
urinary (urologic, urogenital)

and the sub-systems. Amen.

SPIRITUAL ROOTS OF DISEASE
Lists Of Demons
General Diseases

1. **Various:** genetically inherited disease, manic depression, paranoid schizophrenia, Jungian psychology
2. **Depression:** anxiety attacks, use of Prozac and other drugs
3. **Bitterness:** anger, hatred, unforgiveness, resentment, retaliation, violence, murder

Specific Diseases

1. **Various:** scoliosis, sciatica, epilepsy, attention deficit disorder, immune system, Chrons' Disease, ulcerative colitis, diabetes (autoimmune disease), lupus, multiple sclerosis, rheumatoid arthritis, autism, Parkinson's Disease, addictions, masturbation, Alzheimer's Disease, cholesterol, shingles and hives, rosacea, acne, ovarian cysts, breast cysts, systolic acne, endometriosis, herpes, viruses, osteoporisis, spondylolysis, degenerative disc disease, alcoholism, psoriasis, skin diseases, sinus infections, PMS, fibromyalgia, sleep disorders, multiple personality disorder, migraines, allergies, mitral valve prolapse, reflux, CFS (chronic fatigue syndrome), parasites, irritable bowel syndrome, colic, flu, Sjogren's Syndrome, panic attacks, phobias, hypoglycemia, hyperglycemia (diabetes), hypothyroidism (Hashimoto's Disease), hyperthyroidism (Graves' Disease)
2. **Cancer:** colon, skin, liver, breast, ovarian, uterine, Hodgkin's Disease, leukemia, prostate
3. **Arthritis:** involving inflammation of the joints, osteoarthritis
4. **Nonbacterial Inflammation:** interstitial cystitis, prostatitis
5. **Cell Wall Rigidity:** asthma, angina pectoris, hypertension (high-blood pressure), toxic retention
6. **Addictive Personality:** weight, anorexia and bulimia

Fear, Anxiety and Stress Disorders

1. **MCS/EI:** multiple chemical sensitivities / environmental illness, power of the tongue
2. **Endocrine System**
3. **Limbic System:** general adaptation syndrome (GAS), general adaptation syndrome of fear, anxiety and stress
4. **Cardiovascular System:** angina (pain), high-blood pressure (hypertension), heart arrhythmias, mitral valve prolapse (heart valve disease), coronary artery disease, strokes, diseases of heart muscle from inflammation, aneurysms, varicose veins, hemorrhoids, thrombophlebitis (vein inflammation)
5. **Muscles:** tension headaches, muscle contraction backache
6. **Connective Tissue Disease:** rheumatoid arthritis
7. **Related Inflammatory Diseases of Connective Tissue:** prostatitis, interstitial cystitis
8. **Pulmonary System:** asthma (called hypersensitivity reaction), hay fever
9. **Immune System:** immunosuppression or deficiency, autoimmune diseases
10. **Gastrointestinal System:** ulcers, irritable bowel syndrome (IBS), diarrhea, constipation, nausea and vomiting, ulcerative colitis, malabsorption (leaky gut)

11. **Genitourinary System:** diuresis, impotence, frigidity
12. **Skin:** eczema, neurodermatitis, acne
13. **Endocrine System:** diabetes mellitus, amenorrhea
14. **Central Nervous System:** fatigue and lethargy, Type A Behavior, overeating, depression, insomnia

BALDNESS - BEARDS - HAIR
Prayer
Everybody

LORD JESUS CHRIST, I forgive my ancestors and any others for any sin they may have committed that would have brought the curse of baldness on men and my descendants. I ask that you forgive and bless them with long life and a full-head of hair. Forgive me where I have sinned and cursed my head. Forgive me for mocking those with baldness, having a false personality, living in fantasy, trying to be something I am not, and being rejected, bitter and rebellious. GOD please protect every hair from Satan.

Women

Forgive me for my pride, super spirituality, false prophecy, usurping the role of my husband, acting and looking masculine, being haughty, and doing anything that would open me up to baldness and female problems. Please deliver me from psoriasis, female diseases, burning, fear, cancer, baldness, rotting flesh, excessive hair on the face, and female problems. I forgive my father, husband, sons and any other men who have mistreated me.

Men

Forgive me for my pride, letting the wife be head of the home, acting and looking feminine, being false in my position as a man, long hair and vain glory.

Curses

I break the curses of baldness, pride, falseness, fantasy, Jezebel, Ahab and female problems. Heal me of any medical treatment which causes loss of hair.

List Of Demons

Rejection	Bitterness	Rebellion
Baldness	Shame	Ego
Selfishness	Self Pity	Inadequacy
Dying the Hair	Theatrics	Super Spirituality
Haughtiness	Female Cancer	Domination
Disfigurement	Mocking	Pride
Vanity	Jealousy	Envy
Embarrassment	Premature Baldness	Fears
Phobias	Insecurities	Inferiority
Loneliness	Timidity	Shyness
Ineptness	Whipsaw Spirits	False Youngness
Falseness	Playacting	Put On
Affectation	Pretension	Sophistication

Religious Demons Feminine Men Masculine Women
Female Diseases Female Disorders Burning
Diseases of Flesh Jezebel Ahab
Manipulation Control Witchcraft
Excessive Hair on Women
Destruction of Family Priesthood

DRUGS AND MEDICINES
List Of Demons

Appetites & Addictions
Addiction to drugs and many other things
Drugs
Bondage; slavery
Craving for and addiction to cigarettes
Craving for and addiction to alcohol
Cigarette
Nicotine
Amphetamine
Barbiturates
Craving for and addiction to drugs
Downers
Fantasy
Fears
Flashback
Habit
Methodone
Phenobarbital
THC
Hashish
Depressants
Pipe smoking
Unreality and many others
medical and slang names

Various Spirits
Nervousness
Confusion
Mind Control
Tension
Anxiety
Worry

Drugs & Medicines
Apollo and Apollyon
Aesculapuis
Gods and Goddesses
Hippocratic Oath
Caduceus
Pharmakia
Pharmacy
Pharmacist
Witchcraft and Sorcery

Groups of Drugs
Pain Killers
Tranquilizers
Antidepressants
Sedatives
Hypnotics
Hallucinogens

Narcotics
Stimulants

General

Drugs	Witchcraft	Medicines	Poisons
Mania	Madness	Addiction	Charming
Enchantment	Amulets	Potions	Spells
Control	Sorcery	Black Magic	Fascination
Idolatry	Occultism	Charms	Bewitched
Medicine Man	Unsound Mind	Swearing	Taking Oath
Hippocratic Oath	Apollo	Aesculapius	Gods
Goddesses	Mischievous	Peccary	Abortion
Corruption	Seduction	Apollyon	Destruction
Caduceus	Cleverness	Lying	Messenger of Gods
Thievery	Soul Ties	Relievers	Tranquilizers
Uppers	Downers	Spell Giving	Valium
Librium	Aches	Pains	Agony
Diseases	Tension	Worry	Veiling of Mind
Anxiety	Alienation	Pain Killers	Mind Altering
Drugs			
Mind Boggling	Paralyzing	Hypnosis	Instant Witchcraft
Yoga	Hyperactive	Nervousness	T.M.
Confusion	Mind Control	Aspirin	Promethazine
Dull Sensitivity	Vulnerability	Susceptibility	Afflictions
Unreality	Muscle Aches	Spasticity	Withdrawal
Convulsions	Phenobarbital	Alt Perceptions	Impaired
Judgement			
Psychosis	Hallucinations	Psychotic Reactions	Pains
Diarrhea	Loss of Appetite	Impotency	Sterility
Anesthesia	Obesity	Narcolepsy	Encephalitis
Fatigue	Irritability	Insomnia	Nausea
Hypertension	Delirium	Aggressiveness	Alcoholism
Neurosis	Incoherency	Depression	Respiratory Arrest
Vomiting		Tremors	Convulsions
	Blurring of Vision		

DRUNKENNESS AND GLUTTONY
Prayer

We forgive those who have caused you to seek food and drink for comfort. We ask GOD for forgiveness for drunkenness and gluttony, and any other addictions such as drugs and medicines. We break curses and demonic ties on us because of our ancestors who are drunkards and gluttons.

LIST OF DEMONS

Use **Drunkenness and Gluttony**, **Drugs and Medicine**, **Ungodly Spirits** in the **DELIVERANCE MANUAL**, **Mass Deliverance Manual**, Lists of Demons.

- Gluttony
- Nervousness
- Compulsive Eating
- Resentment
- Frustration
- Idleness
- Self-Pity
- Self-Reward
- Caffeine
- Diet Pills
- Indulgence
- Surfeiting
- Addiction to Food
- Cravings for Particular Foods
- Addiction to Any kind of Beverage
- Medications for Drunkenness
- Drunkenness
- Alcohol
- I Like To Eat
- Desire
- Addiction to Alcohol
- Bondage
- Slavery
- Fantasy
- Fears
- Flashback
- Habit
- Unreality
- Craving for Alcohol

HEALING FOR KIDNEYS
Prayer

I forgive anyone who has hurt me and ask forgiveness where I have hurt others for the following: suffers deep within, pierced within; earnestly longs, heart faints within, pain or terror, mourning heart, and hypocrisy and falsehood. I forgive my ancestors, anyone who had spiritual authority over me and myself for generational curses, curses in the immediate family, abuses in the family line, racism, etc.

Please forgive me and I forgive anyone that has affected my will and affections, feelings and emotions, heart and mind, sensitivity, seat of desire, innermost being; knowledge and understanding, center of emotions, reproductive power and seat of generative power.

Please forgive me and I forgive others for unforgiveness; bitterness; rebellion; rejection and self-hatred with guilt; rejection by father, husband/wife or any man/woman in general; self-rejection; bitter-root judgment; speak death; don't love self; blame GOD; be angry with GOD; think and talk death; make a covenant with death; unloving spirit; guilt; fear, anxiety and stress; envy; spirit of death, hell and destruction; jealousy; envy; denominational bondage; false teaching; family alienation, strife and bad blood; mental and emotional abuse; medical personnel speaking a curse; betrayal, abuse and lying; kidney stone; cancer; nephritis; deep hurt; destruction; high blood pressure; trauma; heart disease; broken spirit; unloving spirit; murderous rage; anger; guilt; witchcraft; black magic; hypertension; broken heart and other related ailments.

List Of Demons
Use **BASIC DELIVERANCE** above for deliverance.

DELIVERANCE AND HEALING FOR CANCER AND ARTHRITIS
Arthritis
(Proper Names of Demons)

Bitterness - Root of Bitterness (cause of arthritis): Resentment, Hatred, Violence, Murder, Schizophrenia, Mind Binding, Memory Loss, Recall, Unforgiveness, Temper, Anger, Retaliation, Broken Relationships.

Unforgiveness - cause of arthritis.

Schizophrenia - Schizo, Damnable Seed, a commanding ruler: double mindedness

Rejection - Lust, Fantasy Lust, Perverseness, Jealousy, Paranoia, Self Pity, Depression, Suicide, Guilt, Pride, Vanity, Loneliness, Fears, Attention Seeking, Inferiority, Harlotry, Unfairness, Withdrawal, Fantasy, Daydreaming, Timidity, Self Awareness, Shyness, Sensitivity, Chattering, Nervousness, Vivid Imaginations, Fear Of Germs, Frustration, Impatience, Inordinate Affection For Animals, Intolerance, Insanity, **Self Rejection**, Self Accusation, Tension, Fear Of People, Compulsive Confession, Envy, Fear Of Judgment, False Compassion, **Fear Of Rejection**, False Responsibility, Despondency, Shame, Despair, Discouragement, Hopelessness, Condemnation, Unworthiness, Perfection, Ego.

Rebellion - Fear, Accusation, Selfishness, Pride, Hatred, Resentment, Violence, Murder, Memory Recall Loss, Disobedience, Paranoia, Suspicion, Distrust, Persecution, Confrontation, **Self Will**, Projection, **Stubbornness**, Anger, Judgmental, Self Deception, Self Delusion, Self Destruction, Unteachableness, Control, Possessiveness, Retaliation, False Beliefs, **Anti-Submissiveness**.

CANCER
(Proper Names of Demons)

Termination, a ruler, in charge of terminal diseases.

Optias: puts parasites and organisms into the body; also inserts cancer cells.

Nimo, a controller: deceives, works with **Cancer, Fungus** & **Self-Destruction**.

Blood Cancer (Leukemia) - **Yondacola**: leukemia.

Breast Cancer - **Cerulias**, a ruler, controller **Monroe**: under **Cerulias**.

Verico: mushroom growth type breast cancer.

Taile: lymph glands of the breast.

Colon Cancer - **Blargy**: colon cancer; infection of colon, colitis, diverticulitis.

Cancer of Lymph Glands - **Tatile**: in breast.

Stomach Cancer - **Bozo**: stomach infection, ulcers.

Damulias, a prince: right breast.

Arculias, a ruler: left breast.

Aaile: lymph glands of breast.

Moxie, Maxze: power over chest pains.

Lukoliasn Lukolidus: pain in breastbone, sternum.

Taegy: colitis.

Blargy: infection of colon, diverticulitis, cancer of colon, colitis.

Bozo: stomach cancer, stomach infection, stomach irritation, ulcers.

Carpa: nervous stomach, ulcers.

PERFECTING LOVE
Prayer

Dear HEAVENLY FATHER, I come to you in THE NAME OF JESUS CHRIST to ask for your help and guidance at this time. I want to thank you for loving me enough to die for me so that I might have your life. I thank you for continuing to teach me to understand your love. I thank you for forgiving me for holding unforgiveness against others, you and myself. I do forgive these people (....) freely from my heart, I also forgive myself in like manner. I will forgive all others as THE HOLY SPIRIT reminds me of them. I repent of using the fear of loosing my love to dominate others, to get them to do what I want them to. I repent of manipulating others. I repent of rejecting others, especially those in my family, and causing them to feel the loss of love. I repent of loving the admiration of the world and for doing crazy things to try to get love. I repent of not loving myself properly as one of your creations. I have loved myself and others in the phileo sense and not in an unselfish and Godly way. I let go of all resentment and bitterness which I have held against people for rejecting me. I break the curse of incest, bastard and occult on me and my family line. As I go through deliverance, help me to understand how these demons have worked me in the past and how I have used them to work on others. Help me to make amends where you tell me to. Help me to understand more about your kind of love and help me see how to work this love into my life.

List Of Demons

Lying	Unstable	Fear	Fighting
Fear of loss of love	Unlovable	Pouting	Violent
Fear of being loved	Sly	Cursing	Victim
Demonic manipulation	Cunning	Berating	Alcohol
Drugs	Torment	Suicide	Morbid
Coldhearted	Beating	Lonely	Witchcraft
Unfeeling	Guilt	Inferiority	Uncalled for laughter
Unstable	Destruction	Timid	Silly
Loveless	Jezebel	Shy	Foolishness
Don't Care	Ahab	Suspicious	Pride

ORGANS AND SYSTEMS OF BODY

The following are systems of the body which can be used in deliverance by calling out demons in each organ or system:

1. ORGANS
2. NEUROLOGIC
3. ENDOCRINE
4. REPRODUCTIVE
5. HEMATOLOGIC
6. CARDIOVASCULAR
7. LYMPHATIC
8. PULMONARY
9. RENAL

10. UROLOGIC
11. DIGESTIVE
12. MUSCULOSKELETAL
13. INTEGUMENTARY
14. SUBSYSTEMS

REFERENCES

It is recommended that you purchase and study these books:

Eleven books written by Win Worley, Hegewisch Baptist Church, Highland, Indiana or WRW Publications, Lansing, IL. Most of the medical research was done by J.M. Haggard, (Doctor Veterinarian Medicine).

Healing Through Deliverance - The Practical Ministry by Peter J. Horrobin, Sovereign World

The Hidden Agenda - A Critical View Of Alternative Medical Therapies by David and Sharon Sneed, Thomas Nelson Publishers

Curses and Diseases Listed in Deuteronomy 28:16-68 by Dr. Bill Null, Salina, KS, unpublished

I strongly recommend that everyone purchase these two books and apply them to their lives:

A More Excellent Way - I Corinthians 12:31 - A Teaching on the Spiritual Roots of Disease - The Ministry of Pastor Henry Wright, Pleasant Valley Publications, A Division of Pleasant Valley Church, Thomaston, GA

The Continuing Works of Christ - II Corinthians 5:17 by Art Mathias, Wellspring Ministries of Alaska, Anchorage

SECTION 7 - CHANGE YOUR BRAIN CHANGE YOUR LIFE

CONTENTS
1. PREFACE
2. FIVE OF THE BRAIN SYSTEMS
3. PROBLEMS IN THE DEEP LIMBIC SYSTEM
    1. Deep Limbic Checklist
4. PROBLEMS IN THE BASAL GANGLIA SYSTEM
    1. Basal Ganglia Checklist
5. PROBLEMS WITH THE PREFRONTAL CORTEX
    1. Prefrontal Cortex Checklist
6. PROBLEMS IN THE CINGULATE SYSTEM
    1. Cingulate System Checklist
7. PROBLEMS - DOMINANT (USUALLY LEFT) TEMPORAL LOBE
8. PROBLEMS - NONDOMINANT (USUALLY RIGHT) TEMPORAL LOBE
9. PROBLEMS WITH EITHER OR BOTH TEMPORAL LOBES
    1. Temporal Lobe Checklist
10. THE DARK SIDE
11. BRAIN POLLUTION
12. THE MISSING LINKS
13. HELP!
    1. Relationships
    2. Work
    3. Significant Negative Effects
14. MEDICATIONS
15. REFERENCE

PREFACE

The author, Daniel G. Amen, M.D., went to medical school at Oral Roberts University in Tulsa, Oklahoma. **That Christian school was established to combine the practice of medicine with the practice of prayer for divine healing in the Name of Jesus Christ.**

This book was reviewed to see how it could be used for emotional and physical healing using the practice of Christian deliverance. Healing and deliverance go hand-in-hand. In many cases, the names of symptoms are names of demons. The comments highlighted were added by me.

I highly recommend it for purchase to use as a Christian reference to better understand how to minister to those who have these problems.

FIVE OF THE BRAIN SYSTEMS

The following are five of the brain systems that are most intimately involved with our behavior; listed are some key problems of each system:

Deep Limbic System: moodiness, negativity.
Basal Ganglia: fearfulness, conflict avoidance, nervousness, anxiety, panic.

Prefrontal Cortex: bad decisions, attention span.
Cingulate (sing-u-lat): rigidity, overfocused, getting stuck, worry.
Temporal Lobes: temper flare-ups, rapid mood shifts.

Possible Diagnoses: head trauma, dementia, strokes, seizures, the impact of drug abuse on brain function, and aggressive behavior and mood disorders that are not typical or responsive.

Pseudodementia (depression masquerading as dementia) can cause a person to appear demented **(i.e., having a demon). Dementia can be described variously as madness, insanity, mad, out of one's mind, impairment or loss of mental powers, melancholia, withdrawal, hallucinations, delusions, mental unsoundness, devoid of reason, etc. (Webster's New Twentieth Century Dictionary Unabridged).** The same problems often run in families **(i.e., ancestral curses)**.

PROBLEMS IN THE DEEP LIMBIC SYSTEM

Moodiness, irritability; depression; increased negative thinking; negative perception of events; decreased motivation; flood of negative emotions; appetite and sleep problems; decreased or increased sexual responsiveness; and social isolation.

Deep Limbic Checklist

Feelings of sadness; moodiness; negativity; low energy; irritability; decreased interest in others; feelings of hopelessness about the future; feelings of helplessness or powerlessness; feeling dissatisfied or bored; excessive guilt; suicidal feelings; crying; lowered interest in things usually considered fun; sleep changes (too much or too little); appetite changes (too much or too little); low self-esteem; decreased interest in sex; negative sensitivity to smells / odors; forgetfulness; and poor concentration.

PROBLEMS WITH THE BASAL GANGLIA SYSTEM

Anxiety, nervousness; panic attacks; physical sensations of anxiety; tendency to predict the worst; conflict avoidance; Tourette's syndrometics; muscle tension, soreness; tremors; fine motor problems; headaches; and low / excessive motivation.

Basal Ganglia Checklist

Feelings of nervousness or anxiety; panic attacks; symptoms of heightened muscle tension (headaches, sore muscles, hand tremor); periods of heart pounding, rapid heart rate or chest pain; periods of trouble breathing or feeling smothered; periods of feeling dizzy, faint or unsteady on your feet; periods of nausea or abdominal upset; periods of sweating, hot or cold flashes, cold hands; tendency to predict the worst; fear of dying or doing something crazy; avoidance of public places for fear of having an anxiety attack; conflict avoidance; excessive fear of being judged or scrutinized by others; persistent phobias; low motivation; excessive motivation; tics; poor handwriting; quick startle reaction; tendency to freeze in anxiety-provoking situations; excessive worry about what others think; shyness or timidity; and low threshold of embarrassment.

PROBLEMS WITH THE PREFRONTAL CORTEX

Short attention span; distractibility; lack of perseverance; impulse control problems; hyperactivity; chronic lateness; poor time management; disorganization; procrastination; unavailability of emotions; misperceptions; poor judgment; trouble learning from experience; short-term memory problems; and social and test anxiety.

Prefrontal Cortex Checklist

Inability to give close attention to details or avoid careless mistakes; trouble sustaining attention in routine situations (homework, chores, paperwork, etc.); trouble listening; inability to finish things, poor follow-through; poor organization of time or space; distractibility; poor planning skills; lack of clear goals or forward thinking; difficulty expressing feelings; difficulty expressing empathy for others; excessive daydreaming; boredom; apathy of lack of motivation; lethargy; a feeling of spaciness or being "in a fog"; restlessness or trouble sitting still; difficulty remaining seated in situations where remaining seated is expected; conflict seeking; talking too much or too little; blurting out of answers before questions have been completed; difficulty awaiting turn; interruption of or intrusion on others (e.g., butting into conversations or games); impulsivity (saying or doing things without thinking first); and trouble learning from experience; tendency to make repetitive mistakes.

PROBLEMS WITH THE CINGULATE SYSTEM

Worrying; holding on to hurts from the past; getting stuck on thoughts (obsessions); getting stuck on behaviors (compulsions); oppositional behavior; argumentativeness; uncooperativeness, tendency to say no automatically; addictive behaviors (alcohol or drug abuse, eating disorders); chronic pain; cognitive inflexibility; obsessive-compulsive disorder (OCD); OCD spectrum disorders; eating disorders; and road rage.

Cingulate System Checklist

Excessive or senseless worrying; being upset when things do not go your way; being upset when things are out of place; tendency to be oppositional or argumentative; tendency to have repetitive negative thoughts; tendency toward compulsive behaviors; intense dislike of change; tendency to hold grudges; trouble shifting attention from subject to subject; trouble shifting behavior from task to task; difficulties seeing options in situations; tendency to hold on to own opinion and not listen to others; tendency to get locked into a course of action, whether or not it is good; being very upset unless things are done a certain way; perception by others that you worry too much; tendency to say no without first thinking about question; and tendency to predict negative outcomes.

PROBLEMS - DOMINANT (USUALLY LEFT) TEMPORAL LOBE

Aggression, internally or externally directed; dark or violent thoughts; sensitivity to slights, mild paranoia; word-finding problems; auditory processing problems; reading difficulties; and emotional instability.

PROBLEMS - NONDOMINANT (USUALLY RIGHT) TEMPORAL LOBE

Difficulty recognizing facial expression; difficulty decoding vocal intonation; and implicated in social-skill struggles.

PROBLEMS WITH EITHER OR BOTH TEMPORAL LOBES

Memory problems, amnesia; headaches or abdominal pain without a clear explanation; anxiety or fear for no particular reason; abnormal sensory perceptions, visual or auditory distortions; feeling of deja vu (feelings of being somewhere you have never been) or jamais vu (not recalling a familiar place or person); periods of spaciness or confusion; religious or moral preoccupation; hypergraphia, excessive writing; and seizures.

Temporal Lobe Checklist

Short fuse or periods of extreme irritability; periods of rage with little provocation; frequent misinterpretation of comments as negative when they are not; irritability that ends to build, then explodes, then recedes; person often feels tired after a rage; periods of spaciness or confusion; periods of panic and/or fear for no specific reason; visual or auditory changes, such as seeing shadows or hearing muffled sounds; frequent periods of deja vu or jamais vu; sensitivity or mild paranoia; headaches or abdominal pain of uncertain origin; history of a head injury or family history of violence or explosiveness; dark thoughts, such as suicidal or homicidal thoughts; periods of forgetfulness; memory problems; reading comprehension problems; and preoccupation with moral or religious ideas.

THE DARK SIDE

The violent or aggressive person may have trouble thinking, getting stuck on thoughts, have a short fuse or have anxiety and moodiness.

BRAIN POLLUTION

Caffeine: Heavy daily usage (more than three cups of coffee a day) is a problem and needs to be stopped in order to maintain a healthy brain.
Nicotine: If you want to have full access to your brain, don't smoke.

THE MISSING LINKS

1. Using drugs, especially alcohol, methamphetamines, cocaine, phencyclidine, and anabolic steroids, may directly elicit aggressive behavior.
2. Drug or alcohol usage may impair executive function and increase the likelihood of aggression.
3. Drugs or alcohol may be used as self-medication for underlying brain problems involved in aggression.
4. Cingulate problems, in conjunction with prefrontal cortex and temporal lobe problems, can exacerbate addictions and potentially violent situations.
5. Drug or alcohol usage may be involved in poor decision-making processes or provocative behaviors that put a person in high-risk situations.

HELP!
Relationships

1. Depression can cause a person to feel distant, uninterested in sex, irritable, unfocused, tired and negative. Unless the partners understand this disorder, they often have severe

relational problems. People who suffer from depression have divorce rate six times higher than those who are not depressed.

2. Anxiety causes sufferers to feel tense, uptight, physically ill and dependent, and to avoid conflict. Partners often misinterpret the anxiety as physical symptoms as complaining or whining and do not take seriously the level of suffering.

3. Obsessive or overfocus tendencies, as we have seen, cause rigid thinking styles, oppositional or argumentative behavior, holding on to grudges and chronic stress in relationships. Seeking help is essential to establishing a new ability to relate effectively.

4. Prefrontal cortex problems, such as ADD, often sabotage relationships because of the impulsive, restless and distractible behavior involved. Without help there is a high degree of relational and family turmoil.

5. Temporal lobe problems may be associated with frequent attacks of rage, angry outbursts. mood swings, hearing things wrong and low frustration tolerance. I have seen these problems ruin otherwise good relationships.

Work

1. Depression can cause people at work to be negative, unfocused, tired and unmotivated, and to take things too personally or the wrong way. Such employees may negatively affect others' morale and unknowingly skew everyone's perceptions at work so they see positive things in a bad light. Depressed people have more sick days than people without depression.

2. People with anxiety are often tense, physically sick and conflict-avoidant. Their level of anxiety often cause them to be dependent and require too much supervision. Their anxiety tends to be contagious and those around them may also begin predicting negative outcomes to situations. They can negatively affect a work group and tend to be fearful rather than hopeful.

3. Obsessive or overfocus tendencies cause rigid thinking styles, and employers or employees tend to be more irritable, oppositional or argumentative. They often hold grudges and can be unforgiving, causing long-term workplace problems.

4. Prefrontal cortex problems, such as ADD, cause many problems at work, including chronic lateness, inefficiency, missing deadlines, impulsive decision making and conflict-seeking behavior.

5. Temporal lobe problems often affect work. I am willing to bet that most workplace violence is associated with temporal lobe disorders. More commonly, temporal lobe problems are manifested at work by mood swings or unpredictable behavior, low frustration tolerance, misperceptions, auditory processing problems and memory problems. The anger, misperceptions, and mild paranoia can wreak havoc in a work group.

Significant Negative Effects

1. Depression (limbic system) clouds a sense of accomplishment (even with incredible accomplishment) and causes intense sadness and internal pain. Depression is not the absence of feeling but rather the presence of painful feelings. Depression is one of the most common precursors to drug abuse and suicide. Depression often compromises immune system function, leaving people more prone to illness.

2. The tension and panic associated with anxiety (often a result of basal ganglia problems) can feel like torture. I have known many patients with panic attacks who become suicidal in hope of escaping their fear. Anxiety is often associated with physical tension and an increase in illness. Many anxious people self-medicate by drinking alcohol, taking drugs, overeating, engaging in inappropriate sex and other potentially addictive behaviors.

3. Overfocus (cingulate) issues cause repetitive thoughts and worries that are often self-medicated with drugs or alcohol. Internal torture by constant worry is common. When someone says one negative thing, they may hear it in their minds five hundred times. They cannot get away from negative thoughts.

4. People with prefrontal cortex issues, such as ADD, often feel a tremendous sense of underachievement, repetitive failure, and low self-esteem. People with prefrontal cortex issues may use internal problems for self-stimulation and be chronically upset. The stress associated with these problems is often accompanied by increased illness.

5. Temporal lobe problems can wreak internal havoc. The internal violent mood swings and thoughts often torment the soul. Unpredictable behavior, low frustration tolerance, misperceptions, and memory problems are often associated with an internal sense of damage. Anger often alienates others and loneliness is common.

MEDICATIONS

Stimulants: Adderall, Ritalin, Dexedrine, Dextrostat, Desoxyn, Cylert.
Antidepressants: Norpramin, Tofranil, Wellbutrin, Elavil, Pamelor, Sinequan, Anafranil.
Antiobessives: Prozac, Anafranil, Zoloft, Paxil, Luvox, Effexor, Remeron, Serzone.
Anticonvulsants: Tegretol, Depakene, Depakote, Neurontin, Lamictal, Dilantin.
Blood Pressure: Catapres, Tenex, Inderal.

REFERENCE

I strongly recommend that everyone purchase the book and apply it to their life:
Change Your Brain - Change Your Life, The Breakthrough Program for Conquering Anxiety, Depression, Obsessiveness, Anger, and Impulsiveness by Daniel G. Amen, M.D.

SECTION 8 - SPIRITUAL ROOTS OF DISEASE

CONTENTS
1. DISEASES WITH NO KNOWN MEDICAL CURE
2. SPIRITUAL BLOCKS TO HEALING
3. MASTURBATION, PROSTATE CANCER AND PROSTATITIS
4. FEAR, ANXIETY AND STRESS
5. THE CONTINUING WORKS OF CHRIST
    1. Hypothalamus
    2. Cardiovascular System
    3. Hypertension
    4. Stroke And Aneurysm
    5. Disturbances Of Heart Rhythm
    6. Muscles And Tension Headaches
    7. Muscle Contraction Backache
    8. Rheumatoid Arthritis
    9. Pulmonary System
    10. Immune System
    11. Gastrointestinal System
    12. Genital Urinary System
    13. Skin
    14. Endocrine System
6. REFERENCES

DISEASES WITH NO KNOWN MEDICAL CURE

Pastor Henry Wright says that about 80% of all diseases have no known medical cure. They are psychosomatic, including both psychological and biological diseases. If this is the diagnosis, then try deliverance to rid the person of evil spirits. We know that deliverance from demonic bondage often cures medical or mental problems that have "no known medical cure" in the literature. The person has a spiritual root to the disease or ailment which must be dealt with before the person can be healed.

SPIRITUAL BLOCKS TO HEALING

Prayer may not have any effect if some are just not saved, sometimes the sickness is unto death, and our allotted time in life is fulfilled. 80% of all diseases are spiritually rooted which means that there is a sin behind the disease:

1. Unforgiveness
2. Ignorance Or Lack Of Knowledge
3. No Relationship With God According To Knowledge
4. Personal And Family Sins
5. Not Having Faith In God
6. The Need To See A Miracle
7. Looking For Signs And Wonders
8. Expect God To Heal On One's Own Terms
9. Looking To Man Rather Than God

10. Not Being Honest And Transparent
11. Flagrant Sin Or Habitual Sin
12. Robbing God In Tithes And Offerings
13. Sin Of Our Parents
14. Looking To Symptoms And Not To The Healer
15. Letting Fear Enter Your Heart
16. Failure To Get Away In Prayer And Fasting
17. Improper Care Of The Body
18. Not Discerning The Lord's Body
19. Touching God's Anointed Leaders
20. Immoderate Eating
21. Pure Unbelief
22. Failing To Keep Our Life Filled Up With God
23. Not Resisting The Enemy
24. Just Giving Up
25. Looking For Repeated Healings Instead Of Divine Health
26. Rejecting Healing In The Atonement As Part Of The Covenant For Today
27. Trying To Bypass The Penalty Of The Curse
28. Murmuring And Complaining
29. Hating And Not Obeying Instruction

MASTURBATION, PROSTATE CANCER AND PROSTATITIS

<u>Masturbation</u> can come out of tension and strife leading to uncleanness, guilt and condemnation. <u>Prostate cancer</u> can come out of anger, guilt, self-hatred and self-bitterness. Hate leads to death. When a <u>tumor</u> does not become malignant, it involves bitterness against one's self. When a tumor becomes malignant, it involves bitterness against others. <u>Prostatitis</u> can come from fear, anxiety, self-rejection, self-hatred and guilt.

FEAR, ANXIETY AND STRESS

Many diseases come out of **fear, anxiety and stress**. The family of fear can include many things that a person is afraid of such as the 210 **phobias** recognized by psychiatrists. Fears can include the families of **jealousy, sensitiveness, persecution, paranoia, worry**, and many other spirits.

THE CONTINUING WORKS OF CHRIST
Hypothalamus

The hypothalamus lies just above the pituitary, the main endocrine gland. When the hypothalamus detects certain changes in the body, it releases chemicals called regulating factors that stimulate or inhibit the anterior pituitary gland. The anterior pituitary then releases or holds back hormones that regulate carbohydrates, fats, proteins, certain ions and sexual functions.

1. It controls and integrates the autonomic nervous system, which stimulates muscles, regulates the rate of contraction of cardiac muscle and controls the secretion of many

glands. Through the autonomic nervous system, the hypothalamus is the main regulator of body activities. It regulates heart rate, movement of food through the digestive track and contraction of the urinary bladder.

2. It is involved in the reception of sensory impulses of the fasera.

3. It is the principle intermediary between the nervous system and the endocrine system, the two major control systems of the body.

4. It is the center for the mind over body phenomena. When the Cerebral Cortex interrupts strong emotions, it often sends impulses along tracks that connect the cortex with the hypothalamus. The Hypothalamus then directs impulses by the autonomic nervous system and also releases chemicals that stimulate the interior pituitary gland. The result can be a wide range of changes in body activity. For instance, panic impulses leave the hypothalamus to stimulate the heart to beat faster. Likewise, continued psychological stress can produce long term abnormalities and body function that result in serious illness. These are the so-called psychosomatic disorders and psychosomatic disorders are real.

5. It is associated with feelings of rage and aggression.

6. It controls normal body temperature. Certain cells of the hypothalamus serve as a thermostat.

7. It regulates food intake through two sensors. It contains a thirst center. It is one of the centers that maintains the waking state and sleep patterns. This one gland is the facilitator of something called the Limbic System.

I have just quoted from a medical textbook that tells us that our thoughts and emotions can dramatically effect our health. **The hypothalamus gland is the facilitator and the originator of the following life circumstances, all expressions of fear, anxiety, stress, tension, panic, panic attacks, phobia, rage, anger and aggression are released and facilitated by this one gland. It only responds to you emotionally and spiritually.** The hypothalamus is called the **brain** of the endocrine system, but it is a gland. **It is a responder to thought.** It is a responder to the environment of your life. It only will produce what is happening deep within the recesses of your soul and your spirit.

The endocrine system includes 9 glands that secrete over 23 different hormones and neurotransmitters. Our thoughts and emotions control the secretions from these glands. The over or under secretion of these hormones or neurotransmitters causes most of our diseases.

One of the major emotions that we deal with is anxiety and stress. The Biblical definition of anxiety is fear. Fear is equated in scripture with unbelief or faithlessness. Fear is the opposite of faith. If we are in fear, we are not in faith. If we are in faith, we cannot be in fear. The above textbook teaches that the following organs are targets for anxiety and stress. The words in bold are from the textbook, the non-bold words are my comment.

Cardiovascular System

Coronary Artery Disease: The Bible says, **In the last days men's hearts shall fail them because of fear** (Luke 21:26).

Hypertension

High Blood Pressure: Fear and anxiety is the root for high blood pressure. The Bible ad medical science agree. What we teach is not opposed to medical science. In fact, what I see in the Bible only proves medical science and medical science only proves the Bible.

Stroke And Aneurysm

Strokes and Aneurysms are the result of rage and anger, but behind the rage and anger is also fear. Do you know why people go into rage and anger? First of all, they have a root of bitterness. They are really afraid to deal with issues. Rather than being confronted on an issue and having to deal with it, they just blow up because that is their defensive mechanism. They don't want to be confronted on an issue because they are afraid of men and they are afraid of rejection.

Disturbances Of Heart Rhythm

Rhythmic Problems: Irregular heart beat and Mitral Valve Prolapse are the result of anxiety and stress.

Muscles And Tension Headaches

We rub the back of our necks when we are under stress and tension to relieve the pain. Why not turn to God and deal with the fear and anxiety?

Muscle Contraction Backache

Again anxiety and stress is the issue. I have witnessed many healings when people have repented for the lack of faith in God and then learned to trust Him.

Rheumatoid Arthritis

There is a direct relationship between the tremendous stress of self-hatred and all autoimmune diseases. The person is **afraid of themselves.** They just don't want to face themselves. Out of that comes **self-hatred,** out of that comes **guilt,** out of that comes **conflict** that causes the white corpuscles to attack the connective material of the bones, eat at it and produce rheumatoid arthritis.

Pulmonary System

Asthma and Hay Fever: Johns Hopkins University is now teaching that Hay Fever and Asthma are not caused by air born allergens. It has nothing to do with breathing, dander, dust, pollen, etc. Anxiety and fear cause it. It can be inherited, but it's coming out of **deep-rooted anxiety and fear.** I have proved this many times over.

Immune System

Immunosuppression or Immune Deficiency and Autoimmune Disease: Over secretion of cortisol and catecholamines destroy the immune system, and the result is autoimmune diseases. The Hypothalamus controls over 23 hormones including these two. Autoimmune diseases occur when the white corpuscles attack living flesh and destroy it. **Lupus, Crones, Diabetes, Rheumatoid Arthritis and MS are examples.**

We have learned that the body attacks the body as a person attacks themselves spiritually in self-rejection, self-hatred, and self-bitterness. The body agrees with the mind and starts attacking itself. That is a high price to pay for not loving yourself.

Gastrointestinal System

Ulcers: For years the medical community believed that stress and anxiety caused an irritation in the stomach, which eventually caused the ulceration. Recently they have begun to prescribe antibiotics and are telling us that a bacteria or virus causes ulcers.

People who have ulcers also have compromised immune systems because of the anxiety and stress. When you have a compromised immune system, you don't have the ability to defeat bacteria and viruses. The fear and anxiety come first and the bacteria and viruses show up after the immune system is compromised.

There are a number of gastrointestinal problems that are caused by anxiety and stress. They include **Irritable Bowel Syndrome (IBS), diarrhea, nausea, vomiting and ulcerated colitis.**

Every single malfunction in the gastrointestinal tract is caused by anxiety and stress. The peace of God in your heart regarding issues in your life is the cure with the exception of Crones disease, which is an autoimmune disease.

Genital Urinary System

Diuresis, Impotence and Frigidity are caused by anxiety and fear.

Skin

Eczema, Acne and Dermatitis: Adolescent acne is caused by fear coming from peer pressure. It is not a genetic or biologic problem by itself, but in most cases the kids are afraid of other kids. That level of fear and anxiety triggers increased histamine secretion. It also increases white corpuscle activity in the epidermis thus causing acne.

Endocrine System

Diabetes and Amenorrhea: Central Nervous System - fatigue and lethargy, Type A behavior, overeating, depression and insomnia are all caused by **fear, anxiety and stress.**

REFERENCES

I strongly recommend that everyone purchase these two books and apply them to their lives:

A More Excellent Way - I Corinthians 12:31 - A Teaching on the Spiritual Roots of Disease - The Ministry of Pastor Henry Wright, Pleasant Valley Publications, A Division of Pleasant Valley Church, Thomaston, GA

The Continuing Works of Christ - II Corinthians 5:17 by Art Mathias, Wellspring Ministries of Alaska, Anchorage

SECTION 9 - GODLY PEOPLE STRICKEN BEFORE THEIR TIME

CONTENTS
1. SCRIPTURE
2. LETTER OF OCTOBER 27, 1991
3. REPLIES TO LETTER
4. PRAYERS FOR US
5. OUR MINISTRY
6. FUTURE FOR CHRISTIANS
7. GENERAL COMMENTS
8. ANSWERS TO QUESTIONS
9. GOD IN CONTROL
10. SOVEREIGNTY OF GOD
11. TRIALS AND TESTINGS
12. FAITH OF THE SAINTS
13. CHRISTIAN SCOREBOARD
14. PRESENT CHURCH AGE
15. THIS WORLD
16. TEN THOUGHTS FOR YOU
17. CRUCIFIXION OF THE FLESH
18. SERVANTS OF GOD
19. DELIVERANCE WORKERS
20. APOSTLES SUFFERED
21. PRIDE, EGO AND VANITY
22. CONFUSION OF MIND
23. TESTIMONIES OF OTHERS
24. STANDING WITH EACH OTHER
25. HUSBANDS RESPONSIBILITY
26. HUSBAND'S ASKING WIVE'S FORGIVENESS
27. CREDIT TO OTHERS
28. PRAYERS BY GROUP

LIST OF DEMONS
Diseases Listed In Deuteronomy 28:16-68 By Dr. Bill Null

SCRIPTURE
Gen. 3:15 It shall bruise thy head, and thou shalt bruise his heel.
Deut. 27 Curses are pronounced.
Deut. 28 Blessings for obedience and curses for disobedience.
Ester 2:1-4, 8-9, 12-17 And she obtained grace and favour in his sight.
Book of Job - Disaster falls into our lives because God is testing our faith.
Isa. 53:4-5 Our peace was upon him; and with his stripes we are healed.
Isa. 62:1-4 No more be Forsaken; neither shall thy land any more be desolate.
Matt. 9:22 Daughter be of good comfort; thy faith hath made thee whole.
Matt. 13:21 When tribulation or persecution ariseth, by and by he is offended.

Luke 13:1-5 Think ye that they were sinners above all men that dwelt in Jer.?
Luke 22:31-32 Satan hath desired to have you, that he may sift you as wheat.
John 14:16 And I will pray the Father, and he shall give you another Comforter.
John 16:33 In the world ye shall have tribulation; but be of good cheer.
Acts 3:6 In the name of Jesus Christ of Nazareth rise up and walk.
Acts 14:7-10 Stedfastly beholding him, perceiving he had faith to be healed.
Rom. 5:3 We glory in tribulations; knowing that tribulation worketh patience.
Rom. 8:28 And we know that all things work together for good to them that love.
Rom. 8:35 Tribulation, distress, persecution, famine, nakedness, peril, sword?
Rom. 12:12 Patient in tribulation; continuing instant in prayer.
I Cor. 8:2 And if any man think that he knoweth any thing, he knoweth nothing.
I Cor. 13:12 For now we see through a glass darkly; now I know in part.
II Cor. 1:4 Comforteth us in all our tribulation; we may be able to comfort.
Eph. 2:8 For by grace are ye saved through faith; it is the gift of God.
Eph. 4:11-13 Till we all come unto the measure of the stature of the fullness.
Phil. 4:19 But my God shall supply all your need according to his riches.
Col. 1:27 Which is Christ in you, the hope of glory.
I Thes. 3:4 We told you before that we should suffer tribulation.
I Thes. 5:18 In everything give thanks: for this is the will of God in Christ.
I Tim. 5:23 For thy stomach's sake and thine often infirmities.
II Tim. 2:15 Shew thyself approved unto God, rightly dividing Word of Truth.
II Tim. 3:14 Continue in the things which thou has learned and been assured of.
II Tim. 4:20 But Trophimus have I left at Miletum sick.
Heb. 2:8 But now we see not yet all things put under him.
Heb. 11 What faith is; without faith we cannot please God.
James 5:20 Shall save a soul from death, and shall hide a multitude of sins.
I Peter 2:24 Should live unto righteousness: by whose stripes ye were healed.
I Peter 4:1-2 Christ suffered for us in the flesh, arm yourselves likewise.
Rev. 2:10 Be thou faithful unto death, and I will give thee a crown of life.
Rev. 3:14-21 As many as I love, I rebuke and chasten: be zealous therefore.

LETTER OF OCTOBER 27, 1991

As you know, Earline and I have been in the deliverance ministry for about fifteen years. We have worked with thousands of Christians in the area of healing and deliverance.

Recently, Earline was stricken with kidney failure. Otherwise, she is in fine shape for a woman who is fifty-nine years old.

We have known personally, or have known of men and women of God who have been stricken physically with infirmities. They may have even died before becoming seventy years old. These were people that we felt really tried to follow God and were doing a fine work in His Vineyard. They were also people that believed in the Whole Word of God.

Generally speaking, the ministry teaches the blessings of God and not the justice of God. We get the "bless-me club" personality. Generally speaking, the ministry does not teach about what Christians will go through as they follow Christ and obey His Word. The impression is "Once I become a Christian, I will have no more problems." This seems to be an area of the Bible that is primarily ignored. Many times Christians are taught this philosophy; then when it doesn't work, they leave the church.

My question to you is **Why are these Godly people stricken before their time of seventy years?** In other words, what should we as Christians expect in the battle for the Lord? If we are living a Godly life, should we expect to go through life without having any mental, physical, spiritual or material problems? What does the Bible teach about the lives of Christians? A good example is Paul. **With the Love of Christ, Gene and Earline**

REPLIES TO LETTER

We received replies from the following people to whom we are very grateful: Jo Anne Nystrom, Glen and Erma Miller, Dorthy and Harlan Deem, Ted Haggard, Edwin Edgerton, Frank Hammond, Lorraine A. Kupper, Buz Milosh, Dennis Mulder, Blanche Reynolds, Linda Sutter, Al Dagger, Norman Parish, Martin and Janice Turnbull, and Ann Pigg. We kept the letters and records of telephone conversations. It was quite an effort for those to try to answer our difficult questions. **Thank you for your love and concern!**

PRAYERS FOR US

We want to express our heartfelt thanks for those who have prayed and interceded for us through the years. It is wonderful to hear that we are being prayed for our well being by those who love us and have compassion on us. **Only God knows how your prayers may have helped to sustain us.**

OUR MINISTRY

We have now been in the deliverance ministry for about twenty years. It has been about five years since Earline had her kidney failure. God has seen us through all the difficulties that we have faced in our lifetimes. We have seen God do many wonderful things around the world using us as his servants. Even though we have probably cast out thousands of demons, Satan does not leave us alone. In fact, he probably attacks those who are very active even more because they are a greater threat to his kingdom.

FUTURE FOR CHRISTIANS

The wind may blow in your face to stop your progress now, but may be behind you in the future after you have worked your way through the problem. Move forward with the Lord. Our God is faithful and we must relinquish control to Him. Praise breaks certain bondages put on us by Satan. By all means repent; it is a way of life. We are comforted by the Word of God; standfast and trust in Jesus. Keep on ministering by faith and depend in the leadership of the Holy Spirit. God loves us and cares about us; He has all power and authority to direct our lives.

GENERAL COMMENTS

Earline and I have discussed, thought and prayed about this subject, both before and after Earline's failure of her kidneys, a considerable amount of time. There are many lessons to be learned by us and other Christians in this difficult area. The communications of others helped us to understand what we were going through. It is a real blessing to see what others go through in real life. It is an untruth to tell the Christian world that you, and your family, business and ministry have no problems, and that you are perfect just like Jesus Christ. We are still praying for answers for ourselves and for others. When Earline was in the hospital initially, we read the Book of Job seeking answers. Pay attention to what Job says as well as his so-called comforters.

This lesson was really written by others. We only compiled and edited it so that it could apply to the Body of Christ. It will give you a lot to think about as you ponder your life and the thoughts contained herein. This may be the most profound lesson that we have taught.

ANSWERS TO QUESTIONS

Do you believe that you have all of the answers to the problems we face here on earth? Are you living a perfect life in complete accord with the Bible? We don't believe that anyone has a complete understanding of the Bible. Everyone has problems; if you don't now, you will later. This includes those in the ministry and their families. God is sovereign and we can't change that fact of life. Rest assured that God's Word is a wonderful source of strength and comfort to suffering, hurting, poor people, as well as to those who are wealthy, all around the world. If we want life, we must keep His Commandments. We are all aware that if there was an easy answer, everyone would already know. Volumes could be written to properly answer the question raised, even in a general sense. Word of Wisdom, Word of Knowledge and Discerning of Spirits could be God's way of answering specifically for each of us. Inwardly, there might be the sins of the fathers or some break in Job's hedge; outwardly, there might be an onslaught from some coven or occult source that is getting through; and these are just a few possibilities. There are some valid truths coming from the "bless-me club" but they need to be balanced: God's love balanced by God's justice. There are no pat answers.

GOD IN CONTROL

It may be God's purpose, not some other cause. What lessons can be learned? God can turn it around eventually; the future is in his hands. God understands and is rooting for us. We accept God's dealings with us and resist the Devil. Do not doubt God, who knows what we need. Jesus was not spared from suffering and has compassion on us. He gives us grace and sense to learn; God is teaching us. It may be for our good - for life and death situations. God can do whatever he chooses for greater glory and purpose. Jesus intercedes for us while we are going through the fire. Our peace comes when we rely on Jesus, even if it means that we die.

Satan is not in control. Satan will retaliate; we get wounded. There are occult attacks by witches and warlocks. We must know our enemies. There are curses, hexes and spells that are inherited, as well as received in the nasty now and now. Satan can not kill our spirits or souls, even if he is able to kill our bodies.

What about repressed feelings, used to being blessed, many causes of diseases and judgmental? We are susceptible, sickness is common, not immune to suffering and there are hindrances which may be mysterious or harmful. Do not get impatient. Control your emotions; we can not control the events. Keep our spirits clean before God. Do not go on a guilt trip. It may be a simple lesson of trusting, not just an exercise of faith. We are not immune to attack. It rains on the just and unjust. How do we respond to tragedy? We must have faith that all things work together for good. We will learn or not learn. Wait before God without doubting; die triumphantly. Sometimes it is nothing we do. Good comes out of our experiences. We are more understanding, compassionate and patient, not judging others. Our faith is joined with others. Have conviction that God heals and does recreative miracles.

SOVEREIGNTY OF GOD

God allotted seventy years to all humanity, not just believers, which is about the average age at death. Life may be lengthened or shortened; our body is not redeemed. It is subject to the curse of sin, old nature, physical defects and curse applies to body. Perfect health will come in Heaven. We must relate to the world, demonstrate our faith, believe in redemption and maintain hope. The environment effects our bodies. The dead are all right in God, sleep in Christ and awake to resurrection. Walk by faith; don't worry about tomorrow. God meets our basic needs, not our wants. Food, clothing and shelter are blessings by God's grace. Our bodies are subject to failure. Death has its way with all flesh; God can intervene if He chooses. Pray for God's Perfect Will in our lives. Have an overcoming attitude and draw close to God. There is more to life than just having perfect health. God wants to cleanse us from sin, get our attention and test us to strengthen our faith. Sickness is not immoral and will be in the Millennium. Our spirit and soul are redeemed; our body is not resurrected. Sometimes we may recover from sickness through prayer. It is difficult in dealing with God; his ways are not our ways. Acknowledgment of reality of life is faith. Age brings susceptibility to disease and death.

TRIALS AND TESTINGS

Lord, what do you want us to learn from our trials and testings? Certainly the Bible nowhere promises that Christians will go through life without problems. In fact, a careful reading of the Bible indicates that Christians will face many difficulties and trials. There are at least two biblical reasons as to why Christians suffer. One of them has to do with the fact that we are a fallen human race. The effects of sin, including illness, will come to Christians as well as non-Christian people. The fact that we suffer physical ailments, disease, etc. in some sense has little to do with the fact that we are Christian, it is simply the state of the fallen human race. It is the effects of sin in the world in which we live. Christians are not immune to those effects.

Secondly, there are times when disaster falls into our lives because God is testing our faith. He allows the Devil to have relatively free reign. While at the same time promising that He will never give us a burden too heavy to carry. An obvious example of that would be Job. The Book of Job teaches the above very clearly. Certainly the apostle Paul is a good example. He struggled with a thorn in the flesh all of his life. God chose not to remove that. We may never know the exact reason why, but God had a purpose in doing what He has done.

The Bible does not promise health, wealth and prosperity to all who believe in Christ. There are many Christians around the world who live in poverty. The Bible talks about taking up our cross and following Jesus Christ. In many parts of the world that cross is big and heavy, even to the extent of having to pay for faith, on occasion, with their lives. Those are the kinds of demands and sacrifices that the Scriptures place upon us as Christians. Without question we have been blessed in this country, living in relative freedom and prosperity. God has certainly not promised that we are immune from suffering. In fact, the scriptural teaching is that suffering brings with it many benefits. It is sometimes for those benefits that God allows us to go through these things.

Any Christian who thinks that they will not face tribulation or persecution in this life is sadly mistaken. Satan asked to sift Job and Peter, and he asks to sift the Body of Christ. Consider Job's attitude as well as that of his wife and friends.

FAITH OF THE SAINTS

It takes faith to believe in healing, deliverance and salvation; everything we receive from the Father comes through the Grace and Mercy of God and the Lord Jesus Christ with the interaction of the Holy Spirit. God answers prayer; things happen when we pray that don't happen when we don't pray. We interact with God through prayer. He acts according to His pre-determined will and purpose as we enter into communication with Him through silent and vocalized prayer.

The Lord Jesus Christ is a repository of virtue and righteous power, to meet our needs. It has already been bought and paid for at Calvary; the victory is assured. But it is not automatic without conflict or effort of mind, will, emotions, body strength and spiritual involvement. For instance: fasting, prayer, worship, praise, spiritual warfare, meditating, reading the Word, and submitting to God and one another with a determination to glorify God.

Consider the woman with the issue of blood. The virtue deposited in Jesus for this woman was released through her faith. It brought about the desired results of her being made whole. Consider the man at the gate beautiful. He wanted alms; he didn't appear to have faith for healing. Was anyone else interceding for him? He was caught off guard. Peter reached down and lifted him up. Peter's and John's faith had to be sufficient. God's purpose was to show Himself alive by doing the miraculous. Consider the man crippled from his mother's womb. He heard Paul speaking and Paul perceived he had faith to be healed. He needed to be healed and God purposed a revival.

CHRISTIAN SCOREBOARD

Christians are not any better or worse than anyone else. Job's friends knew that there must have been something wrong in his life, or why else would he have to suffer? Was there a tradition around Israel that the Galileans who suffered such things and the eighteen upon whom the tower of Siloam fell must have been worse sinners than others? But, this is not what Christ taught. We have not come to the measure of the stature of the fullness of Christ. But we have hope for the coming of Christ and his kingdom.

PRESENT CHURCH AGE

Do you believe that we are living in the Laodicean Church age? We think that we are so increased with goods, have need of nothing and we're so rich in the things of God. We don't realize how great our spiritual need really is. Are you prepared for physical death? Which group of the ten virgins do you belong to: those whose lamp is full or those whose lamp is empty? This is an hour that we must use wisely. Return to the simplicity of true devotion to Christ. We should be warriors for Christ.

Jesus has limited His visits to us in relationship to how obediently we provide Him that opportunity by being His Body for Him to fill with His Spirit and presence. As we yield to Him to be locally in fellowship with the other regenerate ecclesians, under His Headship proper and potent healing, etc. will be present in much greater fullness than we presently experience. The problem is we are churchgoing instead of being the local ecclesia and membered together with others by the Holy Spirit. The body is dismembered by locality, hence all the confusions, weaknesses, etc. If we ourselves don't live to enjoy the restored Ecclesia, we should be working on it for our posterity.

The church is full of people who are not well but they are praising God. He is in their midst polishing lively stones for His Tabernacle. God is building a rock house with narrow mortar joints which is pleasing to Him. Have peace in God; there is tribulation in the world.

THIS WORLD

Earth is earth, and does not become Heaven for anyone when one gets saved. In other words, God's perfect plan, the full manifestation of His Kingdom, is fully manifested in Heaven. When we get saved, a ray of his Kingdom shines through our hearts with the provision for that glow to provide healing, deliverance and other manifestations of His Will. Certainly, He wants all to be saved, healed, delivered, filled with His Spirit, etc. and that will all be complete in heaven. Here on earth we get a taste, but not the entire package.

We need to seek God, live saved, be filled with His Spirit, walk in His Fullness all that we possibly can, be as healed as we can, and walk in the greatest degree of freedom and deliverance as possible. But, until Jesus physically returns, we will struggle, suffer and strain for the full manifestation of redemption in our lives.

The Bible reveals God's perfect plan for us in Christ. Now, Christ is here only by His Spirit. Soon we shall see Him face to face. When that happens, all of His Plans for His People will be fulfilled.

So, what should we Christians expect in the battle for the Lord? Exactly that - a battle. As for victory; absolutely. As for timing; some now, the balance later.

Not having any problems is neither biblical nor practical. Living a Godly life means that a person can expect to live a Godly life. As for mental, physical, spiritual and material problems, those all come in varying degrees to all who live. Living a Godly life should minimize those problems and it certainly should open the door for the operation of the Holy Spirit which will help with the solution. But the problems will remain until Jesus settles the sin nature and Satan problem.

This is not defeatist. The powerful manifestation of the Holy Spirit does remarkable things in all of our lives. The authority of the Word of God can do powerful things. The enforcement of God's plans during this present age takes constant prayer, faith and involvement of the Holy Spirit. Hope is there and power is there; but so is the enemy and the world.

TEN THOUGHTS FOR YOU

Each person must seek for himself for a clear understanding of what he believes and how God works in each conflict. We that minister must be careful we do not add to the confusion and minister condemnation:

1. God can and does heal His people.
2. It is God's Will that we be healed for the Glory of God. Therefore, glorify God in your body.
3. There are only two things: blessings and cursings. You are either increasing or decreasing.
4. The pure Word of God without mixture.
5. The non-pure Word of God with mixture.
6. God's medicine for us is His Word for us.
7. God is love.
8. God loves you.
9. You are healed because you were healed by the Stripes of Jesus.
10. Bottom line is agape love in the Master's Service.

CRUCIFIXION OF THE FLESH

Fasting is a way to crucify the flesh and seek God. It is also a way to rid the body of toxins which can kill you. Depression will lower your resistance to disease. We are also required to follow other practices for Christians outlined in the Bible. Doctors may not make any difference if it is time to go and be with the Lord. Fasting may cause the burden to be lifted. Nutrition is a function of healing and a walk of health.

SERVANTS OF GOD

Many have served God faithfully and are in the call of God's purpose for their lives. They know the Gospel, have on the full armor of God, doing spiritual warfare, teaching and demonstrating biblical principles, and are faithful servants. Now the test is on; God removes the consciousness of His presence. The heavens are brass and you can't seem to rouse Him to work for you. You hear condemnation, failure, guilt, what have I done to deserve this, I thought God had a hedge around me and I was untouchable, and on and on until we become filled with despair. Our life is passing from us and there is nothing we can do except turn to the arm of flesh.

We search our souls, examine ourselves and try to find the key that will unlock the mystery of God's Grace. For all we are in Christ, all we do in the kingdom and our ability to stand in the face of the enemy is by God's Grace. The walk we walk is by God's grace: love, mercy, ministry, peace and health. God chose us in trespasses and sin, and seated us in Christ Jesus. He has given us a walk worthy of that Name and armed us to stand against the wiles of the Devil. No one can pluck us out of His Hand. We will not see the death angels, for God's angels will come for us that belong to Him. We will ever be with the Lord.

We can not earn that grace, keep it, improve on it, add to it, take from it or embellish it. Wages are earned and gifts are received. Just praise God and thank Him for Grace. When we are not established in grace, we go into confusion as did Job. He thought he did everything right and believed his works would keep him and his family protected, but it was God who had him hedged about. He could not understand why these things were happening to him and was overwhelmed by confusion.

DELIVERANCE WORKERS

A deliverance worker is a front-line warrior. The front line warrior receives the first strength of any attack. In the case of a couple, it is usually the wife who is attacked first as she is the weaker vessel. Sometimes, it is the man who is called into the ministry and not the wife. She goes along to support her husband, who leans on her for support. It takes a special couple to minister together for years avoiding or defeating Satan's attacks.

Sometimes we get puffed up in the idea of who we really are. We think that we are undefeatable and press on without really taking the time to stop and think that we are just His Servants by grace. We are ministering in His Name, Power, Strength, Might, Suffering, Love and guidance of the Holy Spirit.

Then comes Satan's attack and we get mad at God. This is not supposed to happen to God's warriors. We warriors get wounded. When we fail to turn to the Lord in praise, we stumble. Have you a hole in your armor? Are you spending time in prayer and in the Word everyday? Have idle thoughts found a way to get you to stop praying without ceasing? Have vain imaginations penetrated your armor? Examine your armor for weaknesses.

Continue on to the goal of hearing Jesus say, **Well done my good and faithful servant.** It could be that God is getting ready to do a greater work in your ministry once you overcome this trial. We must praise God in every circumstance. It is the praise, even unto death, that lifts the bonds that hold this earthly body in captivity. No one can separate us from the Love of God except ourselves. Regardless of what happens, we must always follow the Lord in spirit and truth.

APOSTLES SUFFERED

The apostles suffered, were God's saints, were persecuted, weak in body and had infirmities. Consider what Paul and Timothy went through. There are little things that affect the body. It is not a reflection on our spiritual condition if we get sick. Those with bodily weaknesses have been effective witnesses for Christ. The world can identify with their infirmities. They can be strong in the spirit. We are not perfect; we age, die, suffer sickness, are attacked by germs, our cells die every seven years and we are susceptible. Ask God for discernment and do not go on a guilt trip. Do not judge others outwardly; there is only one righteous judge. Show love and compassion; help others who are weaker. The church was persecuted. All apostles were martyred except for John in exile. God's heroes endured by faith even to torture and death.

PRIDE, EGO AND VANITY

God needs to cleanse our lives. Pride stands in our way of obtaining the blessings of God. We need God's wisdom and understanding. We must seek God and search our souls. We will always battle the forces of evil in this world. We need to try to live a balanced life: mentally, physically, spiritually and financially. Anything you neglect in life will cause you problems. Anything you omit in the Bible will cause you problems. Don't be puffed up; pride opens the door to demons.

CONFUSION OF MIND

Many Christians are confused about this subject. Why do they have to suffer in life when it seems that the heathen do not have to suffer? What are God's provisions and promises of healing? The concerns as to why terrible things happen to good people are quite natural and occur to us all. We must have faith and trust in our Heavenly Father, and know that we are loved by Him. The Scriptures are a source of comfort, strength and hope. What lies have we been told by our parents, spouses or children that we believe and affect our lives?

TESTIMONIES OF OTHERS

We hear of stories of those who read the scriptures every day, stand on them and are healed of terminal illnesses. We also hear of those who did the same thing and die. Can you judge and say that one person did not have the faith - absolutely not! There are those who seek the Lord for healing over some period of time, finally yield to surgery and are doing well. Can you condemn them for going to the doctors - absolutely not!

STANDING WITH EACH OTHER

We need to stand with each other, not only as Christian brothers and sisters, but also with other ministries. We are not in competition; there is plenty of work for everyone. This is especially true in the ministry of deliverance; there are few who perform this service. Ministers, just like everyone else, may have a difficult time with stability.

Ministers have a variety of styles and methods of ministry. Just because they don't perform the ministry just like we do, doesn't mean that we can not fellowship with them or support their ministry.

HUSBANDS RESPONSIBILITY

Have respect for your wife for her forced labor in the ministry. Don't put burdens on her so great she can not bear them. Repent to your wife for forced labor. Put her on the altar. God is faithful to honor the husband's proper relationship to the wife.

HUSBAND'S ASKING WIVE'S FORGIVENESS

Husbands and wives please stand together and hold hands. **As your husband, I ask you, my wife, to forgive me for forcing you to labor in this ministry and to do things that God did not call you to do. Forgive me for placing burdens on you that were so great that you could not bear them. Forgive me for not showing the respect for you that you deserve as my wife. I place you on the altar of God and ask that He forgive me for sinning against Him in the way that I have misused you. Lord, help us to have the proper relationship as husband wife in all walks of life including the ministry. Will you, my wife, forgive me? In Jesus Christ's name we pray. Amen.**

CREDIT TO OTHERS

We give credit for this lesson to those who comforted us during our time of illness. We give credit to those who have prayed for us over the years when we have been faced with injuries, illnesses and tragedies. We give credit to everyone who called, wrote or provided material for this lesson. However, we all give credit to the Father, Son and Holy Spirit for working through each of us to bring about God's purpose in our lives. We have taken some editorial liberties with the input to make this into a lesson for others.

PRAYERS BY GROUP

We bind the spirit of infirmity. We command you and all your underlings to leave our bodies now in the name of Jesus Christ. We break every curse of sickness, infirmity and organ failure. We command our bodies to respond to the blessing of healing and health. Our bodies are the temples of the Holy Spirit. We desire a clean temple for the Holy Spirit to dwell in. Father, we confess to you our sins, weaknesses, failures and lack of faith. We ask you to make your grace strong in our weaknesses. Help us to trust you in the things we don't know. We command the spirit of confusions to leave now in the name of Jesus Christ.

Lord, we ask you to grant us the blessings of long life and good health in the service of the kingdom of God. The seventy years, plus blessings, and the abundant life Jesus came to bring is your purpose for believers. We cancel out the purpose and plan of the Devil to kill, steal and destroy. We refuse any part of his plan and send all his curses back to the sender now in the name of the Lord Jesus Christ. In the name of Jesus Christ, we command the body's detoxification system to be healed and every spirit that is working to be destroyed or cause to fail. You must leave us now. All doubt and unbelief must leave. We rebuke you now in the name of Jesus Christ. We loose the ministering spirits for the heirs of salvation to come and minister to us now.

Thank you Lord Jesus for providing us victory over hell, death and the grave, and power over the spirits of sickness and over all the power of the Devil. We ask to live to accomplish all the God has purposed in our lives. Let us be a positive influence for Christ each day.

We break the curses of sickness, infirmity, organ failure, Godlessness, nests of demons, doorways for demons, idolatry of possessions and ungodly holidays.

We break the curses listed in Deuteronomy 27 and 28, in the rest of the Bible, from diseases of Egypt, of every sickness and plague in Book of Law, and every curse and disease not written in this Book of the Law that we have the legal right to do so. Lord we ask that you show us any legal rights that Satan has in our lives so that we may repent and break these curses. In the name of Jesus Christ, we pray.

LIST OF DEMONS

We command that the demonic characteristics and spirits leave in the name of Jesus Christ of Nazareth as your name is called along with your family of repressed feelings, judgmental, impatience, uncleanness, guilt, lack of faith, doubt, unbelief, seat of emotions, hidden spirits, beast nature, bestiality, uncleanness, immorality, unreality, condemnation, failure, despair, idleness, pride, ego, vanity, lying, confusion, overindulgence, selfishness, lust, perversion, greed, lesbian, lawlessness, iniquity, preying, witchcraft, jealousy, dolls with pins, Voodoo, enchantments, serpents in weight, thin veil, poison emotions, demonic reins, retardation, incest, pride, idolatry and condemnation.

Spirits of diseases, susceptible to disease, sickness, poor immunity, death, illness, infirmity, poisons, poor elimination, spirits in stomach - liver - kidney - bladder and other organs, hormone imbalance and related spirits. Every family of disease represented by the thirty-nine stripes that Jesus Christ was beaten with must come out of our bodies.

DISEASES LISTED IN DEUTERONOMY 28:16-68 BY DR. BILL NULL

Cursed in city, in field; cursed shall be basket, store; cursed shall be children, crops, cattle, sheep; cursed going in, coming out; cursing, **confusion** and failure in job and work, **destruction, perishing; plague, pestilence, sickness, death; consumption (wasting disease), fever, inflammation (blood poisoning), extreme burning (high fever), madness (encephalitis),** wars, crop failure, famine, **pestilence,** pursue until perish (harassment); Heaven as brass, no rain (hot sun), earth as iron (hard dry ground); land becomes powder and dust, dust shall cover you (dust storms), **eye trouble from dust, asthma, emphysema, heart trouble;** defeat and terror before enemies; body shall not be buried, wild beast will eat it; **botch (skin ulcers and boils), itch, scurvy, pellagra, beriberi, psoriasis; madness, blindness, astonishment of heart (terror, amazement), tumors, hemorrhoids;** groping at noonday, poverty, oppression, robbed, no deliverance; wife in adultery, raped, home stolen, wages stolen or lost; ox slain, ass stolen, sheep taken, none to rescue; son and daughters run away from home, taken into bondage for sex, **eye and heart fail waiting for their return;** enemies will take your wages and property, oppression and **destruction (crushed); madness,** helpless, hapless, powerless; **boils, ulcers (from sole of feet to top of head), impetigo, eczema;** foreign rulers and Gods; **astonishment,** a proverb among nations, laughing stock, ridicule, belittlement; worms will eat grapes, crop failure, job failure; locust will eat crop, crop failure; olive tree shall fail, job failure; sons and daughters go into captivity, drugs, witchcraft, sex, harlot; crop failure; foreign oppression, debt, poverty; hunger, thirst, nakedness, poverty, **destruction;** defeat by foreign nation; unmerciful enemy; destruction of cattle and crop, robbery of all possessions; siege of cities, destruction of defenses, conquest of land; cannibalism, famine, **distress,** complete poverty; **wonderful plagues, plagues on children, long chronic illness; all diseases of Egypt; every sickness and every plague in Book of**

Law; destruction of race (genocide); plucked off land (exile); dispersion among the nations (exile); **no rest, fearful, terror, blindness, depression, heaviness; fear of death, no assurance; fretting and worry always, constant danger;** bondage, slavery.

And finally, everything (every curse and disease) not written in this Book of the Law, Deuteronomy 28!

SECTION 10 - DIET & HEALING RECOMMENDATIONS

CONTENTS
1. SUMMARY
2. 77 SMART DIET & EXERCISE STRATEGIES
   1. Eat Smart
   2. Exercise Right
3. REFERENCES

SUMMARY

Healing Recommendations are provided because there is a lot of sickness in Christians, even those who believe in divine healing: anointing with oil and praying for the sick. Reading the **PREAMBLE TO HEALING DELIVERANCE MANUAL** will shock you about the physical and mental condition of Americans. The other articles are eye openers too.

America is no longer a Christian nation with a culture of life but now has a culture of death since it has turned against ALMIGHTY GOD. You have to be proactive in your health and educate yourself. Otherwise, you are at the mercy of the world and the world is not merciful about your health. It is not easy to be healthful in America considering what we are exposed to and what we put into our bodies.

Good health requires proper nutrition, supplements to the nutrition, bodily exercise and detoxification of impurities. Supplementation is required because we can not get the nutrition out of the foods we eat. Exercise is a necessity to keep our bodies functioning. Our world is polluted and we must detoxify to remove the chemicals.

There are evil forces at work that want to prevent our obtaining supplementation except from doctors who prescribe supplementation as pharmaceuticals. There are also forces that want to limit the world population and are using methods to do that.

If you can afford the cost of organic food, it is the most healthy but was it grown in depleted soil? Our bodies are not designed to handle the modern pollution and unhealthy food.

The above tabulated information follows after **77 SMART DIET & EXERCISE STRATEGIES**.

77 SMART DIET & EXERCISE STRATEGIES
Eat Smart

Consider calories. Pay attention to portions. Skimp on fat. Fill up on fruits and veggies. Choose whole grains over refined. Eat at home. Set realistic goals. Start the day off with breakfast. Eat soup, lose weight. Steer clear of sodas. Glued to the TV? Mind your eating. Step on the scale. Calorie needs often decrease as you age. Young adults: smart choices start now! Middle years: eat your medicine. Older adults: boost your nutrients, get enough fluids. Opt for produce with a broad range of colors.

Don't think you have to eat individual foods you don't like. Don't rely on a single food for good health. Food - to prevent disease, keep it colorful! Dietary sources of vitamin D. Consume your K. Kick up your calcium. Make magnesium a part of your diet. Get your C's. The Mediterranean diet - a key to longevity? Spice up your food - and boost your health. Research continues to document the anti-cancer benefits of a diet rich in fruits, vegetables, beans, and whole grains. Broccoli: eat it raw. Up your immunity. Get your fiber.

Eat Fish. East good vegetable oils high in unsaturated fat. Avoid trans fats, or partially hydrogenated oil. Limit dietary cholesterol. Cut back on salt. Alcohol - indulge a little. Those nuts. Eat smaller meals. Start the day off with breakfast. Get adequate amounts of vitamins and minerals. East well to sleep well - for increased energy and brain power. Have your iron levels checked. Up your intake of omega-3 fatty acids from fatty fish. Avoid saturated and trans fats. Think about getting extra vitamin B12. Chocolate, wine, and tea for the brain?

Exercise Right

Strength train to get, stay strong. Stay limber for life. Stay limber by doing the following exercises regularly: neck side stretch, wall reach, back-scratch shoulder stretch, back and hip stretch, and hamstring extension. Stretching - do it after exercise. Doing chores. Shopping. Having fun. To shed pounds, get moving! Flex your body's muscles to strengthen your brain's muscles. Work out, think smarter. Get moving to get calm. Take the work out of workouts.

REFERENCES

77 Smart Diet & Exercise Strategies
Eternal Youth Laws
Dietary Changes That Promote Wellness
A Baker's Dozen: Top Nutritious Vegetables
Most And Least Contaminated Fruits And Vegetables
Food, Life-Style And Their Effect On Disease
Improve Your Detoxification Program With Sauna Therapy
Bragg Stay Healthy Books
33 Way The Body Benefits From Rebounding
Messiah's Healing Institute
Prestige Publishing

SECTION 11 - DRUG ADDICTION AMONG CHILDREN

CONTENTS
1. PREFACE
2. INTRODUCTION
3. HOW CHILDREN BECOME MENTALLY ILL
4. HOW THE CHILD IS LABELED
5. WHOSE OPINION COUNTS?
6. GETTING PARENTS TO BUY THE DIAGNOSIS
7. HOW TO PROTECT YOUR CHILD
8. LIST OF DRUGS, SIGNS, SYMPTOMS, REACTIONS AND EFFECTS
9. RECOMMENDED READING LIST
    1. The Citizens Commission On Human Rights
10. REFERENCES

PREFACE

This lesson is meant for ministry to children and also adults who have been treated with drugs to control the mind. It could also apply to **street drugs** which have similar effects on the person.

The saddest thing to us is that the Christian World looks to the psychiatric profession and associated occupations rather than to the Holy Bible and Almighty God about how to handle illnesses of the mind and raise children. God's Word shows you how to do these things.

INTRODUCTION

There are countless children in this country on very dangerous psychiatric drugs. They are the unwitting guinea pigs of an experiment which is turning into a nightmare of monstrous proportions. In the past five years alone, the number of children committing suicide is up over 600%. Evidence is mounting, on a daily basis, that this tragedy is directly related to psychiatric treatment of children at an early age. Even if you have no children, children are the future of this nation. You doubtlessly have been and will be affected by what is going on.

Over the past ten years, psychiatry has shifted its income base from primarily treating adults to primarily treating children. This has been made possible by group medical plans which have recently (over the past 15 years or longer) included coverage for psychiatric **treatments**.

As a result, there are over 400% more children in psychiatric hospitals today than in 1980. It is estimated that the number of school children carrying psychiatric **diagnoses** of **mental illness** is up over 1000% in the same time period. **In today's society, hanging a label of mental illness on a child is like hanging a sign around the child's neck saying, GARBAGE: TAKE IT AWAY!**

HOW CHILDREN BECOME MENTALLY ILL

Under psychiatry's invented criteria, there isn't a single normal childhood behavior which doesn't fall within the broad **symptoms** which comprise so-called **mental illness**.

Psychiatry has implanted into our lives their solution to the age-old problems of life, as well as their solution to the problems encountered in the education of children.

Psychiatry's solution is to medicalize, label and then to cash in on the most common problems of life, including those experienced daily by people who educate and live with children.

HOW THE CHILD IS LABELED

The American Psychiatric Association published a test called the **Diagnostic and Statistical Manual of Mental Disorders**. In the psychiatric industry it is known as the **bible of psychiatry**. It is so highly regarded because if a **mental illness** is not in this book, insurance companies will not pay the bill.

WHOSE OPINION COUNTS?

Whether any of the above CRITERIA fit any particular child, depends only on the subjective opinion of the ADULT making the DIAGNOSIS.

As anyone can observe, some adults are better able to tolerate activity in children than others. This tolerance or intolerance for that matter can even vary, in the same adult, over a period of time.

GETTING PARENTS TO BUY THE DIAGNOSIS

The real trick is to get the parents to buy the DIAGNOSIS of MENTAL ILLNESS. Parents are often told or led to believe that there is a REAL SCIENTIFIC BASIS FOR THE DISEASE. This is an utter falsehood.

The only **criteria** are those listed above and the obvious financial benefits to the psychiatrist and other so-called **mental health professionals**.

The truth is, psychiatrists say they DON'T KNOW WHAT CAUSES CHILDREN TO ACT AS THEY DO. The main criteria for having the **disease** seems to be the parents' willingness and ability to pay for **treatment** and often whether the parents have psychiatric coverage on their medical insurance.

HOW TO PROTECT YOUR CHILD

We also want any parent who still believes a child is too active, to know there are alternatives to drugging the child. In fact, there is extensive information available on handling active children without drugs.

However, the first alternative to drugging a child, which the parent must recognize and choose, is NOT DRUG THE CHILD.

LIST OF DRUGS, SIGNS, SYMPTOMS, REACTIONS AND EFFECTS

This list can be used as names of demons in deliverance. Demons will answer to their medical names or characteristics of how they affect the body:

1. Cylert, Dexedrine, Mellaril, Tofranil, Haldol, Thorazine, Ritalin, Speed and Amphetamine-Like Drugs.
2. Withdrawal, Depressed Mood, Fatigue, Psychotic Episodes, Severe Prolonged Depression, Paranoia, Suicidal, Severe Sleep Disturbances, Bed Wetting, Increased Dreaming with Nightmares.
3. Mental Illness, Crazy, Insanity, Nutritional Deficiencies, Stunting of Growth, Allergic Reactions.
4. Anxiety, Tension, Extreme Agitation, Irritability, Psychosis.
5. Mood Swings, Nervousness, Insomnia, Dizziness, Headache, Appetite Loss, Unexplained Fever, Blurred Vision, Joint Pain, Uncontrolled Movements, Rash, Hives, Sore Throat, Nausea, Abdominal Pain, Chest Pain, Fast/Irregular Heart Beat, Unusual Bruising, Unusual Tiredness, High Blood Pressure.
6. Confusion, Behavior Problems.
7. Tourette's Syndrome, Body Ticks, Spasms, Barking Sounds, Screaming Babble, Screaming Obscenities.
8. Seizures, Epileptic, Convulsions, Fits, Grand Mal, Petit Mal, Body Twitches, Violent Muscular Spasms, Brain Damage, Unconsciousness.
9. Over Stimulation of Central Nervous System, Death, Vomiting, Tremors, Exaggeration of Reflexes, Muscle Twitching, Convulsions, Coma, Euphoria, Confusion, Hallucinations, Delirium Sweating, Flushing, Headache, High Fever, Abnormally Rapid Heart Rate, Irregular Heart Beat, Pounding Heart, High Arterial Blood Pressure, Pupil Dilation, Dryness of Mucous Membranes.
10. Thorazine, Chemical Lobotomy, Thorazine Shuffle, Slack Jawed, Drooling, Palms Turning Back, Arms Hanging Slack, Tardive Dyskinesia, Uncontrollable Muscle Spasm, Tongue Rolled Over, Tongue Protruding, Limbs Shake, Parkinson's Disease.
11. Attention Deficit Disorder, Minimal Brain Dysfunction, Learning Disability, Impulse Disorder.
12. Hyperactivity, Inattention, Impulsivity.

This list can be used as names of demons in deliverance. Demons will answer to their medical names or characteristics of how they affect the body:

1. Cylert, Dexedrine, Mellaril, Tofranil, Haldol, Thorazine, Ritalin, Speed and Amphetamine-Like Drugs.
2. Withdrawal, Depressed Mood, Fatigue, Psychotic Episodes, Severe Prolonged Depression, Paranoia, Suicidal, Severe Sleep Disturbances, Bed Wetting, Increased Dreaming with Nightmares.
3. Mental Illness, Crazy, Insanity, Nutritional Deficiencies, Stunting of Growth, Allergic Reactions.
4. Anxiety, Tension, Extreme Agitation, Irritability, Psychosis.
5. Mood Swings, Nervousness, Insomnia, Dizziness, Headache, Appetite Loss, Unexplained Fever, Blurred Vision, Joint Pain, Uncontrolled Movements, Rash,

Hives, Sore Throat, Nausea, Abdominal Pain, Chest Pain, Fast/Irregular Heart Beat, Unusual Bruising, Unusual Tiredness, High Blood Pressure.
6. Confusion, Behavior Problems.
7. Tourette's Syndrome, Body Ticks, Spasms, Barking Sounds, Screaming Babble, Screaming Obscenities.
8. Seizures, Epileptic, Convulsions, Fits, Grand Mal, Petit Mal, Body Twitches, Violent Muscular Spasms, Brain Damage, Unconsciousness.
9. Over Stimulation of Central Nervous System, Death, Vomiting, Tremors, Exaggeration of Reflexes, Muscle Twitching, Convulsions, Coma, Euphoria, Confusion, Hallucinations, Delirium Sweating, Flushing, Headache, High Fever, Abnormally Rapid Heart Rate, Irregular Heart Beat, Pounding Heart, High Arterial Blood Pressure, Pupil Dilation, Dryness of Mucous Membranes.
10. Thorazine, Chemical Lobotomy, Thorazine Shuffle, Slack Jawed, Drooling, Palms Turning Back, Arms Hanging Slack, Tardive Dyskinesia, Uncontrollable Muscle Spasm, Tongue Rolled Over, Tongue Protruding, Limbs Shake, Parkinson's Disease.
11. Attention Deficit Disorder, Minimal Brain Dysfunction, Learning Disability, Impulse Disorder.
12. Hyperactivity, Inattention, Impulsivity.

RECOMMENDED READING LIST
The Citizens Commission On Human Rights

Psychiatry A Human Rights Abuse And Global Failure
Psychiatry's Betrayal
Psychiatry's Multibillion-Dollar Fraud
Psychiatry Committing Fraud
Psychiatry Shattering Your World With Drugs
Psychiatry Destroys Minds
Psychiatry Destroying Morals
Psychiatry Destroying Religion
Psychiatry Education's Ruin
Psychiatry Victimizing The Elderly
Psychiatry Eradicating Justice
Psychiatry Manipulating Creativity
Psychiatry Rape

REFERENCES
1. **Dr. Caligari's Psychiatric Drugs** from network Against Psychiatric Assault
2. **Drugs** by H. Winter Griffith, M.D.
3. **Physicians Desk Reference** from Medical Economics Company
4. Use a large medical dictionary or standard dictionary.
5. **The Citizens Commission On Human Rights**, CCHR International, Los Angeles, CA.

The above was excerpted from brochures. You can obtain more detailed information from them about drug effects on people.

SECTION 12 - CHILDREN'S DELIVERANCE

CONTENTS
1. **ABUSED CHILD - CHILD ABUSE - RITUAL ABUSE**
   1. Warning Signs Of Sexual Abuse In Children
      1. Symptoms - Observable Behavior
   2. Incest Or Child Abuse
      1. Symptoms
   3. Ritual Abuse
      1. Preface
      2. Characteristics
2. **DEMONIC CHILD ENTERTAINMENT**
   1. Thirteen Doctrines Of The New Age
   2. Twenty Warning Signs Of Satanism
   3. Seven Steps To Overcoming Occultism And Satanic Involvement
3. **CHILDREN DRUG ADDICTS**
   1. List of drugs, signs, symptoms, reactions and effects

ABUSED CHILD - CHILD ABUSE - RITUAL ABUSE
Warning Signs Of Sexual Abuse In Children
Symptoms - Observable Behavior
(A Door Of Hope)

1. Fear of specific persons or situations / strangers. Child verbally declares she doesn't want to go to **grandpa's house** or shies away when around strangers.
2. Nightmares. Usually has dreams of **helplessness** - trying to run away but being caught.
3. Withdrawal (social or emotional). Stays in room; isolates self; is sullen: **Just leave me alone.**
4. Bed wetting / change in sleep patterns. Says, **Mom, I had an accident**, or **I can't sleep.**
5. Personality change. Outgoing child who was a leader type becomes withdrawn; change in school performance.
6. Loss of appetite. **I'm not hungry.**
7. Unprovoked crying spells. Bursts into tears when significant parent goes on routine errands and leaves child, i.e., **Please, Mommy don't leave me.**
8. Clinging to significant adult. Stays in close proximity; needs more physical touching.
9. Excessive washing / baths. Talks of being dirty, feels dirty.
10. Poor self-image / low self-esteem. Increases negative self-incriminations - **I'm no good. I can't do anything right, etc.**
11. Changes in type of fantasy play. Expresses extreme victimization / violence in play.
12. Fear of being alone. **Please, Mommy, stay with me. Don't turn out the light.**

13. Refusal to go to school. expresses dislike; doesn't want to go see friends. **I just want to stay home with you.**
14. Running away. Retreats to **safe** family. **I don't like it here.**
15. Attempt to control environment / fear of unknown. Wants to control excessive environment; often becomes extremely anxious over unknown aspects of life. **What if our house catches on fire?** Or, **Mommy, I'm afraid.**
16. Early sexual precociousness. Practices excessive masturbation; uses sexually explicit words and gestures inappropriate for age.

Incest Or Child Abuse
Symptoms
(Freeing Your Mind)

1. **As A Child:** fear, helplessness, inferiority, blame and guilt, bed wetting, nightmares, hiding away, asthma.
2. **As A Teen:** early rebellion, acute depression, looking downward, feeling worthless, talk of suicide, running away, promiscuity, prostitution.
3. **As An Adult:** gaps in memory, perfectionism, sacrificial work, lack of faith in GOD, repeated victimization, overweight, nightmares, flashbacks, migraines, allergies.
4. **As A Wife:** poor choice of mates, accepting of abuse, frigidity, extreme anger, abusive to children, controlling, lack of emotion, lack of trust, suspicious, promiscuous.

Ritual Abuse
Preface

Ritual abuse is primarily oriented at children and is mainly sexual in nature. It also includes adults but the main emphasis is to affect the lives of children for Satan if they are allowed to live. It is said the this is a three billion dollar business.

We are in a life and death war with the forces of evil. Churches are vandalized, desecrated, and Bibles and churches are burned. Evil people are criminal, stealthily, organized, deadly, selfish, disregard life, devil worshiper, lust, unrestrained indulgence and forbid things of GOD. This is clearly demonic influence.

Many churches and youth groups are clueless and powerless, and kids are toxic. Since there is no power in the churches, the youth look to Satanism for power. The children are lonely, hurt, crying, fearful, lost and looking for love with anyone who will give it to them. Hurting teenagers are rejected from church because they don't fit the mold. Churches fall into sedition, gossip, false teaching, secretiveness, exclusivity, pride and arrogance.

Characteristics

1. Ritual abuse, sexual abuse, child abuse, spouse abuse
2. Sacrifice of animals, children and adults
3. Blood ritual, death ritual, cattle mutilation, drink blood
4. Teen Satanist, teen vampire, teen bisexual

5. Sex with corpse, snuff death film
6. Pedophile, child molestation, child pornography, child trading, sexual predator, child sex toy
7. Children considered animals, killing babies
8. Rape, torture, death, suicide, murder
9. Criminal occultist, pedophile, pornography, trader
10. Victimization, government programming, high-tech harassment, fragmenting mind, mind control
11. Babylonian witchcraft, Egyptian black magic, black arts.
12. Wiccan, white magic
13. The Necronomicon, Book of Shadows
14. Satanic cult, Druid
15. Adult sexual orgy, pimp, street drugs

DEMONIC CHILD ENTERTAINMENT
Thirteen Doctrines Of The New Age

(1) The children of the future will serve a One World (Planetary Government) and live in a One World Culture. **(2) Patriotism to one's country must be abolished and all national barriers destroyed in order to build a New One World Order.** (3) Children will accept that Eastern mystical religion is to be married to the Christianity of the West to forge a new, unified social and religious order of Universal Truths. **(4) Teenagers and youth will rebel and revolt against their parents and against authority to help usher in the New Age World Order.** (5) Youth and all of humanity must accept that the time will inevitably come when grown-ups who refuse to become part of the New Age will have to be killed. They are to be considered as lowly germs, an infection or blot on humanity that must be stamped out and eradicated. **(6) The traditional family unit is not desirable for the Aquarian, or New Age. Children belong to the government, to the world and the community--the human group--not to their parents. A new kind of family unit must inevitably come into existence.** (7) Young people must be taught to believe in reincarnation and karma (the Law of Rebirth) rather than the resurrection and judgment teaching of the Bible. This belief must guide behavior, especially the sexual conduct.

(8) Absurd and immature notions of sin and guilt must not be imparted to children by parents, teachers, pastors and other adults. A more permissive and worldly attitude must be adopted. (9) Children are to be taught that all religions--Christianity, Witchcraft, Hinduism, Buddhism, Islam, Judaism, Paganism, etc.--are equally worthwhile and that it doesn't matter in which God one believes. **(10) The new generation of youth must recognize that Jesus did not come to save or convert anyone; because no one is lost.** (11) Christian doctrines, such as that of heaven, hell, and judgment, must be discarded and theology of the Old Testament must be repudiated. **(12) A New Age World Religion must be established without Jesus Christ as Lord and Savior. The Christian Church is dead and must be replaced.** (13) The coming New Age World Religion will emphasize the unity of all religions while rejecting Jesus Christ's profound Biblical statement, **I am the way, the truth and the life.**

They plot to decompose and destroy the family unit, subvert Bible doctrine, and promote a One World New Age Religion and Government. The roots of New Age occultism can be traced all the way back to ancient Babylon. The unholy trinity has three divinities: Father, Mother, Son. We see in these events the roots of several **cardinal New Age doctrines: evolution, human divinity, spirit worship, reincarnation, and sexual license.**

Many other doctrines, rituals, practices and symbols have been revived from the past by the New Age movement. There is a gigantic conspiracy underway. Billions will join the Jesus-hating forces of the New Age Beast. **Regrettably, most Christian leaders do not even understand the most basic rudiments of what the New Age is all about.** The word occult simply means hidden or concealed, kept from view.

Here is just a partial list of ancient satanic teachings, practices and symbols now in vogue and being pushed on the children and teens: **color therapy, heavy metal music, unisex dress, sadism, sorcery, incest and immorality, hypnotism, New Age mood music, palmistry, rebellion, astral travel, mystery teachings, ESP (psychic powers), God as Mother, astrology, nature worship, rhythmic breathing, visualization, psychedelic drugs, sodomy, feminism, necromancy, dragons, pyramids, chanting, yoga, demonic music, fortune telling, levitation, self-love, fire walking, body tattoos, numerology, pedophilia, mental imagery; the unicorn, pegasus and other magical beasts; communication with the dead; mediation (other than on God's word); and satanic symbols (pentagram, triangle & circle, etc.).**

Twenty Warning Signs Of Satanism

(1) A sudden or rapid change in attitude toward authorities. (2) A rebellious, sullen spirit toward parents. **(3) Possession or intense interest in occult and magical books; The possession of the Satanic Bible or a similar book on rituals is of special importance.** (4) A philosophy or attitude that shows a reversal of norms; for example, bad is good and good is bad. **(5) Animosity and cynicism towards Christianity, including GOD, JESUS CHRIST, The Bible, The Church, pastors, youth leaders, and Christian ideals and ethics.**

(6) Severe mood swings, a drop in grades, intense introspection, depression, loss of sleep, frequent nightmares, paranoia or excessive fear, restlessness. **(7) Possession of specific Satanism-related items, which might include knives (especially daggers and knives with bizarre or medieval handles and blades), small pots, cauldrons, or incense burners; special salts or herbs; bells or gongs; tribal drums; animal parts; bones; candles; incense; amulets; talismans; charms.** (8) Intense interest in, study of, or dabbling in New Age philosophies, practices, and rituals, such as ESP powers, spirit channeling, crystals, acupuncture, reflexology, reincarnation and karma, etc.

(9) Morbid fascination with the dead or with death. (10) Self mutilation, including cutting oneself or marking with tattoos or body paint. **(11) Black colored clothing, when worn almost exclusively, or when combined with the wearing of jewelry, buttons, or paraphernalia with occult symbology. Also, the wearing of such jewelry and**

paraphernalia with any clothing, T-shirts with pictures of heavy-metal album covers or Satanic symbols, and black fingernail polish. (12) Intense interest in heavy-metal rock music, including the worship or admiration of rock stars, and the hanging of posters of these stars and their albums. Also, interest in New Age mood music.

(13) Use of illegal drugs of any kind, or alcohol abuse. (14) Obsession with fantasy role-playing games, such as Dungeons & Dragons. (15) Unusual body movements and effects such as twitching, tics, rocking, glazed eyes, head banging, moaning or groaning, chanting. (16) Lack of empathy toward the hurts in other people's lives. (17) Cruelty or inhumane acts against people and animals, or acts of vandalism. (18) Fascination or obsession with horror, slasher and occult movies, or with occult symbols. (19) Use of Satanic nicknames. (20) Fascination with blood.

Seven Steps To Overcoming Occultism And Satanic Involvement
(1) Confess the involvement. (2) Break the contact--and contract--with evil. Renounce your involvement by first identifying each and every act or behavior, then stating aloud to God that you permanently renounce and cast away from your life anything connected with Satan. (3) Get rid of all Satanic articles and items.

(4) Ask the Lord Jesus Christ to forgive you and cleanse you of all the sins in your life. (5) Acknowledge to God verbally the He is your deliverer. Praise Him for your deliverance. (6) Pledge to obey God, to read your Bible, to pray frequently, and to witness to others. (7) Stand daily against Satan, always with the full assurance that God is almighty and that His strength is always sufficient. Lean on God and he will protect, inspire, and lead you to victory in all things.

CHILDREN DRUG ADDICTS
List Of Drugs, Signs, Symptoms, Reactions And Effects

This list can be used as names of demons in deliverance. Demons will answer to their medical names or characteristics of how they affect the body:

1. Cylert, Dexedrine, Mellaril, Tofranil, Haldol, Thorazine, Ritalin, Speed and Amphetamine-Like Drugs.
2. Withdrawal, Depressed Mood, Fatigue, Psychotic Episodes, Severe Prolonged Depression, Paranoia, Suicidal, Severe Sleep Disturbances, Bed Wetting, Increased Dreaming with Nightmares.
3. Mental Illness, Crazy, Insanity, Nutritional Deficiencies, Stunting of Growth, Allergic Reactions.
4. Anxiety, Tension, Extreme Agitation, Irritability, Psychosis.
5. Mood Swings, Nervousness, Insomnia, Dizziness, Headache, Appetite Loss, Unexplained Fever, Blurred Vision, Joint Pain, Uncontrolled Movements, Rash, Hives, Sore Throat, Nausea, Abdominal Pain, Chest Pain, Fast/Irregular Heart Beat, Unusual Bruising, Unusual Tiredness, High Blood Pressure.
6. Confusion, Behavior Problems.
7. Tourette's Syndrome, Body Ticks, Spasms, Barking Sounds, Screaming Babble, Screaming Obscenities.

8. Seizures, Epileptic, Convulsions, Fits, Grand Mal, Petit Mal, Body Twitches, Violent Muscular Spasms, Brain Damage, Unconsciousness.
9. Over Stimulation of Central Nervous System, Death, Vomiting, Tremors, Exaggeration of Reflexes, Muscle Twitching, Convulsions, Coma, Euphoria, Confusion, Hallucinations, Delirium Sweating, Flushing, Headache, High Fever, Abnormally Rapid Heart Rate, Irregular Heart Beat, Pounding Heart, High Arterial Blood Pressure, Pupil Dilation, Dryness of Mucous Membranes.
10. Thorazine, Chemical Lobotomy, Thorazine Shuffle, Slack Jawed, Drooling, Palms Turning Back, Arms Hanging Slack, Tardive Dyskinesia, Uncontrollable Muscle Spasm, Tongue Rolled Over, Tongue Protruding, Limbs Shake, Parkinson's Disease.
11. Attention Deficit Disorder, Minimal Brain Dysfunction, Learning Disability, Impulse Disorder.
12. Hyperactivity, Inattention, Impulsivity.

SECTION 13 – CURING AND HEALING THE BODY BY DELIVERANCE

CONTENTS
1. LIST OF SCRIPTURE
2. STUDY OF CURE - CURED - CURES
    1. Action by God or Physicians
    2. Old Testament (Medicine and Healing)
    3. New Testament (Relieving and Making Whole)
    4. Conclusion
3. EXCERPTS FROM THE BIBLE
4. POSSIBLE ROOTS OF INFIRMITY
4. ALTERNATIVE HEALTH PRACTICES
6. ACUPUNCTURE
7. SICKNESS AND DEMONIC SYMPTOMS
    1. Epilepsy
    2. Schizophrenia
    3. Coprolalia
8. MUTILATION
9. SPIRIT OF PARALYSIS
10. WITCHCRAFT AND SORCERY: PHARMACY - MEDICATION - POISON
11. BIBLICAL CURSES OF SICKNESSSES AND PLAGUES
12. REFERENCES

LIST OF SCRIPTURE

There are many healing scriptures in the Holy Bible; the following is good list:
Ex. 15:26; 23:25-26
Num. 12:13; 16:46-48; 21:7-9; 23:19
Deut. 7:15; 28:15-61
II Kings 5:14; 20:5
II Chron. 16:12-13
Job 2:6-7; 5:26
Psa. 27:1; 30:2; 34:19-20; 37:25; 42:11; 91:10, 14-16; 103:1-3; 105:37; 107:20
Prov. 3:7-8; 4:20-22; 12:18; 13:3; 16:24
Isa. 53:4-5; 58:6,8; 59:19; 61:1
Jer. 8:22; 16:19; 17:14; 30:17; 33:3,6
Matt. 4:23-24; 7:7-8; 8:8,13, 6-17; 9:2, 5-6, 20-22; 9:27-30, 32-35; 10:1; 7-8; 12:13,15,22,24; 13:15; 14:14,36; 15:28; 17:14-21; 18:19-20
Mark 1:22-25,40; 2:5,9,11; 3:10-15; 5:23,28-31,34,36;6:1-6,13,56; 9:23-25; 10:46-47,52; 11:20-24; 16:14-20
Luke 1:37-38; 4:8-32,35,39,41; 5:9-13; 6:19; 7:21-23; 8:28-30,36; 9:1-2; 6:37-42; 10:8-9,17-20; 11:14; 13:11-17; 17:11-19; 18:35-43
John 4:47-53; 5:5,14; 6:2,63; 8:32,36; 10:10; 14:12-16; 15:5,7; 16:23-24
Acts 1:8; 3:4-6; 4:9; 5:12,14-16; 8:5-8; 9:18,34; 10:38;14:8-11; 16:18; 19:11-16; 28:8-9

I Cor. 12:9-10
II Cor. 9:8; 10:4-5; 2:14
Gal. 3:13
Eph. 3:20; 6:10-18
Phil. 2:27; 4:13
II Tim. 1:7
Heb. 2:4; 11:1,6,11,34; 12:2,6-8: 13:8
James 4:7; 5:13-16
I Peter 1:3-7; 2:20,24; 4:12-19; 5:7-8,10
II Peter 1:3-4
I John 4:4; 5:4,14-15
Rev. 12:10-11

There are also scriptures for destruction of the flesh:
I Cor. 5:4-8 The destruction of the flesh for sin.
II Cor. 12:7-9 The messenger of Satan to buffet Paul to keep him humble. (It is a very good virtue to be humble before GOD; pride is an abomination to Him.)

STUDY OF CURE - CURED - CURES
Action By God Or Physicians

Jeremiah 33:6 Behold, I will bring it health and cure.

Jeremiah 46:11 In vain shalt thou use **many medicines** - not to be cured.

Hosea 5:13 Yet could he not heal you, nor cure you.

Matthew 17:16 And they could not cure him.

Matthew 17:18 And the child was cured from that very hour.

Luke 7:21 Cured many of their **infirmities and plagues**.

Luke 9:1 **Power and authority over all devils, and to cure <u>diseases</u>.**

Luke 13:32 **Behold, I cast out devils, and I do I do cures.**

John 5:10 The Jews therefore said unto him that was cured.

Old Testament (Medicine And Healing)
1. A medicine, healing (cure).
2. To mend, to heal (cure).
3. Heal it, to remove (cure).
4. Bandage as placed on a wound (cured).

New Testament (Relieving And Making Whole)
1. To **relieve of disease**.
2. To attend (cure, cured).
3. Healing, **make whole** (cures).

Conclusion
I made a study of cures in the Bible; here is what I found. Either you can pray to God or you can go to the physicians to be cured. Medicine is used to relieve diseases. God is displeased when Christians do not seek God first for their cures. We have

found that demons come into a person when they **have an operation and are given an anesthetic**. Demons also come into the child during birth by operation and drugs.

EXCERPTS FROM THE BIBLE
The following are excerpts from the Bible that show how **the body can be cured and healed by the casting out of demons**:
Matt. 4:23-24 **Torments, lunatic,** possessed with devils - healed.
Matt. 8:16-17 Possessed with devils - healed sick.
Matt. 12:22 Possessed with devil, **blind and dumb** - healed him.
Matt. 17:14-21 Rebuked the devil - child was cured.
Luke 4:38-39 Rebuked the **fever** and it left her - healed.
Luke 6:17-19 Vexed with **unclean spirits** and they were healed.
Luke 7:21 And **plagues and of evil spirits** - cured.
Luke 8:2 Of **evil spirits and infirmities** - healed.
Luke 9:37-42 Rebuked the **unclean spirit** - healed the child.
Luke 13:11-17 **Spirit of infirmity** - healed.

Apparently the casting out of demons is considered healing by the Bible; it frequently says that demons were cast out and they were healed. Other verses make a strong reference to this phenomenon.

Demons can lie dormant while waiting for the right opportunity to strike. They can be in the body due to inherited sins from the ancestors.

POSSIBLE ROOTS OF INFIRMITY (EXCERPTS)
John 10:10 **The thief cometh not, but for to steal, and to kill, and to destroy.** We have seen people exclaim they were healed when the casting out of demons is taking place and there was no prayer for healing. There are **evil forces (demons)** behind many illnesses from minor to life threatening.

Behind a screen of bitterness, rebellion, ingratitude, and rejection hide evil spirits which work on the mind and on body chemistry and cause disturbances in physical, mental and emotional health.

God has designed all the parts of the human body to work in harmony.

In some cases a person will repent of their sins, forgive all who have hurt them and receive healing, **but will later allow themselves to get into a pattern of unforgiveness again and allow the problem to reoccur.**

Here are a few scriptures which show the correlation between attitudes, sins and actions with sickness or disease:

Proverbs 12:4; 14:30 Rottenness in bones - **incurable disease, stink, cancer, etc.**
Psalms 6:7 **Eyes dim because of grief. While I was grieving for Earline, my wife, Marie, my daughter, said that my** skin turned grey.

II Chronicles 21:12-15 **Intestinal disease** because of **idol worship and murder**.
Isaiah 3:16-26 Ladies who are **haughty, undisciplined, flirtatious, and proud** may suffer **scabs** on the crown of heads, **stench of rottenness** and/or **baldness and poverty**.
Deuteronomy 28:21-35 **Disobedience** brings many consequences; some are **physical and mental illnesses**.

ALTERNATIVE HEALTH PRACTICES
Healing Through Deliverance

Alternative medical practices are not necessarily spiritually dangerous. **Whether they are spiritually safe or not, depends on the beliefs of the practitioner and the spiritual history of the practice.**

The following are some of the alternative medical practices which are known to have spiritual origins or guiding principles of New Age, Occultic or otherwise non-Christian nature:

Acupuncture, Aromatherapy, Bach Flower Remedies, Color Therapy, Crystal Therapy, Faith Healers, Guided Imagery, Homoeopathy, Hypnotherapy, Iridology, Kinesiology, Magnetic Healing, New Age Medicine, Past Lives Therapy, Psychic Healers, Psychic Surgery, Pyramid Healing, Radiesthesia, Rebirthing, Reflexology, Spiritualist Healing and Zone Therapy.

The Hidden Agenda

There have always been healers proclaiming the message of herbal remedies, spiritual healing guides and a distrust of Western medicine. We recognize them as witch doctors, shamans and medicine men who practice primitive healing methods in remote tribal areas of the world.

Today the homeopath, psychic healer or alternative physician promoting visualization, acupuncture, crystal healing, iridology, reflexology or many other methods of today's alternative medicine movement would have us embrace unproved unscientific methods and occult philosophies.

These alternative health practices run the gamut from innocent, even scientifically proven beneficial techniques such as hypnosis, biofeedback and natural foods, to outright occult practices, such as spirit guides and psychic surgeons. The holistic health industry includes Rolfers, colonic hygienists, shamans, faith healers, herbalists, polarity therapists, reflexologists, naturopaths, homeopaths and psychic surgeons.

Many alternative practices are heavily steeped in false spirituality, Eastern mysticism and New Age thought. From acupuncture and aromatherapy to shamanism, yoga and Zen macrobiotics, alternative medical practices span the alphabet. They run the gamut from clever blending of fact and fancy to complete foolishness.

Failure to diagnose and treat, physical threats, toxic effects, emotional harm, wasted money, diverted resources and loss of reality can hurt or kill due to mystical interpretation of reality and pursuit of occult practices.

Are these therapies scientifically proven, medically safe and spiritually sound? See **The Hidden Agenda** and its Appendix for more detailed answers. The fact that doctors are combining occultic spiritual practices with modern healing produces medical quackery and false spirituality. Just because something works doesn't make it right especially for Christians.

Natural Therapies - Ayurveda, Colonics, Herbalism, Naturopathy, Homeopathy, Macrobiotics and Osteopathy.

Manual Therapies - Massage, Rolfing, Trager Work and Chiropractic.

Mind Therapies - Hypnosis, Biofeedback, Christian Science, Dreamwork, Transcendental Meditation and Yoga (power of mind over sickness, pseudo-sceientific, dynamic relaxation, altered consciousness, guided imagery, visualization, shamanic trance, New Age religions, Science of Mind religions, body/mind integration techniques).

Energy Manipulating Therapies - Acupuncture, Applied Kinesiology (muscle testing), **Crystals, Flower Remedies, Iridology** (iris of eye), **Reflexology, Reiki, Therapeutic Touch and Universal Energy** (New Age, self-transformation, metaphysical, electromagnetic, polarity, quasi-religious, oriental wisdom, cosmic radiant energy, chakras, ancient sacred knowledge, Eastern mysticism and religious concepts, Chinese and Indian philosophy, Buddhist spiritual principles, Taoism, Confucianism, Monism, Legalism, esoteric occultism, prana, face reading, hydrotherapy, manipulative, bio-force, chi, jin shin do, physiotherapy, prophetic healing, trigger point therapy, sorcery, white magic, wizardry, Acupressure).

Supernatural Therapies - Channeling, Psychic Surgery, Shamanism, Spirit Guide and Visualization (occult, spiritual and faith healing, spiritual awareness, demonic influence, clairvoyance, psychokinesis, crystal ball, fortune telling, witchcraft, tarot cards, phrenology, worship of nature, spiritual attunements, yin and yang, astral projection, alchemy, out-of-body experience, communication with dead, spiritists, spirit guide, seance, create own reality, magical healing, seeking forbidden knowledge, psychoanalysis, hypnotherapy, rituals, somatic therapy, magic, metaphysical, past life incarnation / regression, UFO contact, sacred science, palm reading, aura, pendulum, witch doctor, medicine man, past-life regression).

ACUPUNCTURE

Stay away from **Acupuncture, Acupressure, Spiritualism and Christian Science** for healing. According to recent medical reports, it has been found that treatment by acupuncture brought relief to only one-third of the people who have used this procedure to cure chronic pain. (Does that make it all right?)

According to **Encyclopedia Britannica**, acupuncture comes from two Latin words **acus** meaning needle and **pungere** to prick. Five thousand years ago, the Chinese used this method to relieve pain. According to **The New Family Encyclopedia** it is the <u>yin/yang</u> theory and many investigators attribute its effects to <u>hypnosis</u>. This information alone should warn a Christian not to allow these methods to be used on them. The practice of medicine was limited to the **occult priests** in the **Hindu religion**; the oldest recorded medical information comes from them. Because of this we know acupuncture is <u>**Witchcraft**</u>. The ancient Chinese were expert in the use of Acupuncture and Acupressure. Acupressure which uses pressure points and massage instead of needles, but is still based on the occult.

Often when a person receives a healing through some **occult practice**, they will soon find themselves with a greater illness. **My (Earline's) father used an occult practice of <u>tying knots in a string and burying it in the drip of the house</u> to cure one of my brothers, Wilburn, of warts. Later he had spinal meningitis which killed him. He went to Heaven and GOD sent him back to earth. This could have been the swap of <u>demon of warts for demon of spinal meningitis.</u>** (Can you be healed by witchcraft? Yes, but you swap a lesser demon for a greater demon.)

SICKNESS AND DEMONIC SYMPTOMS
Call out the symptoms of the disease as names of demons. Some examples are as follows:

Epilepsy
According to **Taber's Cyclopedic Medical Dictionary** epilepsy is a recurring paroxysmal disorder of cerebral function characterized by sudden, brief attacks of altered consciousness, motor activity, or sensory phenomena. Convulsive seizures, hyperpyrexia, metabolic disturbances, recurrent attacks of abdominal pain, headaches, falling, dizziness, vomiting, emotional instability, fainting spells and the like. Psychomotor attacks cause mental confusion, staggering, purposeless movements, may make unintelligent sounds, may have occasional outbursts of irrational and even violent behavior.

Schizophrenia
One out of eight people probably have some degree of Schizophrenia. Since Schizophrenia starts with the families of Rejection then Bitterness and then Rebellion, probably everybody has some degree of Schizophrenia. This personality problem begins when a person withdraws from friends, has morbid introspections, reduced initiative, strange behavior, delusions, hallucinations, and thought disturbances. Three main groups: **Catatonic** will have one or more of the following problems: catatonic stupor, mutism, negativism, rigidity, excitement, and violence. **Paranoid** will have these problems: delusions of grandeur, persecution, jealousy, or hallucination of these. **Undifferentiated** will have some of these: delusions, incoherence, and grossly disorganized behavior. We have seen all these types of schizophrenics freed by the casting out of demons. Most of the time the thoughts these people have are the thoughts of demons and are always meant to incapacitate the individual. In James 1:8, the Bible calls this double mindedness.

Coprolalia

This disease was recognized by Gilles de la Tourette a, French neurologist. It is the compulsion to scream obscenities. The afflicted person may have a lack of muscle coordination, involuntary purposeless movements, facial and muscle ticks, incoherent grunts and barks may accompany the obscenities. They may appear to be very vulgar, drunk or psychotic. There is little or no help in medicine. This ailment usually begins in childhood with uncontrollable twitching, especially of the facial muscles. **This is usually helped by repentance and deliverance from spirits** of swearing, hate, obscenities, etc.

MUTILATION
(Written by Earline Moody)

It is strange that some people seem to be needing operations on a fairly routine basis. There have been a number of times we have found **Mutilation** to be the ruler. He often has a partner named **Accident Prone**; they seem to work together to bring a person accidents and operations. **(Earline had many operations until the demon of Mutilation was cast out.)**

Traumatic Shock opens the way for many demons to enter. Some of the natural ones are **Paranoid Fear, Depression, Despair, Discouragement, Suicide, Paralysis, Affliction, Death, Fear of Death**, etc.

I (Earline) was prayed for many times in an attempt to overcome demons who had come in at our son's death. These demons strengthened those already in my mind and body. Every Sunday for almost two years I was prayed for and the demons would be quiet for a week or less. I became convinced that my problems were too much for God, I had not repented enough or God hated me. After God told me to ask Gene to pray for me in deliverance, only then did I realize I had not been prayed for correctly. Prayers of faith don't do much good unless when deliverance is needed.

SPIRIT OF PARALYSIS (EXCERPTS)

It is not strange that in the realm of healings there are relatively few among the paraplegics and quadriplegics? Although demons do not know everything about the future, they certainly know a great deal more than we do.

Spirits called **Accident and Accident Prone** work with others named **Bone Breaker and Back Breaker** to open the way for a character called **Traumatic Shock**.

Once the base is established and the headquarters in the nervous system is secured, **Paralysis** calls in spirits of **Crippling, Deformity, Atrophy, Depression, Discouragement, Hopelessness, Despair, Suicide, Death** and many others, and begins the systematic destruction of the victim.

Paralysis sneered at the many preachers and others in healing ministries who had prayed for this man in the wheelchair and others in similar bondage with little or no

results. He called them fools because they refused to recognize the presence and the work of demons, and thereby could not deal with the problem adequately.

Apparently, there were ruling demons of **Paralysis, Affliction and Spinal Cord Scar Tissue** present. I'm sure that there are others yet to be rebuked and cast out.

I am convinced that some people have such a strong gift of faith for healing that when they pray, evil spirits are literally thrown out whether the person praying knows this or not. On the other hand, if the demons are only stunned or immobilized temporarily by believing prayer, then there is always a possibility of a later revival of their work and activity. **(And there is the possibility of the demons coming back in again if the sin has not been dealt with in the person's life.)**

WITCHCRAFT AND SORCERY: PHARMACY - MEDICATION - POISON

Now the works of the flesh are manifest, which are these: adultery, witchcraft, fornication, uncleanness, lasciviousness, idolatry, hatred, variance, emulations, wrath, strife, seditions, heresies, envying, murders, drunkenness, reveling, and such like: of the which I tell you before, as I have also told you in time past, that they which do such things shall not inherit the kingdom of God (Galatians 5:19-21).

That word witchcraft is not the word that is used in the Hebrew. It is found only one time in the New Testament. It is the Greek word pharmakeia, Strong's number 5331. It means medication **(pharmacy, sorcery)** and is taken from the Greek root word 5332 pharmakeus, which means a drug, a druggist **(pharmacist or poisoner, that is sorcerer)**.

Pharmakeia is used in Ex. 22:18, Gal. 5:20-21, Rev. 9:21, 21:8 and 22:15. The literal meaning **primarily signified the use of medicine, drugs, spells; then poisoning; then sorcery. It most commonly means medicine, drugs, spells and poisoning.** This is where we get **pharmacy** (pharmakeia).

Put pharmaceuticals in Rev. 9:21: **Neither repented they of their murders, nor of their pharmaceuticals (sorceries), nor of their fornication, nor of their thefts**.

BIBLICAL CURSES OF SICKNESSSES AND PLAGUES

But it shall come to pass, if thou wilt not hearken unto the voice of the Lord thy God, to observe to do all His commandments and His statutes which I command thee this day; that all these curses shall come upon thee, and overtake thee (Deut. 28:15).

Also every sickness, and every plague, which is not written in the book of this law, them will the LORD bring upon thee, until thou be destroyed (Deut. 28: 61).

REFERENCES

It is recommended that you purchase and study these books: **Conquering The Hosts Of Hell** by Win Worley, WRW Publications, Lansing, IL
Healing Through Deliverance - The Practical Ministry by Peter J. Horrobin, Sovereign World

The Hidden Agenda - A Critical View Of Alternative Medical Therapies by David and Sharon Sneed, Thomas Nelson Publishers

Curses and Diseases Listed in Deuteronomy 28:16-68 by Dr. Bill Null, Salina, KS, unpublished

SECTION 14 - CANCER AND ARTHRITIS DELIVERANCE
(Teach with BASIC DELIVERANCE SUMMARY)

CONTENTS
1. LIST OF SCRIPTURE
2. ANALYSIS OF MATTHEW 5:44
3. ANALYSIS OF MATT. 18:21-35
   1. Law of Forgiveness
   2. Kingdom of Heaven Is Likened To
   3. Value of Money
   4. Value of Your Salvation
4. UNFORGIVENESS
   1. Spiritual Bondage
   2. Consequence of Unforgiveness
   3. Pattern for Being Delivered and Healed
5. FORGIVENESS
6. TESTIMONIES
   1. Earline's Testimony About Indian Curses
   2. Earline's Testimony About Heart Condition
   3. Earline's Testimony About Eating
   4. Our Testimony About Marie's Broken Shoulder
7. GENERAL OPERATING PROCEDURES
8. REFERENCES

LIST OF SCRIPTURE

Psa. 85:2 Forgiven iniquity and covered sin - God.
Psa. 86:5 Ready to forgive and plenteous in mercy - God.
Psa. 103:3 & 12 Forgiveth all & removed as far as east from west - God.
Isa. 1:18 Sins shall be as white as snow - God.
Isa. 43:25 Blotteth out and will not remember - God.
Matt. 5:44 Forgive your enemies - man.
Matt. 6:14-15 Forgive men or not be forgiven by God - man.
Matt. 18:21-35 Law of Forgiveness - man.
Mark 11:25-26 Forgive men or not be forgiven by God - man.
Luke 17:3-4 Rebuke man and forgive seven times a day - man.
Eph. 4:32 King, tenderhearted, forgiving as God does - man.
Col. 2:13 Forgiven you all trespasses - God.
Col. 3:12-13 Mercies, kindness, humbleness, meekness, long-suffering, forbearing and forgiving one another - man.
Heb. 8:12 Merciful to unrighteous and remember not sins - God.
Heb. 10:17 Remember not sins and iniquities - God.
I John 1:9 Confessing, forgiveness, cleansing from unrighteousness.

ANALYSIS OF MATTHEW 5:44

But I say unto you, Love your enemies, bless them that curse you, do good to them that hate you, and pray for them which despitefully use you, and persecute you.

1. **Love your enemies.** We do not have to love Satan! Love in a social or moral sense: beloved. Enemy is an adversary: foe.

2. **Bless them that curse you.** Speak well of: thank or invoke a benediction upon. Curse is to execrate: to doom.

3. **Do good to them that hate you.** Do good honestly: full well. Hate is to detest: especially to persecute.

4. **Pray for them that despitefully use you and persecute you.** Pray earnestly for: supplicate. Despitefully is to insult: slander and falsely accuse. Persecute is to pursue: to suffer.

5. Forgive your enemies; there are no excuses! Whites forgive blacks, blacks forgive whites and other races forgive each other.

6. **You would have a lot fewer infirmities, weaknesses, sicknesses and diseases if you would forgive your enemies.**

ANALYSIS OF MATT. 18:21-35
Law Of Forgiveness

1. Forgive your fellowman 70 x 7 = 490 times. Actually there is no limit to forgiving others. How would you like it if God only forgave you for 490 sins?
2. God sends demons to torment these with unforgiveness.
3. Tormentors are Satan and his demons.
4. Prison is being in jail with Satan as Warden and his demons as guards.

Kingdom Of Heaven Is Likened To

The parable is: God **(is The King)**, the Rich Man **(is You)**; and the Poor Man **(is anyone you have not forgiven)**.

Value Of Money

Talent = 750 oz. of silver; Pence = 1/8 oz. of silver.
10,000 talents x 750 = 7,500,000 oz. = $52,800,000.
100 Pence x 1/8 = 12-1/2 oz. = $44.00.

Value Of Your Salvation

Your salvation is worth $52,800,000.
Your unforgiveness is worth $44.00.
This is a ratio of 600,000 to 1.
God forgave you 600,000 times as much as you are willing to forgive others.

UNFORGIVENESS
Spiritual Bondage

Generally a person's demons can not be cast out if he has unforgiveness in his heart!

This is the crucifixion of the flesh until you come to your senses and forgive your fellowman and then ask God to forgive you!

Consequence Of Unforgiveness
The consequence of unforgiveness is the most important lesson that God has taught us about deliverance. The corollary is the importance of forgiveness.

Cancer, arthritis and certain other diseases can come in through the sin of unforgiveness. If you know a Christian with cancer and arthritis, see if they have unforgiveness. They cannot be healed if the demons have a legal right before God to be there.

Pattern For Being Delivered And Healed
Forgive ancestors, descendents and others, ask God for forgiveness, and forgive self. Cast out the family of bitterness. Cast out cancer and arthritis. Anoint with oil and pray for healing. **Try this pattern on all diseases: first do deliverance then pray for healing.**

FORGIVENESS
(Conquering The Hosts Of Hell)
Forgiveness is hard to give because it hurts to extend it to undeserving and hard-hearted ones. To release a wrong-doer instead of exacting a just penalty requires that we reach out in love, rejecting the temptation to hold bitterness and resentment. This is contrary to our natural inclinations, thus the old adage, **To err is human, to forgive divine.**

Forgiveness is not forgetting the wrong done; some hurts are so deep that this would be impossible. We can forget the anger and hurt we felt, but the act is branded in our minds. Forgiveness takes place when the victim accepts the loss and/or injury done him and deliberately cancels the debt owed him by the offending person. **This is an act of your will and God will honor it.**

Anger must be dealt with openly and honestly, not denied or ignored. Either it must be vented in retaliation or the injured party must accept his own anger, bear the burden of it, and confess it in prayer to release himself and to set the other party free. **Revenge always hurts the revenger far more than the one at whom it is leveled!**

In other words, our pattern must be the grievous and substitutionary death of Christ. He willingly received the hurt and evil of the entire human race in His own body on the tree (I Peter 2:21-24) to pay the debt for our guilt. He now offers what He has wrought as a free gift to undeserving and guilty persons so they can be free (Rom. 6:23; John 10:28-30).

As nothing else will, forgiveness takes us into the mysteries of grace where God forgives unconditionally on the basis of the substitutionary payment by another (Mark 11:25-26).

One of the fruits of the Holy Spirit's work in a life is the quality of meekness. It is a quality which is nurtured and abetted by practicing forgiveness.

This highly prized quality will cause us to be able to accept God's dealings with us as good, without disputing or resisting them. Meekness will also cause us to be able to **bear one another's burden's** cheerfully and for Jesus' sake, enabling us to enter into the mystery of Christ's sufferings.

Because unforgiveness, and the resentment and bitterness it generates is so deadly, it is not optional, but necessary that it be dealt with. Cancer and arthritis spirits definitely root into this fertile ground. To be bitter and unforgiving costs far more than it is worth.

Husbands forgive your wives. Wives forgive your husbands. Children forgive your parents. **In Jesus' Name, I forgive my wife or husband my parents. Amen.**

TESTIMONIES

Our testimonies are found in the **Deliverance Manual** and are illustrative of deliverance and healing. They were written by Earline or myself about our experiences.

Earline's Testimony About Indian Curses

What are the effect of curses? I had a heart condition which was unusual. It never occurred with regularity nor under any specific condition.

While taking a tread mill test, I experienced tremendous pain in the chest, arms and neck. Having been examined by a "heart specialist" in Minneapolis, who told me that my heart was good but he had written "death by heart attack" on many people's certificates like myself. These were people who didn't really have anything wrong with their hearts.

A year or so after my dad's death I found my heart acting up again. Sometimes one to five years would elapse between seizures. I began to ask God to show me why my brothers, dad, dad's brothers and his dad all had heart problems.

He showed me **Ezekiel 18 & Exodus 20**. He told me to repent for my ancestors and myself for the sin of idol worship in **Leviticus 26:40-41**. The curse of idol worship follows the blood line. I did these things and have been free for over eleven years. I was only the second generation from previous generations that sinned before God.

Earline's Testimony About Heart Condition
Earline's Comments
(How many of you have Indian Ancestors?)

I had a heart condition which was unusual. It never occurred with regularity or under any specific condition.

God gave me a vision of a shaman or witch doctor at an elevated funeral pyre which was burning dead bodies. He was chanting and waving, and saying on the descendents and descendents. This was supposed to be a blessing, but in actuality was a curse, because Indians worship demons. This was a curse that came down on my family causing heart problems.

Gene's Comments
This is a sign of demonic symptoms of disease brought about by a curse. It doesn't follow the medical guidelines. All they can say is that it is inherited.

Earline's Comments
While taking a tread mill test, I experienced tremendous pain in the chest, arms and neck. I was examined by a **heart specialist** in Minneapolis who told me that my heart was good but he had written **death by heart attack** on many people's certificates like myself.

Gene's Comments
These were people who didn't really have anything wrong with their hearts physically but had a spiritual root to the disease. The prayer of faith will not heal a disease that has a spiritual root that must be dealt with as sin to be confessed. Then the curse can be broken and the person prayed for to be healed.

God is beginning to show the Christian world spiritual roots of various diseases. Pastor Henry Wright of Molena, Georgia is a pioneer in this area. Also Art Mathias who is in Anchorage, Alaska.

Earline's Comments
A year or so after my dad's death, I found my heart acting up again. Sometimes one to five years would elapse between seizures. I began to ask God to show me why my brothers, dad, dad's brothers and his dad had heart problems.

God showed me Exodus 20 and Ezekiel 18. He told me to repent for my ancestors and myself for the sin of idol worship in Leviticus 26:40-41. The curse of idol worship follows the blood line down to the descendants. I did these things and have been free from these attacks for over twenty years. I was only the second generation from previous generations of Indians that sinned before God.

Gene's Comments
You have to forgive your ancestors and ask for forgiveness for yourself. Earline took her older brother, Clyde, through breaking the curse and he is still alive after a heart attack.

Exodus 20 lists the Ten Commandments which are still applicable today. The scriptures about worshipping other Gods are verses 3, 4 and 5. This outlines the curse for idol worship which lasts three or four generations according to God's purposes. (Does anybody know why God curses some sins for three generations and some sins for four generations?)

Ezekiel 18 shows the equity of God's dealings with us. The sin of idol worship is defined as eating upon the mountains (in the groves), lifting up the eyes to the idols (worship), and not walking in God's statutes and judgments (disobedience).

This was a **revelation of the sins of the ancestors** that God gave Earline through prayer about why her family was plagued by heart attack and death by heart attack. This was primarily the men that were attacked but even Earline, a woman, was attacked. The revelation was the effect of the sins of the ancestors in her family coming through the Indians to cause heart problems and early death. The sin was disobeying the Ten Commandments of having no other Gods before you, which is idol worship, that the Indians committed. Up to that time, we had never heard about the sins of the ancestors.

Earline had Cherokee Indian ancestry coming through her father and mother. We were raised in and around Chattanooga, Tennessee which was not far from Cherokee, North Carolina which had a demonic draw upon Earline. We were drawn to make a pilgrimage to the Smokey Mountains every year although we did not make it every year. In the fall, Earline would long to go to the mountains. After Earline was delivered from Indian spirits, she did not have that draw to go to the Smokey Mountains.

When you are a person of mixed races, you inherit the curses coming down through the different races, languages, customs, religions and nationalities. If you have Indian ancestry and are Caucasian, you receive the curses from the Indians and the Caucasians.

The curse would come from those ancestors that had sinned. This means that you can be cursed for ten generations (2046 ancestors) from both sides of your family.

Which of your ancestors didn't sin or that you know didn't sin? It is a good assumption that you have the curse of incest and the curse of the bastard on you. It could come from any of 2046 ancestors back to the tenth generation that sinned assuming it has not been properly broken. You will see the sin repeating itself generation after generation such as bastard after bastard.

We worked with one Indian woman who was a Christian. She had a hard time getting free of Indian curses and demons brought upon her by her ancestral lineage and sexual abuse. She was cursed by being an Indian and by incest which is very hard on a woman being abused by her blood relatives.

Earline's Testimony About Eating

1. I was sitting on the couch after eating a good breakfast. I had this urging to go and get more food, but I was not hungry. I asked The Lord why and He forced the demon within me to say, **My name is "I Like To Eat", go and get me some food.**
2. After casting out the demon, **I Like To Eat**, I told God how I had tried dieting and I knew that was hopeless.
3. I was told **Obedience is better than sacrifice, and I knew how to eat but was not doing it. Plenty of fresh fruits and vegetables, not much meat and very little sweets is the basis of a proper diet.**
4. **Asked if I'd do what I was told, I assured God that I would. He said that food can be divided into two groups: God's and Devil's. Devil's foods include sweets to excess, junk food, and liquids which are mostly empty calories.**

5. It's not bad manners not to eat sweets or any other food when you know your body has not used up the last meal. I was intelligent enough to know if I truly needed food.

6. Here are the rules in summary:
   a. Eat fruits and vegetables; include leafy greens.
   b. Do not eat much meat - three or four servings weekly.
   c. Don't eat unless you truly need to.
   d. Don't let others stuff you.
   e. Seldom eat sweets.
   f. Almost never eat junk food.
   g. Remember those whose God is their belly.
   h. Cook all foods simply.
   i. Use little fat and cut fat from the meat.

Gene's Comments

1. Earline lost about seventy pounds and weighed less than she did when we got married and before she had two children. She weighed 100 to 110 pounds which was less than Marie, our teenage daughter, who had not had any children. It was like having a new wife!

2. Do you realize that the body has enough energy for you to fast for forty days? Marie fasted for forty days on water taking only vitamins, minerals and supplements.

3. You must take care of your spirit, soul and body. You can not neglect any part of your tripartite being and be in health. You can not neglect your body and expect God to take care of it or heal you every time that you pray. One of Earline's sayings is, **If you don't brush your teeth, God will let them rot out of your mouth.**

4. Healing and deliverance go hand in hand. You can get healed by anointing with oil and praying the prayer of faith, or by casting out demons of infirmities. The Lord told me to take a person through deliverance and then pray for healing. You have a double possibility of getting the person healed.

5. Sometimes the demon of infirmity manifests as it is being cast out and you know that there was an infirmity demon in the person. If the infirmity is there because of sin, you won't get healed by the prayer of faith, because the demon has a legal right to be there. You must take away the legal right and then cast out the demon.

Our Testimony About Marie's Broken Shoulder

One Sunday after going to church, we decided to get Marie's horse, King Fox, and go to the park. After enjoying an afternoon in the sun, we told Marie to ride back and stable the horse so that we could go to Sunday evening services. She rode thru the woods and we rode around the woods in our car.

When we got back to the stables, the horse was tied up and Marie was lying in a car. She had fallen off King Fox and broke her arm. Her face was white and her lips were blue. This shocked Earline and I, but we had the presence of The Holy Spirit, so we prayed for Marie; nothing happened outwardly.

After putting the horse in the stable and Marie in our car, we headed for home. We didn't know whether to take her to the hospital or to the doctor or to depend upon God for healing. As we rode back home, the Lord quickened this verse to my mind, **The steps of a good man are ordered by the Lord: and he delighteth in his way** (Psalm 37:23). I asked God to order our steps about what to do.

After we reached home, Marie sat in the car and felt the bones in her arm. She could feel the dislocated broken bones. We called our family doctor, but he was out and his backup was not to be found either, which was good because we sought The Lord about what to do, PRAISE GOD!

Earline said that one of us should be in the car with Marie. I said I would go and went back to my study to get the anointing oil. As I came out, Earline said, Go get your oil and pray for Marie. God had given us a Word of Wisdom, one of the nine gifts of the Holy Spirit, **For to one is given by the Spirit the word of wisdom; to another the word of knowledge by the same Spirit** (I Cor. 12:8).

We were familiar with anointing with oil and praying the prayer of faith. **Is any sick among you? let him call for the elders of the church; and let them pray over him, anointing him with oil in the name of the Lord: And the prayer of faith shall save the sick, and the Lord shall raise him up; and if he have committed sins, they shall be forgiven him.** (James 5:14-15). I then anointed Marie's forehead, held her hand of the broken arm, and we all prayed again. **Her arm tingled and she could feel the bones moving within the arm, PRAISE THE LORD!**

We then took her to the hospital where she was x-rayed and attended by a bone specialist. He was very talkative and showed us the x-ray. He could see a complete break thru the shoulder socket. The bone was perfectly set and a chipped bone was perfectly in place. We told him about praying for her arm and he said that it was unusual to see that type of break and not have to set the bone.

He put a cast just past Marie's elbow and said come back in three weeks. Earline and Marie prayed that she would be completely healed by then. He examined her and took another x-ray to prove she was not healed. **PRAISE THE LORD, she was healed, the cast was taken off, and she rode King Fox three weeks after the arm was broken!** Any doctor will tell you that it takes six to eight weeks to heal an ordinary break and longer for complicated breaks.

We had memorized a verse in church the Sunday before the accident, **Behold I am the Lord, the God of all flesh: is there anything too hard for me?** (Jer. 32:27). The answer naturally is, No!

Since then I have heard of three other cases where God set the bones, I personally know two of the individuals.

The Lord taught us a number of lessons:
1. Anointing with oil is important to Him.
2. Pray The Blood Of Jesus over your family everyday.

3. He will heal injuries as well as sicknesses.
4. Be ready to pray at all times.

To God be the glory, honor, praise and credit for everything that was done!

GENERAL OPERATING PROCEDURES

Work this lesson with **Deliverance Manual** or **How To Do Deliverance Manual**. I can not say that all cancer and arthritis is demonic, but I can say that some is the result of sin. Holding **Bitterness, Resentment, Hatred, Unforgiveness,** Violence, Temper, Anger, Retaliation and Murder in your heart are sins in the Sight Of God and you will pay a bitter price for those sins. Either you forgive others or God will not forgive you. Arthritis and cancer take root in bitterness; this is fertile ground for diseases to grow in.

When I was in Florida and Alaska, God showed me that we had setup a hospital with an operating room and a recovery room in the church to spiritually operate on the people in deliverance and healing. Think of this as God's Hospital with His Operating Room and His Recovery Room. In individual deliverance, I have cast out cancer and arthritis spirits. I know they were spirits because they manifested when their names were called out.

1. Anoint yourself, deliverance team and the patient with olive oil which is symbolic of The Holy Spirit. This is not magic.
2. Have one of the deliverance team open up with prayer. Train the deliverance team and give them a chance to minister.
3. Ask the patient about bitterness, resentment, hatred and unforgiveness against others, husband or wife, and themselves.
4. Ask the patient if they know of any open door for Satan to attack them with cancer or arthritis. Were there any traumatic events in their life that left scars especially in the emotions?
5. Ask the medical name of the cancer or arthritis so that it can be specifically called out. It is more powerful to call out specific rather than generic names of demons. They want you to call out their name, probably due to pride. It doesn't do any good to say that **I command every demon to come out of this person in The Name Of Jesus**.
6. If it is female cancer, did she have an abortion? Breast cancer can be a result of an abortion. Female diseases can be a result of a promiscuous life style.
7. Ask the patient if the deliverance team and minister can lay hands on them. You need their permission and cooperation.
8. For more power, the deliverance minister shall place their hands on the front and back of the patient's head while casting out demons. You can cast out demons from across the room.
9. Women can lay hands on women, and men on men in places where it would be inappropriate for the opposite sex to do so. Sometimes I will ask women to lay hands on a woman's chest or stomach for more power.
10. Start with Basic Deliverance: Rejection, Bitterness and Rebellion families.
11. After calling out a family of demons, have the patient take three deep breaths to help expel the demons.

12. Observe the manifestations of demons and alter the deliverance process as the need arises. Be led by The Holy Spirit.

13. Leave infirmities, weaknesses, sicknesses and diseases for last. Go after cancer and arthritis in particular. The unusual names are the spiritual names of demons known to them in the spirit world. Call out spirits of death.

14. If the situation is appropriate, take the patient through Fifty-Three Common Demon Groupings found in **How To Do Deliverance Manual**, Prayers And List Of Demons For Mass Deliverance or found in the book, **Pigs In The Parlor**.

15. Have one of the deliverance team pray the prayer of faith for healing. They need the practice of praying for others.

16. Have the deliverance team take the patient into the recovery room and continue working with the person so that you can start with the next patient.

17. In this manner of operation, the deliverance minister can work with a lot of people. Time periods can be two hours, one hour, thirty minutes or even fifteen minutes as the situation dictates.

REFERENCES

Deliverance Manual, **Spiritual Warfare Manual**, **How To Do Deliverance Manual**, **Sexual Deliverance Manual**, **Witchcraft Deliverance Manual**, **Curses Deliverance Manual** and **Healing Deliverance Manual** by Gene and Earline Moody.

Conquering The Hosts Of Hell and **Proper Names of Demons** by Win Worley, Hegewisch Baptist Church, Highland, IN.

SECTION 15 - HEALING FOR KIDNEYS AND OTHER DISEASES

CONTENTS
1. FATHER'S BLESSING
2. SCRIPTURE FOR REINS
3. DEFINITION OF REINS
4. DEFINITION OF KIDNEY
5. DEFINITION OF LOINS
6. EFFECT ON THE BODY
7. PREFACE
8. SPIRITUAL PRINCIPLES
9. SPIRIT - SOUL - BODY
10. SIN'S EFFECTS
11. SPIRITUAL WARFARE
12. KIDNEY DISEASE
13. DIABETES
14. HIGH BLOOD PRESSURE
15. PLEASANT VALLEY CHURCH
16. SPIRITUAL ROOTS OF DISEASE
17. WELLSPRING MINISTRIES OF ALASKA
18. OTHER DISEASES
19. VICTORIA WEST
    1. Conversation
    2. Positive Actions
    3. Negative Actions
    4. Effect of Others
    5. Names of Demons
20. MEDICAL DICTIONARY
21. NEPHROLOGY FAMILIES OF DISEASES
22. WORK BOOKS
23. REFERENCES

FATHER'S BLESSING

I am an ordained minister, apostle, teacher and counselor. I have been a spiritual father to many through the years. I am now a spiritual grandfather due to my age. Many problems are caused in the spiritual realm because the person did not have a father or the father did not act the way he should have. This starts a cycle of problems for the person that will go throughout their life if not dealt with spiritually.

My child, I love you! Your are special. You are a gift from God. I thank God for allowing me to be a father to you. I bless you with the healing of all wounds of rejection, neglect and abuse that you have suffered. I bless you with overflowing peace, the peace that only the Prince of Peace can give, a peace beyond comprehension. I bless your life with fruitfulness--good fruit, much fruit and fruit that remains. I bless you with success. You are the head and not the tail; you are

above and not beneath. I bless you with health and strength of body, soul and spirit. I bless you with overflowing prosperity, enabling you to be a blessing to others. I bless you with spiritual influence, for you are the light of the world and the salt of the earth. You are like a tree planted by rivers of water. You will prosper in all your ways. I bless you with a depth of spiritual understanding and a close walk with your Lord. You will not stumble or falter, for the Word of God will be a lamp to your feet and a light to your path. I bless you with pure and edifying relationships in life. You have favor with God and man. I bless you with abounding love. You will minister God's comforting grace to others. You are blessed, my child! You are blessed with all spiritual blessings in Christ Jesus. Amen!

SCRIPTURE FOR REINS

Job 16:13	He cleaveth my reins asunder.
Job 19:27	Though my reins be consumed within me.
Ps. 7:9	God trieth the hearts and reins.
Ps. 16:7	My reins also instruct me in the night.
Ps. 26:2	Try my reins and my heart.
Ps. 73:21	And I was pricked in my reins.
Ps. 139:13	For thou hast possessed my reins.
Prov. 23:16	My reins shall rejoice.
Is. 11:5	Faithfulness the girdle of his reins.
Jer. 11:20	That trieth the reins.
Jer. 12:2	And far from their reins.
Jer. 17:10	I try the reins.
Jer. 20:12	And seest the reins.
Lam. 3:13	Of his quiver to enter his reins.
Rev. 2:23	I am he which searcheth the reins.

DEFINITION OF REINS

1. **nephros**, a kidney (nephritis, etc.), is used metaphorically of **the will and the affections**. The feelings and emotions were regarded as having their seat in the **kidneys**.
2. **kidneys and loins**, nephros - kidneys, loins - waist - heart - mind, pierced within or inward parts.

DEFINITION OF KIDNEY

To the Hebrews, the kidneys, because of their sensitivity, were believed to be the seat of desire. Scripture contains many eloquent assays referring to this. When a man suffers deep within himself, he is **pierced within**; when he rejoices, it is within his **inmost being**; and when he earnestly longs, his **heart** faints within. The kidneys also seem to provide knowledge and understanding where THE WORD is rendered **mind**. **Job complains that God has split his kidneys open**.

DEFINITION OF LOINS

Ancient people commonly used **loins** figuratively for the center of emotions such as pain or terror. It is used by euphemism for the reproductive power. The loins were especially dressed with sackcloth symbolizing a mourning heart.

Loins is used in the natural sense as **the seat of generative power**, metaphorically of girding the **loins** in readiness for active service for the Lord with truth. Bracing up oneself so as to maintain perfect sincerity and reality as the counteractive in Christian character against hypocrisy and falsehood; of girding the **loins** of the mind, suggestive of the alertness necessary for sobriety and for setting one's hope perfectly on **the grace to be brought at the revelation of Jesus Christ**.

EFFECT ON THE BODY

In the above biblical definitions of reins, kidney and loins you can see the importance of various effects on the body: **will and affections**, feelings and emotions, heart and mind, pierced within or inward parts, sensitivity, seat of desire, suffers deep within, **pierced within**; within **inmost being**; earnestly longs, **heart** faints within, knowledge and understanding, **mind**, center of emotions, pain or terror, reproductive power, mourning heart, **seat of generative power**, and hypocrisy and falsehood.

From these effects come diseases of the body and soul (mind, will and emotions). You can see how your thoughts can affect your being mentally, physically and spiritually.

PREFACE

Kidney failure is a very difficult area to work in. I have found little in the medical or Christian literature about healing of kidneys when they fail. You can go on dialysis or have a kidney transplant but this does not heal the kidneys, it only maintains life. There are side affects associated with these methods of treatment. I am not aware of anyone who has been healed supernaturally, when the kidneys failed completely, by the prayer of faith and/or the casting out of demons.

It only takes 25% of one kidney to maintain life. Less than 25% results in death unless one of the two treatments is used. The accumulated toxins and fluid in the body kill the body.

If the kidneys have not failed completely, there is more possibility of being healed. This may take the form of diet and/or alternative medicine, pharmaceutical medicine and/or operation, anointing with oil and/or the casting out of demons or some combination of these methods.

SPIRITUAL PRINCIPLES

The teaching contained in this lesson could be applied to other diseases. **The principles are the same but the individuals are different and have different diseases.** Each person is unique with unique problems. Each person needs to be ministered to as an individual given special attention.

SPIRIT - SOUL - BODY

We are a tripartite being composed of a body which contains the soul and spirit. When we die our spirit and soul will go to be with THE LORD. To be in complete health, you must take care of these three parts. You can not neglect any one of these and be in health.

The spirit comes from GOD and will go back to GOD. Your soul is your mind, will and emotions, and all that they contain. Your body is the physical part which contains your brain where the soul resides.

To take care of the spirit requires first becoming a Christian and then following THE HOLY SPIRIT in living a holy life free of sin. To take care of the soul requires training the brain how to follow GOD and THE HOLY BIBLE and then disciplining your body. To take care of the body requires proper use of the body and feeding the body with proper food.

A lot can be said about taking care of the body. THE BIBLE has dietary laws which are worth studying. Are you feeding your body with healthy food and drink? Are you exercising and using the body correctly in areas of sex and other areas? For instance, THE BIBLE forbids the eating of blood. What effect could eating blood have on the person: mentally, physically or spiritually?

SIN'S EFFECTS

THE BIBLE teaches that if you sin it will affect your body. Many times the cause and effect is clearly presented. For instance, consider the occult, witchcraft or Satan worship. These will affect your spirit, soul and body here on earth and eventually send you to Hell. **If you repent over THE SCRIPTURES for some particular part of your body, you may be healed.**

SPIRITUAL WARFARE

We are in a life and death battle with the forces of Satan. It is necessary not only to pray but to enter into spiritual warfare where you fight against the forces of evil. This should be done on a daily basis.

Spiritual Warfare Personal shows how I apply these principles to my life. **Spiritual Warfare General** shows how anyone can apply these principles to their lives. I use these almost daily.

KIDNEY DISEASE

Some medical terms for this disease for you to research are glomerulonephritis, kidney and nephritis. Renal means kidney. There are a list of names pertaining to symptoms of disease in each category.

DIABETES

Diabetes is called autoimmune disease, hyperglycemia and diabetes mellitus. The spiritual root behind **diabetes: <u>extreme rejection and self-hatred</u> coupled with <u>guilt</u>**. There is **direct rejection by a father and sometimes, a husband, or a man in general. <u>Fear, anxiety and stress</u> is a root cause and the <u>unloving spirit</u> that allows <u>self-hatred, self-rejection and guilt</u>.** Fear can be inherited. Scripture: Eze. 18:17, Exe. 20:4-5.

HIGH BLOOD PRESSURE
It is caused by <u>fear and anxiety</u>. High blood pressure is hypertension caused by <u>fear, anxiety and stress</u>. Scripture: II Tim. 1:7.

PLEASANT VALLEY CHURCH
A letter from the church stated, **We are still learning, but so far our experience with kidney failure is that the spiritual dynamics behind it can be <u>rejection, self-rejection, envy, bitterness, fear, and a spirit of death, hell and destruction</u>. These are some areas you might want to explore.**

Pleasant Valley Publications has some books and tapes that are recommended for purchase. The church also conducts training and seminars.

SPIRITUAL ROOTS OF DISEASE
GOD has shown Pastor Henry Wright of Pleasant Valley Church about spiritual roots of disease. **If there is a spiritual root to the disease, the person can not be healed but has to be delivered.** The sin that opened the door to the disease must be dealt with first. This is either the sins of the ancestors, someone who had spiritual authority over the person, the person or some combination of these open doors to disease.

WELLSPRING MINISTRIES OF ALASKA
I had a telephone discussion with Art Mathias, author of **Biblical Foundations of Freedom**. He stated that kidney failure may be from many different causes; he had nothing specific. He suggested working through his book and also the book, **A More Excellent Way**. **Start with bitterness which is an open door to diseases such as cancer and arthritis.** Bitterness is a strong demon, a principality.

OTHER DISEASES
(The Continuing Works of Christ)
Cardiovascular System, Coronary Artery Disease: The Bible says, **In the last days men's hearts shall fail them because of fear** (Luke 21:26).

Hypertension: High Blood Pressure. Fear and anxiety is the root for high blood pressure. The Bible and medical science agree. What we teach is not opposed to medical science. In fact, what I see in the Bible only proves medical science and medical science only proves the Bible.

Stroke and Aneurysms: Strokes and aneurysms are the result of rage and anger, but behind the rage and anger is also fear. Do you know why people go into rage and anger? First of all, they have a root of bitterness. They are really afraid to deal with issues. Rather than being confronted on an issue and having to deal with it, they just blow up because that is their defensive mechanism. They don't want to be confronted on an issue because they are afraid of men and they are afraid of rejection.

Disturbances of Heart Rhythm: Such things as rhythmic problems. Irregular heart beat and Mitral Valve Prolapse are the result of anxiety and stress.

Muscles and Tension Headaches: We rub the back of our necks when we are under stress and tension to relieve the pain. Why not turn to God and deal with the fear and anxiety?

Muscle Contraction Backache: Again anxiety and stress is the issue. I have witnessed many healings when people have repented of the lack of faith in God and then learned to trust Him.

Rheumatoid Arthritis: There is a direct relationship between the tremendous stress of self-hatred and all autoimmune disease. The person is **afraid of themselves**. They just don't want to face themselves. Out of that come **self-hatred**, out of that comes the **guilt**, out of that comes the conflict that causes the white corpuscles to attack the connective material of the bones, and eat at it, and produce rheumatoid arthritis.

Pulmonary System: Asthma and Hay Fever. John Hopkins University is now teaching that Hay Fever and Asthma are not caused by air born allergens. It has nothing to do with breathing, dander, dust, pollen, etc. Anxiety and fear cause it. It can be inherited, but it's coming out of **deep-rooted anxiety and fear**. I have proved this many times over.

Immune System: Immunosuppression or Immune Deficiency and Autoimmune Disease: Over secretion of cortisol and catecholamines destroy the immune system, and the result is autoimmune diseases. The Hypothalamus controls over 23 hormones including these two. Autoimmune diseases occur when the white corpuscles attacks living flesh and destroy it. Lupus, Crones, Diabetes, Rheumatoid Arthritis, and MS are examples.

We have learned that the body attacks the body as a person attacks themselves spiritually in self-rejection, self-hatred, and self-bitterness. The body agrees with the mind and starts attacking itself. That is a high price to pay for not loving yourself.

Gastrointestinal System: Ulcers. For years the medical community believed that stress and anxiety caused an irritation in the stomach, which eventually caused the ulceration. Recently they have begun to prescribe antibiotics are telling us that a bacteria or viruses cause ulcers.

People who have ulcers also have compromised immune systems because of the anxiety and stress. When you have a compromised immune system, you don't have the ability to defeat bacteria and viruses. The fear and anxiety come first and the bacteria and viruses show up after the immune system is compromised.

There are a number of gastrointestinal problems that are caused by anxiety and stress. They include **Irritable Bowel Syndrome (IBS), diarrhea, nausea, vomiting, and ulcerated colitis.**

Every single malfunction in the gastrointestinal tract is caused by anxiety and stress. The peace of God in your heart regarding issues in your life is the cure. (With the exception of Crones disease, which is an autoimmune disease.)

Genital Urinary System: Diuresis, Impotence, and Frigidity are caused by anxiety and fear.

Skin: Eczema, Acne, Dermatitis: Adolescent acne is caused by fear coming from peer pressure. It is not a genetic or biologic problem by itself, but in most cases the kids are afraid of other kids. That level of fear and anxiety triggers increased histamine secretion. It also increases white corpuscle activity in the epidermis thus causing acne.

Endocrine System: Diabetes and Amenorrhea

Central Nervous System: Fatigue and lethargy, Type A behavior, overeating, depression, and insomnia are all cause by **fear and anxiety and stress.**

PASTOR RON TIFFIN

I had a telephone discussion with Pastor Ron Tiffin of British Columbia, Canada concerning the healing of chronic kidney disease of various people that the church has ministered to; they had amazing success. God showed him that kidneys are mentioned as **reins in THE BIBLE**. **The deep roots are <u>jealousy, envy and rejection</u>** which must be overcome.

You are set free by THE TRUTH OF THE BIBLE which is an ongoing process of learning: line upon line, precept upon precept, a little here a little there. The person must be taught THE TRUTH OF GOD, ministered what was taught and prayed for. John The Baptist said to clear the pathway for JESUS CHRIST. As we follow the pathway to GOD, we rectify sins and clean up our lives opening the pathway for healing. Through the teaching of THE WORD OF GOD, a person needs to know how they got into trouble and how they got out of trouble, or they will go back into trouble.

You must turn to GOD rather than man. **THE BIBLE IS first and foremost** rather than men's books which are to only be used as support for THE BIBLE. You must agree with THE TRUTH OF GOD and receive it into your heart.

<u>**You need to believe that you are accepted, loved and worthy.**</u> Every person needs individual ministry. You can not heal a broken heart; it must be mended by a **father's love** either by GOD or man. This could be a pastor or minister with the **heart of the Father**.

There is tremendous turmoil and need in THE BODY OF CHRIST JESUS. Many times it is father or mother who didn't do their parenting properly and the person has turned against them in some way. There can be denominational bondage due to false teaching. There are generational curses, abuses in the family line, racism, and other means that opens the person's spiritual armor to penetration by diseases and demons.

The person needs to recount their problems to the minister. This is the spiritual profile of the individual who must be brutally honest.

VICTORIA WEBB
Conversation

I had a telephone discussion with Victoria Webb of British Columbia, Canada who had a healing of her kidneys. She used the methods of her church and Pleasant Valley Church along with THE HOLY SPIRIT teaching her. Kidney disease is like a planter wart with many spiritual roots. This is a delicate and difficult matter. She received a Miracle of Mercy.

Positive Actions
Positive things to do are: line up with GOD in repentance, live up to GOD's WORD, walk in resurrection life, die to self, live for Him, agree with THE WORD, exercise the power of prayer, control your reins, read scripture and pray. Get the elders of the church to anoint with oil, lay hands on the sick, have the church to pray for healing and receive beauty for ashes.

Negative Actions
Negative things not to do are: make a bitter-root judgment, speak death, don't love self, blame GOD, be angry with GOD, think and talk death, and make a covenant with death.

Effect Of Others
You can be affected by your family or others who have spiritual authority over you: generational curses and curses in immediate family; family alienation, strife, bitterness and bad blood; mental and emotional abuse; medical diagnosis speaking a curse; living in a death world; and betrayal, abuse and lying.

Names Of Demons
She mentioned the following which can be used for names of demons: root of bitterness, kidney stone, cancer, nephritis, unforgiveness, deep hurt, self-hatred, rejection, bitterness, destruction, high blood pressure, fear, trauma, heart disease, broken spirit, unloving spirit, murderous rage, anger, guilt about bondage, rebellion, witchcraft, black magic, hypertension, broken heart, and other related ailments. Assume the names of what is wrong with the person are the names of demons.

MEDICAL DICTIONARY
A handy tool to use in deliverance is a medical dictionary. You can look up the name of the disease and its symptoms. Use the name as the ruler demon and the symptoms as the lesser demons. Think of it as a family with a head and members of that family. This method has proved successful in some instances.

NEPHROLOGY FAMILIES OF DISEASES
Kidney failure has certain families of diseases. Consider these families because they have different symptoms in each grouping. These come under the category of nephrology. The following are conditions: **acute glomerulonephritis, chronic glomerular, hypertension nephrosclerosis, nephritis, acute interstitial nephritis, acute renal failure, acute tubular necrosis, chronic renal failure, diabetic nephropathy, hematuria, ischemic nephropathy, kidney stones, nephrotic syndrome, polycystic kidney disease, proteinuria and microalbuminuria, renal artery stenosis and renal vascular hypertension.**

The kidneys can be affected by high blood pressure and diabetes which destroy the nephrons in the kidney and cause fluids to be retained in the heart. Other families that need to be considered are **hypertension and diabetes.**

WORK BOOKS

THE BIBLE is your main book. You have to study the whole BIBLE for mental, physical, spiritual and material health. It is recommended that you work your way through the books, **A More Excellent Way, Biblical Foundations of Freedom,** and **Deliverance Manual.** Healing and deliverance go hand-in-hand together; they compliment each other. You can be healed by deliverance, divine healing or a combination of both. Completely read the books and follow the instructions. The time spent is worthwhile if you want to be delivered and healed. **It may be the only way to rid yourself of disease because these are complex areas and humans are complex beings.**

REFERENCES

I recommend the purchase of the books from Pleasant Valley Publications, at least one medical dictionary and the **Deliverance Manual**.

A More Excellent Way (I Corinthians 12:31 - A Teaching on the Spiritual Roots of Disease - The Ministry of Pastor Henry Wright), Pleasant Valley Publications, A Division of Pleasant Valley Church, Inc., Thomaston, GA 30286
Biblical Foundations of Freedom (Destroying Satan's Lies with God's Truth) by Art Mathias, Pleasant Valley Publications
Taber's Cyclopedic Medical Dictionary, F.A. Davis Company
PDR Medical Dictionary, Medical Economics
Vine's Complete Expository Dictionary of Old & New Testament Words by W.E. Vine, Merrill F. Unger and William White, Jr.
The New Unger's Bible Dictionary by Merrill F. Unger
The New Strong's Exhaustive Concordance Of The Bible by James Strong
Deliverance Manual by Gene and Earline Moody. Also **Spiritual Warfare Manual, How To Do Deliverance Manual, Sexual Deliverance Manual, Witchcraft Deliverance Manual, Curses Deliverance Manual** and **Healing Deliverance Manual** are additions to the **Deliverance Manual** which may assist you in being delivered and healed.
The Father's Blessing - Imparting The Blessings Of God To Your Children by Frank D. Hammond
The Continuing Works of Christ by Art Mathias, Wellspring Ministries of Alaska, Anchorage, AK

SECTION 16 - TESTIMONY - JESUS SET MARIE'S BROKEN ARM

One Sunday after going to church, we decided to get Marie's horse, King Fox, and go to the park. After enjoying an afternoon in the sun, we told Marie to ride back and stable the horse so that we could go to Sunday evening services. She rode thru the woods and we rode around the woods in our car.

When we got back to the stables, the horse was tied up and Marie was lying in a car. She had fallen off King Fox and broke her arm. Her face was white and her lips were blue. This shocked Earline and I, but we had the presence of The Holy Spirit, so we prayed for Marie; nothing happened outwardly.

After putting the horse in the stable and Marie in our car, we headed for home. We didn't know whether to take her to the hospital or to the doctor or to depend upon God for healing. As we rode back home, the Lord quickened this verse to my mind, **The steps of a good man are ordered by the Lord: and he delighteth in his way** (Psalm 37:23). I asked God to order our steps about what to do.

After we reached home, Marie sat in the car and felt the bones in her arm. She could feel the dislocated broken bones. We called our family doctor, but he was out and his backup was not to be found either, which was good because we sought The Lord about what to do, PRAISE GOD!

Earline said that one of us should be in the car with Marie. I said I would go and went back to my study to get the anointing oil. As I came out, Earline said, Go get your oil and pray for Marie. God had given us a Word of Wisdom, one of the nine gifts of the Holy Spirit, **For to one is given by the Spirit the word of wisdom; to another the word of knowledge by the same Spirit** (I Cor. 12:8).

We were familiar with anointing with oil and praying the prayer of faith. **Is any sick among you? let him call for the elders of the church; and let them pray over him, anointing him with oil in the name of the Lord: And the prayer of faith shall save the sick, and the Lord shall raise him up; and if he have committed sins, they shall be forgiven him.** (James 5:14-15). I then anointed Marie's forehead, held her hand of the broken arm, and we all prayed again. **Her arm tingled and she could feel the bones moving within the arm, PRAISE THE LORD!**

We then took her to the hospital where she was x-rayed and attended by a bone specialist. He was a very talkative and showed us the x-ray. He could see a complete break thru the shoulder socket. The bone was perfectly set and a chipped bone was perfectly in place. We told him about praying for her arm and he said that it was unusual to see that type of break and not have to set the bone.

He put a cast just past Marie's elbow and said come back in three weeks. Earline and Marie prayed that she would be completely healed by then. He examined her and took another x-ray to prove she was not healed. **PRAISE THE LORD, she was healed, the**

cast was taken off, and she rode King Fox three weeks after the arm was broken! Any doctor will tell you that it takes six to eight weeks to heal an ordinary break and longer for complicated breaks.

We had memorized a verse in church the Sunday before the accident, **Behold I am the Lord, the God of all flesh: is there anything too hard for me?** (Jer. 32:27). The answer naturally is, No!

Since then I have heard of three other cases where God set the bones, I personally know two of the individuals.

The Lord taught us a number of lessons:
1. Anointing with oil is important to Him.
2. Pray The Blood Of Jesus over your family everyday.
3. He will heal injuries as well as sicknesses.
4. Be ready to pray at all times.

To God be the glory, honor, praise and credit for everything that was done!

SECTION 17 - FAMILY TESTIMONIES

CONTENTS
1. **BYRON'S DEATH**
   1. From Death Into Real Life
   2. Gene's Testimony About Byron's Death
   3. Earline's Testimony About Byron's Death
   4. Earline's Testimony About Grief Over Byron's Death
2. **EARLINE'S DEATH**
   1. Gene's Testimony About Earline's Homecoming
      1. Job's Test
      2. Hospital Experience
      3. The Perfect Number Seven
      4. The Future
   2. Gene's Memorial For Earline
      1. Persecution
      2. Testimony About How GOD Taught Us Deliverance
      3. Declaration
3. **OUR DELIVERANCE TESTIMONY**
   1. General
   2. Pigs In The Parlor
   3. Faith Tabernacle
   4. Can A Christian Have A Demon?
   5. All Christians
   6. Our Family
   7. Our Ministry
4. **GENE'S TESTIMONY**
   1. Gene's Testimony About Ahab Characteristics
5. **EARLINE'S TESTIMONY**
   1. Earline's Main Testimony About Deliverance
   2. Earline's Testimony About Rejection
   3. Earline's Testimony About Ancestral Background
   4. Earline's Testimony About Heart Condition
      1. Earline's Comments
      2. Gene's Comments
   5. Earline's Testimony About The Curse Of The Bastard
   6. Earline's Testimony About Eating
      1. Gene's Comments
   7. Earline's Testimony About Maintaining Deliverance
   8. Earline's Testimony About Schizophrenia Deliverance
   9. Earline's Testimony About Deliverance From Indian Curses
6. **MARIE'S TESTIMONY**
   1. Earline's Testimony About Marie's Salvation
   2. Our Testimony About Jesus Setting Marie's Broken Shoulder
   3. Marie's Testimony About Experience With Demonic Objects

7. PSYCHIC PRAYERS
1. OUR TESTIMONY ABOUT PSYCHIC PRAYERS
1. Gene's Comments

BYRON'S DEATH
From Death Into Real Life

This is the testimony of my family: Earline, my wife; Marie, my daughter; and Byron, my son. We were married in 1955 by Dr. Lee Roberson, who had a practice of not marrying anyone who was not a Christian. Little did we realize then what a difference it makes for both spouses to be Christians and for God to control your family. We give God the credit for our successful marriage of 25 years.

We were average Christians who never had really done anything very bad or very good. Although I had held most of the positions in the church, there was not much love in my heart for others. Nor did we see much love in the many churches we attended as I moved around the United States following the engineering profession. Worship services were more of a formality.

Earline had a number of miscarriages. Thyroid and parathyroid were completely removed as a teenager. The doctors said that we could not have any children. Earline began praying, and in 1960 God rewarded us with a beautiful baby boy we named Byron. Two years later, God gave us a beautiful baby girl we named Marie. They were all the children we could have because of Earline's health.

We went to traditional churches. They did not teach us about the miracle-working God. We did not see the miracles of God for twenty years. After several medical checkups culminating in a $500 one in 1973, it was conclusively proven that Earline had no thyroid or parathyroid. According to the doctors, she could not be alive, but was doing fine at 40 years of age. We later recognized that our children were medical miracles.

We had a near perfect family for 12 1/2 years, then tragedy struck. Byron climbed a tree and touched a 4000-volt power line and fell 50 feet. We really began to see God at work in our lives. I would like for Earline to tell what happened. We still don't understand why it had to happen or what all God has done for us.

On May 22, 1973 my world came to a crushing halt! As the children played, two neighbors came over to join me for tea. The children came in for cookies and went out again. Byron stood by my chair, his arm on my shoulder, gave me a little hug and said some day he would climb a tree to the very top. Turned, on the run, and said, "You're a nice mom", went out the door and climbed a tall cottonwood.

Soon, one of the children said that Byron had fallen out of the tree. One look at Byron and I knew only God could help him. Marie and I began to pray as never before. Nothing in my life had prepared me for this moment. No faith in God rose to meet this crisis.

On the way to the hospital, we became sure that God didn't love us or He would never have let this happen. Having nothing else to cling to, we clung to God anyway (Ps. 50:15).

At the hospital, I accused God of not living, not caring, not being. He so lovingly said, **"I love you, Gene and Marie more than you love each other, more than you love yourselves. I love Byron more than you do".** I couldn't believe Him. I told God, if He didn't do something to prove He loved us and that Byron was in Heaven, I would kill them and myself. I told Him if Byron was not in Heaven I didn't want any part of it either.

With all this fussing at God, I could only feel love coming to me. He said **"All things are His including the tree, the power line and all the earth"** (Ps. 50:10-12).

I heard myself telling Satan to remove death from Byron in the name of Jesus. Byron lived on as a miracle. I didn't know this was possible (rebuking Satan in Jesus' name).

After Gene arrived, I told all God had said. We could not believe that God really was talking. We didn't know He talked today.

As we prayed together, God assured us of His love and His everlasting knowledge. He knew Byron's future and asked if we did or would be responsible for it. A real belief and reliance in God's words sprang up in us and we were able to give Byron into the hands of this loving God. At that moment, he died.

One glance at the doctor's face and we knew before he spoke "death". I had been in the hospital with an extremely rapid heart beat. Now I could hardly see and my heart had gone mad - beating wildly. As I stood, God acted. Something very wonderful began at the top of my head, eyes were suddenly clear, heart suddenly regular. I was so calm I was startled. Peace had come over me so that I could hardly bear it. I didn't understand **"peace that passes understanding"** (Phil. 4:7). Now I knew this peace and understood Jesus more.

People came to console us. All we could do was tell them about this Jesus we had just experienced and all He had done for us. We had no need for the pills that were offered. We had just met the God of power and were sure we could rely on Him for all things. God had become greater than our loss and fears. He is real, He is alive, He has power, He loves us.

We saw visions, had dreams and interpretations of dreams, and had words of knowledge and words of wisdom. We didn't know where these things came from. In John 16:13 we found the answer. Later on we met people who could explain the Baptism of the Holy Spirit. We received this Baptism, a prayer language, a new joy in reading the Bible and understanding. Isaiah 16:14 is a promise which God has richly kept.

Once it seemed that Byron visited me - whether in a dream or vision I'm not sure. I asked about his death; he said it was terribly cold but now everything was fine. I asked if he had seen Jesus; he said Jesus was nearly always with the children but was not there - and then Byron left.

God came to Marie in a terrible dream that showed Byron coming out the casket, sitting in a wheel chair and talking out of the side of his mouth. God gave me the interpretation. If we had not let God's perfect will be done, Byron would have been a living vegetable. We would have regretted praying for him to live.

God did many kindnesses for us to show that He was alive and loved us. Before we knew about raising our hands and praising God, He held our hands and walked with us. God spoke audibly to Earline several times. Byron had only been dead a short time when God told us that we must share what He had done for us with others. God told us when Byron accepted Christ and that Proverbs 20:11 changed him from death to life.

Jesus Christ was Savior but not Lord and Master for 20 years. We dedicated ourselves totally to God in 1973 and things began to happen. We had never tithed. We started tithing 10% after deductions and God cut my salary to 10 times the tithe. After we searched the Bible and found out that we owe God a tenth of gross income, then God found me another job. He had cut my salary $2,000 a year but he gave back $5,000 a year after my heart was right.

God has given our family divine health for the past seven years. The first major miracle was to heal Earline's back. She had been losing calcium for five years and was becoming a cripple. In addition to healing her back, God lengthened her leg 1/2". Then God healed Earline of her allergies. She went to a world renowned doctor, Dr. Browning, who found that she had 175 allergies and he said that she could never be cured. One night when she was about to take her shot, God spoke and said she didn't need her shots. She has not taken a shot since and is completely healed. When I saw God heal Earline, I decided by faith to stop taking my shots; God faithfully healed me from my allergies. Marie has been healed of many minor ailments by prayer such as a broken tail bone and ear ache. We could spend many days telling about people that we have seen God heal.

One Sunday afternoon, Marie decided to get her horse, King Fox, and go riding. When we got back to the stables, Marie had fallen off King Fox and broken her arm. This shocked Earline and I but we had the presence of the Holy Spirit so we prayed for Marie.

We didn't know whether to take her to the hospital or to the doctor or to depend upon God for healing. As we rode back home, the Lord quickened Psalm 37:23 to my mind, **"The steps of a good man are ordered by the Lord".** I asked God to order our steps.

Marie sat in the car, she could feel the dislocated broken bones. We called our family doctor, Dr. Lee. He was out and his backup was out too.

I went to my study to get the anointing oil. As I came out, Earline said, "Go get your oil and pray for Marie". God had given us a **"Word of Wisdom"** (I Corinthians 12:8). We were familiar with James 5:14 and 15 about anointing with oil and praying the prayer of faith. I then anointed Marie's forehead, held her hand of the broken arm, and we prayed again. Her arm tingled and she could feel the bones moving within the arm.

We then took her to Doctor's Memorial Hospital where she was x-rayed and attended by Dr. Kilroy, a bone specialist who showed us the x-ray. We could see a complete break through the shoulder socket; the bone was perfectly set. He said that it was unusual to see that type of break and not have to set the bone.

Earline and Marie prayed that she would be completely healed in three weeks. The doctor took an x-ray to prove she was not healed. PRAISE THE LORD, she was healed, the cast was taken off, and she rode King Fox three weeks after the arm was broken! Any doctor will tell you that it takes six to eight weeks to heal an ordinary break and longer for complicated breaks.

Jeremiah 32:27 says, **"Behold I am the Lord, the God of all flesh; is there anything too hard for me."** God is only limited by our faith. Since then, I have learned of three other cases where God set the bones. To God be the glory, honor and praise for everything that was done.

We were baptized in the Holy Spirit at the Full Gospel Business Men's Fellowship International meeting in Baton Rouge. We have received the fruit of the Spirit: love, joy, peace, long suffering, gentleness, goodness, faith, meekness and temperance. Spiritually God has filled our cups to overflowing with His love and grace. Materially God has met all of our needs out of His riches in Glory through Christ Jesus.

The first year after the Baptism we went to as many meetings as we could attend to learn and be blessed. Then God began to deal with us about helping others. Now, we minister to whoever God puts in our path. We pray for the sick and those needing deliverance. We have seen the sick healed and God grow out arms and legs as much as 2". We have seen demons cast out and the dead raised (Matthew 10:78).

Gene's Testimony About Byron's Death

After Byron's death, the world seemed unreal. I wanted to leave this world and I asked God to kill us. This was an improper prayer and it was a selfish action on my part. Losing Byron was like losing an arm or a leg. We searched the Bible to see if we could commit suicide, go to heaven and be with Byron, and also to be out of our misery. The Bible says that you have no right to commit suicide and you may end up in Hell. We prayed that the plane would crash in the Atlanta Airport. There were one-hundred tornadoes in Atlanta that day and the plane shook on its take-off. My grief really was for my loss and for myself. God told us that Byron was in Heaven. I would sit and hold Byron's picture and cry; I did this many times. I felt like I had to grieve over Byron's death or I was not showing proper love for him. I would drive to work praying and crying. I cry often now but they are tears of joy. I have found that there is nothing wrong with a man crying in the sight of God.

I did not want to work but God told me that I must support my family. I tried to go to the mission field but nobody wanted me; they only wanted me to go to the seminary. God told me to continue to be an engineer and to start helping others who were in need.

After Byron's death we really started seeking God. Jesus was our Savior but He became our Lord and Master also.

Byron's death caused us to reach out and help others who were experiencing death in their families. God has helped restore our lives as we have helped others. Now we have a ministry of helping others centered around deliverance.

It took four years to write our testimony "From Death Into Real Life" and to overcome our grief. I handled my grief by the following steps: **I quit looking back at Byron's death, I ministered to the needs of my family, and I went on with what the Lord wanted me to do.**

Earline's Testimony About Byron's Death

There are days you never forget . Some are joyful, happy, fun days and others are terrifying, horrible days. May 22, 1973 was one of those terrifying days.

It started off as a lovely day. Spring in Minnesota is a beautiful, delicate time of year. It begins in lovely pastels and flows into stronger hues. This day was so lovely in its beginning. The children are off to school. I spend some time reading my Bible and praying for the members of my family. Then it's time for the housework. I've been busy all day and in a hurry to finish so that I'm free by the time the children come home from school.

Here they are at the door eager to get in and tell all about the day's events. Byron hits the back steps on the run with the usual "Hi Mom!" Marie is not far behind. They have some snacks, change clothes, and run out to play.

Our pastor's wife and children, and a neighbor come by. I make tea for the adults and the children go off to play. Byron comes in, hugs me where I sit, tells me "I'm a good Mom," and sneaks a cookie out of my saucer. Tells me as he rushes out the door that, "Someday I'm going to climb to the top of a tree". He's gone but I hear me saying, "Don't climb the tree at the top of the hill". He doesn't hear.

The talk among adults begins again, pastor's wife leaves, and neighbor stays. The door slams and the pastor's son says "Byron fell out of the tree". I rush up the hill to where he lays. One look and I know there is no hope except in God. We begin artificial respiration but there's no response. I hurry to call the rescue unit. They are here in no time. The route to the hospital is cleared; we're there in a matter of minutes. All the way Marie and I pray begging God to help him, to heal him.

Now he's in the emergency room; they are trying so hard to help him. We're in the waiting room praying; praying as we have never prayed before. They've called Gene; I'm praying for him. His children are the light and joy of his life, and now only God can restore his son. Oh God, please help him!

During this wait, I hear myself thinking, "Where in God's Word can I find help?" By a miracle He has given this child, how can He let him die? How can I let him die? I hear my voice asking God, "How can you say you love him and us if you will not hear and heal?" And God said, "I love him more than you do". I tell God I don't understand it. I reason with Him that Jesus didn't have children here so how can He understand? All He says is, "I love you, Gene and Marie more than you do. I know the present, past and future of all things". Not once did I feel He did not love me or them but I truly could not understand.

Gene is here now; a moment I've desired and dreaded. He is told everything; I tell him what God has said. We still cannot say "Lord we trust you, have your way here".

As in a distance, I hear myself tell the Devil to remove death from this child; that in Jesus' name he cannot have him. And Byron lives on in a coma.

As time passes, God's love and assurance penetrates us; at least we are able to say, "He is yours". At this moment God removed his spirit. We never had been able to dedicate our children to God. Somehow we were afraid of God. He had not become a God of love and power to us but He is becoming so now.

Now I am letting all my fear out to God. I tell Him, "If this child dies, I will kill myself, Gene and Marie because I know with certainty that I cannot help it". Even knowing what the Bible says about suicide and murder, I know I cannot help myself.

Byron had never been down the church isle nor had he joined the church. When he was a baby, he was loving and a joy to behold. All of his life he excelled in all things: school, sports, etc. Instead of growing away from his family, he seemed to grow closer.

In the year before his death, he was happiest when we did things as a family. At night he would study or pretend to until Gene finished his work in the study and came down to the den. He had a favorite chair. He would get up and walk around the room and his dad would sit in Byron's favorite chair Byron jumps in his dad's lap and sits there during the news. He's 12 years old and we're wondering when he will start to rebel.

I'm remembering how Byron, Marie and Gene play together, and now one will not be present anymore. The pain is so great that I tell God, "If Byron does not make it into Heaven, I don't want any part of your Heaven". I tell Him that He must do something for me so I will know where Byron is and that God himself really exists and has a personal love for each of us because if He does not I don't need Him or want Him.

For 2 ears before Byron's death, I had begun to feel there must be more to being a Christian than I saw in myself or in any other Christian I ever knew. If there was no more than what I had and had seen in others, it was not enough.

One Sunday I issued God an ultimatum; He had three Sundays to do something to prove His existence. Now I couldn't see that He performed at all that first week nor the second week. At last the third week came and I was truly expecting something to happen. I didn't know what but something--nothing happened. I quit church that day spiritually.

Friends had started a Bible study group. They were going to skip around and study different books of the Bible. I told them, "No, I'd quit". Their shocked faces amazed and amused me. They didn't seem to have anymore of God in their lives than I did. I retorted that, "If I ever read again in that Book, I'll start with Genesis, and go all the way through the Book. If I found no more than I had before, I'd burn the Book and think of it no more".

Well, they started in Genesis and found some very interesting things. Like that group in the desert that was at least as big a group as all the people in Houston (where we lived at that time) plus all the surrounding area. Now Houston had 2 million people there.

That set me off. I had just been hearing how much water we used in Houston including food, clothing, etc. I was in amazement at how God cared for the people. I got my Bible and I read, "Did your clothes get threadbare or your shoes wear out?" I then am truly amazed because I do already know about the manna and quail. Well, I didn't stop going to church but I did begin to look at the Bible differently. I learned a lot about the Bible and believed in God more.

But here I am living by Baptist standards and by then my child may be on his way to Hell; only God knows and I must know. I asked God for a sign or I told Him that I would die and my family also.

The doctor comes in now. One look at his face and I know his words will be "death". As I try to get up, I realize my heart is beating so hard I cannot see. As I stand up and grab for his jacket to hold on to, something begins to happen. I can see and besides there is a sweet, sweet peace coming over my head. It's down to my shoulders and now my heart instantly begins to beat properly. The sweet peace continues until I am strengthened even to my feet.

At the moment the doctor says he is gone, that sweet peace begins to flow down over me--assurance unshakeable that comes from God. Byron is with Him, God exists, Hallelujah! He loves us, will strengthen us, will be with us, and preserve us. No one has ever been able to shake this answer in my mind or spirit.

As we go in to tell Byron good-bye, our hearts realize that he is already with God--what can I say to his body? I love him so much I cannot cry. I want to scream it cannot be so. I want to grab him up and run away where no one can take him from me but that sweet,

sweet peace comes. I cannot shake it--I want to--I don't want to. We are told we must leave. It is like ripping us into shreds but we know we must go.

There are things we must take care of. As the problems appear, we pray that God shows us what to do. Where do we bury Byron? Our home then was in Minnesota but we didn't believe we would stay there long. We could not bear to leave him there. God gives me a vision of a place I had not seen since I was about five years old; didn't know where it is or even if it exists. Mother tells me it is where my grandparents on my dad's side are buried. It's a family plot in Tennessee. As questions come up, God gives the answers.

As we are going through the church services, I am numb. I can only feel pain and that sweet, sweet peace. All the children from his school come to the funeral. Gene has asked the pastor to tell the children of God's love and Jesus' provision for salvation. God anoints the pastor and it is a truly inspired service. It is over; I still am numb and in great pain but that sweet peace refuses to leave.

We fly to Tennessee to complete the service of burial; now it's over. Still I cannot sleep; I pray and wait. I cannot see how I can go on living. I'm always asking God just to give me strength in body, soul and spirit for the next job and after that the next.

I am very pained because we had planned for Byron to have a jet ride; now he is but he cannot see or enjoy it. The pain is too great to cry--only moans come out. Marie reminds me that his spirit has already flown higher than jets.

I don't want to go home to Minneapolis but I know I must. I'm the type that if I run from pain or unpleasantness, I will continue running. This is why I have to guard against anything which gives artificial help like drink, drugs, people, etc.

We drive to Atlanta to the airport. Atlanta has over one hundred tornadoes that day-- some big, some small. The plane sits on the ground for hours. At take-off it labors and shakes until we are beginning to wonder if it will make it. I'm thinking that maybe God will answer my prayer and help us to get to Heaven together: all three of us right now. So I don't pray for the plane or even the other people because my pain is too great.

Later on I ask God to reveal to me when and how Byron was saved. He flashed an incident across my memory. Byron had read Proverbs 20:11 one day in Sunday school. The lesson was not interesting so he read on in his Bible. On arriving home (then I'm suffering from allergy) he was glowing and he told me this verse. From then on his life was changed.

I am sharing these events in my life with you so that you may know of the love of God for your personally. He has asked all saved people to tell others of this great love which welcomes all people regardless of condition to the Savior who loved us so much that he died on the cross to redeem us to Himself.

In a few nights I'm praying and asking God if I might see Byron in a dream or vision if it wasn't against His rules. As I was sleeping this night I heard a loud sound like a knife falling on concrete. I think I'm awake; even now I'm not sure. I feel this presence at the head of my bed. I cry out, "what are you?" Byron says, "It's me, Mom". I immediately asked Him, "How is everything with you?" He says, "It's fine, so very fine". Then I asked him if Jesus is there. This had been an important question on my mind and only Jesus could answer it. He said, "Jesus was not there just then but was there most of the time". I asked, "How was death?" He said "It was so cold and terrible when the accident happened", but hastened with much joy to add that "everything is wonderful and fine now".

A few days later I am so close to the brink of despair or insanity. I asked God why He let this happen to us. I know a family with several children they do not want. The children are pitiful in every way. "God why didn't you take one of them?" He only answered, "I began to prepare your family for this time 2 years ago. I drew you back, Gene back, and Marie was saved. I love and prepare my children for all things." But why he died, God did not say.

We knew nothing of the Gifts of the Holy Spirit, yet they were operating in our lives then. I had dreams, Marie had a vision, and Gene had the interpretation.

There were many times I would reach points of no return knowing that easing into insanity was next and that was welcome. I'd just scream "Jesus" until it became a whisper, and peace and strength would return. There is more power in that name than any man has yet understood.

It is now four years later. We have found out much more about the God of love and power. About 1 years to 2 years after Byron's death, we were still earnestly seeking God. We had discovered that God heals and baptizes in the Holy Spirit. Now we know He loves us, cares for us, and protects us.

I received a healing in my back in 1975. Later on in that year God told me that I need not take any more allergy shots. I had 175 severe allergy problems and had been treated over five years by doctors. I didn't take any more shots. Now in 1986 I am still healed--Praise The Lord!

Earline's Testimony About Grief Over Byron's Death

I grieved over Byron's death and worried over my family. I became a dominating Jezebel, trying to fix everything for everyone except myself. This action tended to make everything worse, even creating more problems. I prayed and fasted a lot to get God to straighten them out, but forgot to ask for wisdom and understanding to straighten myself out. I did not follow I Peter 5:7-11. I would cast my cares upon Him but because there was no quick-fix, I took them all back and did not follow on to believe v.9, that after a while He would finish the work He planned in us. We would be established, secure, settled and strengthened

I had been taught about good confessions. I confessed, until I was worn out, that the problems would be taken care of by God. Things got worse rather than better. I did not take scriptural care of my part of the problem. I was ignorant of the Bible's instruction so God could not act. I did not qualify due to ignorance and disobedience (Hosea 4:6). I began to say to God, "If I must go through this, please teach me all that I need to learn. I don't want to go through this over and over."

Grief is a normal reaction to loss or pain . It is not normal grief when two, five or ten years later, it is as great or greater then when it happened. **Grief becomes rebellion when it controls our action to the point we do not obey God.**

In John 10:10 we find out who wants to kill, steal and destroy us. The Devil never lets up when you have trouble; that's when he pounces the hardest through his demons.

EARLINE'S DEATH
Gene's Testimony About Earline's Homecoming
Job's Test

When Earline had kidney failure, the LORD impressed me to read the Book of Job in the hospital to Earline. We didn't realize that GOD was telling us that we were going to be put through a major test, especially Earline. We were at the height of our ministry but we did not spiritually discern what was happening. After Earline's death, GOD told Marie, our daughter, that He had put Earline through a seven-year Job's test for rewards in Heaven. Earline had suffered for seven years from kidney failure, kidney transplant and related problems from not having a naturally-functioning kidney. She also had a broken hip, two broken arms and a broken elbow. It seemed like she had one problem after another which never ended. It seemed many times that prayer or deliverance did not work. Now we can look back and see that GOD was allowing these things to happen to test Earline's faith.

Hospital Experience

We were told that Earline would be able to recover from fluid in the lungs. Marie and I started fasting for Earline after she had a near-death experience in the hospital. We had turned Earline over to GOD. We wanted His Perfect Will to be done. We told GOD that we would serve Him even if He did not heal Earline. Earline would not have wanted to be in a wheelchair. There were two times in the hospital that Earline seemed to indicate that she wanted to go and be with the LORD.

Many people came to comfort the family and to pray for us and Earline. Earline was anointed with oil, and healing and deliverance were prayed for her. There were other people around the nation and on the Internet that were praying for Earline. There was sufficient prayer power to heal Earline or to raise her from the dead.

The presence of GOD was wonderful in the hospital and the power of GOD was there to heal. We were having a prayer circle in the waiting room. GOD sovereignty chose to heal Marie's neck. She had injured her neck ten years ago when she fell off a horse and hit a post. Spiritually you felt good due to the presence of the LORD. Physically you were crying for Earline as you watched your loved one die.

After death, we spent a day at home praying for Earline to be raised from the dead. Earline's spirit was with us until we finished praying.

Sometime after the burial, we had a family prayer meeting. GOD healed Marie of TMJ, a jaw problem, which had been bothering her for some time. He then healed Nat, my grandson, of allergies. GOD was showing us that He still healed people. He could have healed Earline or raised her from the dead, but He chose to take her to be with Him.

We kept waiting for Earline to sit-up in bed or sit-up in the casket. It seemed like our faith was high for GOD to heal and to raise Earline from the dead. We had a wonderful funeral celebrating Earline's homecoming. It was like no other funeral that I know about. The burial in the family cemetery plot was good with a gentle alter call made by Clyde, Earline's brother. Many good things have come out of Earline's death. There was reconciliation in the Moody and Chauncey families from previous hurts.

The Perfect Number Seven
The number seven was prominent in Earline's death. From kidney failure to Earline's death was seven years. Earline had seven different kinds of doctors trying to keep her alive. Earline was buried seven days after her mother was buried. Marie and I fasted seven days to Earline's death. Everything seems to indicate that it was GOD's PERFECT WILL for Earline to be taken to be with Him.

The Future
The LORD has told me to spend more time with my family, and to continue the ministry and the business. He said that He has a lot for me to do. I have chosen to be a spiritual eunuch, THE BRIDE OF CHRIST, and devote my time to THE LORD.

Gene's Memorial For Earline
Persecution
I am going to pass out our more complete family testimony. On the front is listed a website for our ministry and other ministries. You can look these up on the Internet to access our **Deliverance Manual**, **Spiritual Warfare Manual**, **How To Do Deliverance Manual**, **Sexual Deliverance Manual**, **Witchcraft Deliverance Manual**, **Curses Deliverance Manual** and **Healing Deliverance Manual**, and other information.

I want to honor Earline for her ministry and the persecution that she received primarily from Christians about deliverance. **Yea, and all that will live Godly in JESUS CHRIST shall suffer persecution** (II Tim. 3:12).

Testimony About How GOD Taught Us Deliverance
After Byron, our only son died, our marriage was breaking up and Marie, our daughter, was in rejection and rebellion because she felt that we did not love her. We were all

trying to recover from Byron's death. We fasted, prayed and sought the LORD for about two years for GOD to help us in our terrible situation.

One night, Earline told me that she threw her BIBLE across the family room into the corner and told GOD that she was going to quit Christianity if He didn't do something for our family. **The LORD then appeared to Earline in a series of visions. A window shade came down and He told Earline to get me to pray deliverance.** She argued with GOD; she didn't want me to pray or anyone else. Many people had prayed for us with no results. **The window shade came down the second time and GOD repeated the command.** Earline argued with GOD again. **The window shade came down a third time; GOD laughed at Earline and told her, "Didn't I tell you to get Gene to pray deliverance?"** She came back to the bedroom where I was in bed, but not asleep, and told me what GOD had said.

I made my arguments too about not knowing about deliverance and why not get our pastor to do it. Finally, I gave in and prayed in English and then in Tongues, The Heavenly Language. Then THE HOLY SPIRIT began to call out names of demons through my voice which then came out of us. Marie was in the next bedroom but she also received deliverance. The next day she was a smiling teenager. Deliverance saved our marriage and family, and began our ministry.

THE HOLY SPIRIT personally taught us basic deliverance, **the families of Rejection, Bitterness and Rebellion**, in the middle of the night in the middle of our bed. We did not learn from reading a book or listening to someone teach us. We did not receive any books or teaching by man until about six months after our supernatural deliverance by GOD. Then we heard Frank and Ida Mae Hammond teach about deliverance and discuss the book, **Pigs In The Parlor**. The churches we went to did not teach deliverance which was about a third of JESUS CHRIST's ministry here on earth.

People wanted to know what had happened to us; we were different. Then GOD began to send people to us for help. We knew very little about deliverance and GOD began to teach us as we helped others. That started us in a deliverance ministry about twenty-five years ago.

Earline gave her deliverance testimony in public. Women would look at her and say "She had a demon!" This was hard on her to be ridiculed in public. People began to talk about us in charismatic Christian circles. We were made fun of from the pulpit by pastors.

Persecution is harder on the woman than it is on the man. **Likewise, ye husbands, dwell with them according to knowledge, giving honour to the wife, as unto the weaker vessel, and as being heirs together of the grace of life; that your prayers be not hindered** (1 Peter 3:7).

After Byron died in Minneapolis, we really started trying to follow GOD. We moved to Baton Rouge and went to many Christian meetings in our area to be fed spiritually.

We gave our testimony in public and became popular. After GOD taught us deliverance, we went from being two of the most popular Christians to two of the most unpopular Christians. We were no longer sought to give our testimony but were shunned. We were pioneers for the LORD to bring deliverance to the Greater Baton Rouge Area in our time.

It was very hard on Earline what people said about her. She decided that she would not say anything about deliverance to stop the talk. GOD spoke to her and said that if she denied her deliverance that she would lose it. She decided not to deny her deliverance but to speak about it as GOD directed.

Marie decided not to follow deliverance because of the persecution that we received. After Marie and Nathan were married, GOD brought her back into deliverance and then her family into deliverance.

What Satan fights hard against is the question, **"Can a Christian have a demon?" The answer is yes, absolutely. Christians have many demons.** Deliverance is growing around the world as the Church rediscovers what the early Christians practiced regularly.

At first, the LORD used deliverance to save our marriage and family. Then we began to help people in our home. Then we began to have meetings in homes, motels and churches. Then we started to go to Lake Hamilton Bible Camp for a month out of the year. We would spend about two months out of the year in the ministry. We did this until Earline had kidney failure.

After Byron had been with the LORD for about four years, we wrote our family testimony. Then the LORD led us to start writing the **Deliverance Manual** which took about twenty years to write. It took about a year of my life and a year of Earline's life to complete.

Out of our teachings came audio tapes, video tapes and booklets. These were sent around the world. We see the tip of the spiritual iceberg here on earth about what GOD is doing in our lives. I feel confident that GOD, through us, has helped thousands of people around the world. Earline has an equal share of the ministry and will get her rewards in Heaven.

Declaration

All the credit, honor and glory goes to GOD. We glorify THE FATHER GOD, JESUS CHRIST THE SON, AND THE HOLY SPIRIT. Finally, we honor Earline for her ministry, the persecution that she received, and the many people that GOD has used her to help. Her ministry will live on through her writings and teachings, and continue to help people around the world.

OUR DELIVERANCE TESTIMONY
General

1. Pray and bind spirits over spirit, soul and body.
2. Read Matt. 10:7-8; Mark 16:17-18; II Tim. 2:19-22.

3. Testimony of ten years in deliverance.
4. Jesus: Savior, Baptizer, Healer, Deliverer and Prosperer.

Pigs In The Parlor
1. Every Christian should have a copy.
2. Read cover.
3. Seven Ways to Determine the Need for Deliverance, Seven Steps to Deliverance and Seven Steps for Retaining Deliverance.
4. The deliverance prayer (salvation and deliverance).
5. 53 Common Demon Groupings
6. Three R's: Root of Bitterness, Rejection and Rebellion
7. Schizophrenic - Paranoid: Satan's Master Plan

Faith Tabernacle
1. Wednesday - Basic deliverance.
2. Thursday & Friday - Schizophrenic Personality: Inward and Outward Signs
3. Saturday - Coming out party (demon manifestations).
4. Sunday - How to stay delivered.

Can A Christian Have A Demon?
Human: Spirit - Soul - Body
Temple: Holy of Holies - Inner Temple - Outer Temple
Spirits: Holy Spirit - Unholy Spirits
Control: Possession - Oppression by Demons
Realms: Mental - Physical - Spiritual - Material

All Christians
1. Demons come out of Spirit-filled Christians.
2. All Christians need deliverance: II Tim. 2:19-22.
3. We must also cleanse our houses of anything displeasing to God.

Our Family
1. Earline delivered Marie in Mexico.
2. Earline and I had problems for 1 1/2 years.
3. "I Like To Eat Spirit" - Lost 70 pounds.

Our Ministry
1. Our Family - Common Demon Groupings.
2. Week Nights - We have seen many demons leave.
3. Infirmity - Disease and sickness yield to deliverance rather than healing prayers.
4. Individuals or families.
5. Group mass deliverance.

GENE'S TESTIMONY
Gene's Testimony About Ahab Characteristics
1. Leaving spiritual leadership up to Earline about how to raise our children.

2. Breakdown of communications between Earline, Marie and me as I pursued spiritual goals but neglected my family.
3. Fear of getting hurt by others especially by my family and Earline's family.
4. God of Jobs at one time when I put my job first, family second and God last. Now it is reversed: God first, family second and job last.
5. Leaving spiritual things of God to wife occurred partially such as receiving the Baptism. I suggested that Earline receive it first.
6. I came from a poor family and had a materialistic drive until Byron died.
7. We had many misunderstandings as Ahab husband Jezebel wife.
8. I did not believe in having an argument with my wife. So, I would go into my room, study engineering, and not talk to Earline.
9. We even came close to separation and divorce at our low point about twenty-five years ago after Byron died.
10. I was somewhat unemotional and could not show love the way I should.
11. The greatest blessing was that God kept us from whole-heartedly pursuing fame and fortune before Byron died.
12. Earline said I acted like an Ahab but did not give in anytime!
13. Do you have divine order in your home? Are you Ahab men and Jezebel women?

EARLINE'S TESTIMONY
Earline's Main Testimony About Deliverance

In July of 1975 I came into deliverance. **Do you know it is truly possible to have peace in your mind?** For most of my life, I was your average daughter, wife, mother and woman. In my mind there was never any real peace, only a sort of make-believe peace. I was not particularly moody, not often angry and not often depressed.

Life for me after I married was a continual move - new places - new people - new houses, all of which I enjoyed. Our homes were among the best and most beautiful around. Decorating them was a lot of joy for me. Taking my children to new places and introducing them to new experiences was exciting. We toured all of the U.S., Canada and Mexico. The greatest fun was watching the children enjoy all the new and unusual things we came across. Life was very exciting.

On May 22, 1973 we were devastated. Our son died from an accident at play. Now all of these lovely homes, beautiful furniture, exciting places, fun people and fun times seemed like trash. At this time we came to know the love of Jesus and the power of God. Never would we be the same again.

After five months passed, we returned south from Minneapolis. In Baton Rouge at the Full Gospel Business Men meetings, we heard about divine healing and the Baptism in the Holy Spirit; I needed both. In time I was healed of my allergies, bad back, etc. and got the Baptism in the Holy Spirit.

Gene and I went to meetings, testified and prayed for people, and saw miracles of healing and Baptisms. For about six months things went fine but as time passed, some attitudes and hurts began to show up and I was very unhappy, moody, and depressed.

I spent hours telling Gene how badly he had treated me. I came to believe he had done things that he had not. If you look at my previous statement, you'll see I enjoyed moving. One time when I was ill, I didn't want to move. The rest of the time I enjoyed it. So, I let myself come to believe that he moved just to hurt me and to make life bad for me. I accused him of shutting Marie and me out of his life since Byron died. Gene never knew what to expect when he got home -- maybe a frying pan on the noodle. No amount of Bible reading, prayer or fasting helped for more than a week or two at the most.

I was trying to help Marie who was going through all kinds of adjustments to her brother's death but only made matters worse. She also became full of resentment and hurt, and was bitter and angry.

Gene, Marie and I fasted, prayed and talked. I was fasting and praying that God would fix Gene up. I was so blind I was sure that I was perfect - well almost.

After a year or so, I was sitting reading Psalm 91. I had always loved it but suddenly like a bucket of ice water it hit me. The Psalm was not true for me. I had no peace, and was always angry and moody. I (when you are persuaded by the Devil to look on others as the problem) was even beginning to wonder if God was just being bad to me.

I sat on the couch and began to pray: "God if you don't help me tonight I am going out of church, and into the world for good". I told God that Gene is worse off than me; he's all of my problems. **God just stopped talking** so I started praying again the same prayer. **God said again, "Get Gene to pray deliverance for you".** I asked about having our pastors do my deliverance. **God didn't answer; it was like he pulled down a shade or veil.** Being one of determination I started out again "God I must have help tonight; if I don't get it, I flat quit. **He said, "Get Gene to pray deliverance for you". God was not harsh, neither was he condemning. He seemed to be pleased that I had finally asked for help and really meant it.**

I called Gene; he didn't seem particularly impressed. He also suggested the same people and the same excuses. But the best one was "I don't know what deliverance is; I don't know how to do that".

After some discussion, we decided to go to the bedroom and get in the middle of the bed. We were sitting facing each other, Gene starts praying, and my mind starts wandering. He prayed a while in tongues and started saying strange things such as, "You come out of my wife in the name of Jesus". One thing I remember well was that at the beginning when each demon was named, I had a thought, "I don't have that".

As he called out Rejection, its hurts and kindred spirits, I was being shown by the Holy Spirit how these spirits had gained entrance into me, and how they had checked and bound me in all attempts to be myself. Rejection kept me just short of my goals in life. Mostly it kept me from doing what God said to do due to a fear that the other person would disagree or reject me and my idea. I always worked better and succeeded best in those things that I did alone.

Next came Bitterness; I never even considered myself bitter. But as he called out demons under this ruler, I saw hate, violence and anger. I had much trouble with temper. Not that I was always violent, on the contrary I was seldom angry to the observer. When I did get angry or lose my temper, my husband children usually found some other more suitable place to be.

At the naming of Rebellion, I thought I surely don't have this spirit. As he called it out again, I balled up my fist, drew back to back-hand him, and was consumed with a fit of coughing and mucus.

As this was going on, I was shown how there is only one real rebellion, and it is pointed toward God. Even if we say, "My husband just does not accept God's way so I am going to---". In the end when it's traced back, it is rebellion to God for God gave directions about how to live with an unsaved mate. If it is against circumstances, God says, **"This is the will of God in Christ Jesus concerning you. In whatever circumstances, I am therewith to be content".**

One of my rebellions was against circumstances. I had always had such lovely homes with rooms to spare, so that Gene always had an office, and I always had a sewing and craft room. When we came here, Gene bought a three bedroom house with only two baths. His reason was that I couldn't set up Byron's bedroom; I became bitter. I said, "Yes, but you still have your office; I don't have a room. You always get what you want." And I became more rebellious.

When I first moved here I didn't hate this house but little by little it crept up on me. At first it was just the things packed together. Then it grew until I hated the house twenty-four hours a day. Then my ingratitude reached other branches of my life. My wheels were the wheels of a camper truck. I didn't like the truck anymore. Next came Gene, and then living in this bug-infested hot climate with people who can't speak good English. Next the ungrateful person begins to blame others even if he sees it's as much his fault as the other persons. He lies to himself until in his eyes, at least, the other person is entirely at fault.

God showed me my attitude in light of His attitude letting me know that He could take even this house away; that He had provided it and I was ungrateful for His provision. Oh my, this really was sobering me up. After these three main ruler demons were cast out, I gave up if he called a demon out. I just agreed and became free of it.

I had a habit of getting my work done as fast as I could because I didn't like being in the house alone. So, I roved all over this town looking for plants and cloth to work on the house, but I never worked on it. I did a lot of visiting with other Christian women which is not necessary.

Since neither Gene nor I knew anything about this turn of events, I asked God to teach me so I wouldn't go backwards. I rather liked the changes in my mind and attitude.

I found Romans 12 contained my answer. In verse 2, I am told to renew my mind and attitudes with God's instructions. By doing this, I would prove for myself what is the good and acceptable and perfect will of God. In response to your obedience and surrender, God will help you change bad attitudes and habits.

Attitudes submitted to God's word will follow with actions of obedience.

In studying Eph. 5:25-32, I saw how my home was meant to show Christ's relationship with the Church. To my dismay, I saw it reflected my relationship with Christ. It was not a relationship to bring others to Christ.

I also saw how the Church is rebelling against Christ just as in our family members were in rebellion.

The morning after this experience I came down the hall to the kitchen and was greeted pleasantly by my daughter. Now, this was a surprise because she was not so pleasant at that time either. I noticed that she began to change. I asked God about this often and learned that my condition had put such a strain on her that she was being broken under it. I didn't tell her about my deliverance; I didn't know I should. She became a very obedient and joyful person. I began to enjoy Marie and not worry about her so much.

Earline's Testimony About Rejection

Rejection is the basic cause of abuse. All types of rejection work to destroy the mental and emotional health of an individual.

I had often wondered about certain problems I had: (1) an inordinate desire to please, (2) inability to say no to things I didn't want to do, (3) always setting goals, working hard to accomplish them and then stopping short of success, (4) always feeling I had to do things better than anyone else, and (5) trying to make everything around me and about me look better than I thought it was.

I cut off part of my finger in an accident loading a horse into a trailer. **It was the first time I had need of a hospital in many years.** I was put to sleep and my finger was sewn into my palm. The next day I was supposed to be quiet and take it easy.

For five years, I had been trying to help my mom get resettled after my dad's death. At times she would tell me what she wanted me to do and I would start to do it. **Right in the middle of my doing it, she would suddenly, without telling me, change her mind and have one of my brothers doing an entirely different thing.**

Two years ago I took her to Maine to see my brother. Back in Chattanooga she accused me of wanting and trying to kill her. This really puzzled me because I thought we got along very well.

After the operation, I was being still on the sofa praying. I asked God **Why can't I help mom? Why does she think I want to kill her?**

I had a vision. (Have you had visions?) I was standing in the room I had as a child. I was high near the ceiling. I was witnessing a terrible thing. A woman was beating, not whipping, a child. I went down to see who this was and to stop it; I saw it was my mom. I went beside the bed, bent down and looked; the child was me.

Thinking I was hallucinating because of the drugs from the operation the day before, I quickly decided to get up and get busy. One-handed work was hard to find, so I swept the carport.

My brother called me or I called him. Since I sounded a little funny, he asked what was wrong. I told him next time they could sew me up awake. Then I related this story to him. He was silent, then he asked me if I remembered that day.

He said he had told my dad that if my mom didn't stop beating me for no reason, he would kill her. The only words said in the scene were by my dad; he said to my mom that he would kill her if he ever heard of this happening again. I was not a small child. I was ten or twelve years old when the beatings stopped.

For some reason, I simply cannot remember this today. He thought her fear that I wanted to kill her came from the guilt for what she did to me.

About eight to nine years before this incident, Gene and I had fasted and prayed for me for two years. When I got the Baptism of the Holy Spirit, there was only initial joy. Immediately, I began to have more fears than before, my emotions were out of control and I couldn't think clearly. God does not give us a spirit of fear but a spirit of power, love, calm, well-balanced mind, discipline and self control.

Neither of us knew about deliverance from demons, so God had to teach us. After a long time of praying one night, Gene began to call out **Rejection, Rebellion, Bitterness, etc.** I was very different after this.

I had to learn how to stay free by studying the Bible. No one in our town believed a Christian could have a demon, so we had to rely on God and His Word.

I was doing very well until the scene passed before my eyes and I learned of my early life. Immediately, I began to have times of panic for no apparent reason. I was hostile. I noticed a panic when those who had authority over me were present. I would become fearful if a policeman came near me, and when the pastor or principal came into my school room. I felt I had to challenge Gene's decisions.

We prayed and felt that I needed more deliverance. Gene was led to call out the same things as before. **We realized at this point that we were working on my subconscious mind.**

Earline's Testimony About Ancestral Background

The following testimony will help you understand how the soul (mind, will and emotions) works. It will also show you how Satan attacks the physical body with demons by curses.

I have an Indian - English - German - French background. There are curses on each of these people. Indians worshipped demons; some English and Europeans were Druids - they worshipped Satan.

In innocence, my father participated in some occult practices: **wart removal** and water witching. From my father came curses of Masons and Indians. Physical problems came as a result of curses on Indian worship: inactive thyroid, female disorders and heart disease.

My father removed the warts from my brother by mountain medicine (witchcraft). This occult practice was something in the order of tying strings, going out under the drip of the eave and burying the strings. The occult practice removed the warts but he got spinal meningitis. **Apparently, a demon of spinal meningitis was swapped for a demon of warts.**

Satan doesn't give anything away for free; there is a greater price to pay. Spinal meningitis killed him. He went to Heaven and saw two siblings which had died early in life; God sent him back to earth. I had to nurse him back to health.

My mother was a paranoid schizophrenic with an Indian - English background. Her emotional illness caused me to need a lot of deliverance from emotional problems.

Earline's Testimony About Heart Condition
Earline's Comments

I had a heart condition which was unusual. It never occurred with regularity or under any specific condition.

> God gave me a vision of a shaman or witch doctor at an elevated funeral pyre which was burning dead bodies. He was chanting and waving, and saying on the descendents and descendents. This was supposed to be a blessing, but in actuality was a curse, because Indians worship demons. This was a curse that came down on my family causing heart problems.

Gene's Comments

This is a sign of demonic symptoms of disease brought about by a curse. It doesn't follow the medical guidelines. All they can say is that it is inherited.

Earline's Comments

While taking a tread mill test, I experienced tremendous pain in the chest, arms and neck. I was examined by a **heart specialist** in Minneapolis who told me that my heart was good but he had written **death by heart attack** on many people's certificates like myself.

Gene's Comments

These were people who didn't really have anything wrong with their hearts physically but had a spiritual root to the disease. The prayer of faith will not heal a disease that has a spiritual root that must be dealt with as sin to be confessed. Then the curse can be broken and the person prayed for to be healed.

God is beginning to show the Christian world spiritual roots of various diseases. Pastor Henry Wright of Molena, Georgia is a pioneer in this area. Also Art Mathias who is in Anchorage, Alaska.

Earline's Comments

A year or so after my dad's death, I found my heart acting up again. Sometimes one to five years would elapse between seizures. I began to ask God to show me why my brothers, dad, dad's brothers and his dad had heart problems.

God showed me Exodus 20 and Ezekiel 18. He told me to repent for my ancestors and myself for the sin of idol worship in Leviticus 26:40-41. The curse of idol worship follows the blood line down to the descendants. I did these things and have been free from these attacks for over twenty years. I was only the second generation from previous generations of Indians that sinned before God.

Gene's Comments

You have to forgive your ancestors and ask for forgiveness for yourself. Earline took her older brother, Clyde, through breaking the curse and he is still alive after a heart attack.

Exodus 20 lists the Ten Commandments which are still applicable today. The scriptures about worshipping other Gods are verses 3, 4 and 5. This outlines the curse for idol worship which lasts three or four generations according to God's purposes. (Does anybody know why God curses some sins for three generations and some sins for four generations?)

Ezekiel 18 shows the equity of God's dealings with us. The sin of idol worship is defined as eating upon the mountains (in the groves), lifting up the eyes to the idols (worship), and not walking in God's statutes and judgments (disobedience).

This was a **revelation of the sins of the ancestors** that God gave Earline through prayer about why her family was plagued by heart attack and death by heart attack. This was primarily the men that were attacked but even Earline, a woman, was attacked. The revelation was the effect of the sins of the ancestors in her family coming through the Indians to cause heart problems and early death. The sin was disobeying the Ten

Commandments of having no other Gods before you, which is idol worship, that the Indians committed. Up to that time, we had never heard about the sins of the ancestors.

Earline had Cherokee Indian ancestry coming through her father and mother. We were raised in and around Chattanooga, Tennessee which was not far from Cherokee, North Carolina which had a demonic draw upon Earline. We were drawn to make a pilgrimage to the Smokey Mountains every year although we did not make it every year. In the fall, Earline would long to go to the mountains. After Earline was delivered from Indian spirits, she did not have that draw to go to the Smokey Mountains.

When you are a person of mixed races, you inherit the curses coming down through the different races, languages, customs, religions and nationalities. If you have Indian ancestry and are Caucasian, you receive the curses from the Indians and the Caucasians.

The curse would come from those ancestors that had sinned. This means that you can be cursed for ten generations (2046 ancestors) from both sides of your family.

Which of your ancestors didn't sin or that you know didn't sin? It is a good assumption that you have the curse of incest and the curse of the bastard on you. It could come from any of 2046 ancestors back to the tenth generation that sinned assuming it has not been properly broken. You will see the sin repeating itself generation after generation such as bastard after bastard.

We worked with one Indian woman who was a Christian. She had a hard time getting free of Indian curses and demons brought upon her by her ancestral lineage and sexual abuse. She was cursed by being an Indian and by incest which is very hard on a woman being abused by her blood relatives.

Earline's Testimony About The Curse Of The Bastard

Great grandfather marries great grandmother in church. All seems well; they have three children. Great grandfather dies. Great grandmother discovers she can not get his railroad pension because she is his fifth wife. My grandfather becomes very bitter and a little paranoid. My mom is paranoid and schizophrenic (like father - like daughter). She abused me physically.

Here are some of the problems created for me by this bastard curse. Never feeling at home in any church for long. Never feeling good about myself. Being ashamed for people to look at me even though I didn't know what I wanted to hide, overriding fear, striving excessively to succeed and stopping short of realizing the goal, fear of failure, fear of authority, resisting authority, fighting verbally and physically, demonic pressure to sexual activities, and not much joy in natural or spiritual life.

(Raise your hand if you were born out of wedlock (marriage). Raise your hand if you conceived a child out of wedlock. Raise your hand if your child conceived a child out of wedlock. Notice the continuation of the curse of the bastard.)

Earline's Testimony About Eating

1. I was sitting on the couch after eating a good breakfast. I had this urging to go and get more food, but I was not hungry. I asked The Lord why and He forced the demon within me to say, **My name is I Like To Eat, go and get me some food.**

2. After casting out the demon, **I Like To Eat**, I told God how I had tried dieting and I knew that was hopeless.

3. I was told **Obedience is better than sacrifice, and I knew how to eat but was not doing it. Plenty of fresh fruits and vegetables, not much meat and very little sweets is the basis of a proper diet.**

4. **Asked if I'd do what I was told, I assured God that I would. He said that food can be divided into two groups: God's and Devil's. Devil's foods include sweets to excess, junk food, and liquids which are mostly empty calories.**

5. It's not bad manners not to eat sweets or any other food when you know your body has not used up the last meal. I was intelligent enough to know if I truly needed food.

6. **Here are the rules in summary:**
   a. **Eat fruits and vegetables; include leafy greens.**
   b. **Do not eat much meat - three or four servings weekly.**
   c. **Don't eat unless you truly need to.**
   d. **Don't let others stuff you.**
   e. **Seldom eat sweets.**
   f. **Almost never eat junk food.**
   g. **Remember those whose God is their belly.**
   h. **Cook all foods simply.**
   i. **Use little fat and cut fat from the meat.**

Gene's Comments

1. Earline lost about seventy pounds and weighed less than she did when we got married and before she had two children. She weighed 100 to 110 pounds which was less than Marie, our teenage daughter, who had not had any children. It was like having a new wife!

2. Do you realize that the body has enough energy for you to fast for forty days? Marie fasted for forty days on water taking only vitamins, minerals and supplements.

3. You must take care of your spirit, soul and body. You can not neglect any part of your tripartite being and be in health. You can not neglect your body and expect God to take care of it or heal you every time that you pray. One of Earline's sayings is, **If you don't brush your teeth, God will let them rot out of your mouth.**

4. Healing and deliverance go hand in hand. You can get healed by anointing with oil and praying the prayer of faith, or by casting out demons of infirmities. The Lord told me to take a person through deliverance and then pray for healing. You have a double possibility of getting the person healed.

5. Sometimes the demon of infirmity manifests as it is being cast out and you know that there was an infirmity demon in the person. If the infirmity is there because of sin, you won't get healed by the prayer of faith, because the demon has a legal right to be there. You must take away the legal right and then cast out the demon.

Earline's Testimony About Maintaining Deliverance

The scriptural basis for giving a testimony is found in Rev. 12:11 where we overcome Satan by three things: **the blood of Jesus, our testimony, and not loving our lives to the death. God told me that if I was unwilling to tell about my deliverance, I would lose it. And furthermore, if I was ashamed of Him and His provisions, He would be ashamed of me in Heaven.**

In James 4:7 we are told how to make the Devil flee. We often quote part of the verse **"resist the devil and he will flee from you"**. This gives us a false sense of security. The truth is you must first submit yourself to God. This is not a careless submission but true submission to God which requires us to read, study and obey the Bible. As we submit this way to God and then resist the Devil, he will indeed flee from us. God does not require us to know all the Biblical requirements before He will help us but we must be making every effort to obey all that we have learned, and be diligent about learning and applying more.

After all deliverances, some decisions must be made and never changed no matter how much pressure is applied to you from whatever source to change or go back to old sins. **Here are some decisions which must be made: 1. Study God's Word and accept His principles as your own. 2. Discipline your life and accept responsibility for your actions and thoughts in the areas where you have been delivered. 3. Enter His presence with thanksgiving for all with which He has blessed you. 4. Joyfully obey God's direction even if you have to force yourself in the beginning.**

The day after I received my main deliverance, I had an empty feeling and did not know what to do. My reaction was to ask God continually for direction.

We cannot do what God directs if we never apply His Word to our life. If we do not apply His Word to our thoughts and actions we are not truly subject to God. Therefore the Devil will not flee from us and we are only fooling ourselves if we think the demons will leave us alone. While we kid ourselves, the Devil and his demons eat our dinner and by the time we face the truth dinner is nearly over.

I learned that I didn't really know God's Word. I didn't know how to use God's Word or how to use my mind. I asked God to take my thoughts. **He told me that He wouldn't touch my thoughts with a ten foot pole; that His thoughts were higher than mine and that I must control my thoughts bring them into submission to Jesus Christ (II Cor. 10:5).**

I started marking everything that God said in the Bible in red. I found there is much said about the mind in Deuteronomy and throughout the Bible. Next I was impressed to underline every verse in the New Testament that told me something that I should do.

I soon realized that I really didn't know what I should think with my mind. It occurred to me that my mind is to be an instrument for my spirit's use and not the other way around.

The hands, feet, eyes, ears and body obey, so why not make the mind obey? To make the mind obey, I needed to know what to make it do.

I had to learn how to tell the difference between God's and the Devil's thoughts. The battleground for the Christian is primarily for his soul, not body or spirit. The demons want to re-enter through your mind.

See Romans 6;16-18. Do you not know that if you continually surrender yourselves to any one to do his will, you are the slaves of him whom you obey, whether it be to sin, which leads to death, or to obedience which leads to righteousness - right doing and right standing with God. But thank God, though you were once slaves of sin you have become obedient with all your heart to the standard of teaching in which you were instructed and to which you were committed. And having been set free from sin, you have become the servants of righteousness - of conformity to the divine will in thought, purpose and action.

How do we yield ourselves to anyone (God or Devil)? Is it not in the mind? A human always plays with sinful thoughts, then he acts it out. It is not by accident we sin. A lot of people do not want to accept the responsibility for their sinfulness and want to blame it on someone else. The only trouble with this idea is that God will not be fooled by it neither will your enemy, the Devil.

Temptation - **1 Cor. 10:13 For no temptation - no trial regarded as enticing to sin (no matter how it comes or where it leads) - has overtaken you and lied hold on you that is not common to man - that is no temptation or trial has come to you that is beyond human resistance and that is not adjusted and adapted and belonging to human experience, and such as man can bear. But God is faithful to His Word and to His compassionate nature and He (can be trusted) not to let you be tempted and tried and assayed beyond your ability and strength of resistance and power to endure, but with the temptation He will (always) provide a way out - the means to escape to a landing plane - that you may be capable and strong and powerful patiently to bear up under it.**

This tells me temptation in common to mankind, therefore it is common for the Devil and the demons to use it. If they tempt us, we have not sinned. We have sinned when we enjoy and continue to invite the temptation, then yield and obey. the temptation. It also shows we were not watchful for the escape route and we did not take it.

Situations around you will not necessarily change immediately now that you have changed. Just as you practiced obedience to the demons' words, now practice obedience to God's Word.

This is my first encounter with the Devil after I was delivered. Before I was delivered, I would get very angry and depressed when I cleaned house. At that time, we had wall-to-wall furniture. The living room was really badly cluttered. Each piece of furniture had to be moved to vacuum around it. I was happy and didn't hate this house anymore.

As I was vacuuming the living room, I dropped a table on my toe and was having trouble getting the vacuum nozzle under the sofa. I raised up and let out a loud "I hate this---". **God quickly warned me that "life and death is in the tongue, and they that love it will eat the fruit thereof" (Prov. 18:21). God also told me at this time that He had given it to my family. If I didn't have an attitude of gratitude about the house and furniture, He could easily remove them from me.** I knew that I must not complete the sentence or I would be back where I started from. I repented and repeated until I believed it, "I love this house and I thank God for it".

Another of Satan's tactics is to use gradualism on us. He will give us a sin to look at and consider. He will cover it over with pretty lies (pretty young people smoking, never an old person dying of lung cancer). He will use rejection to trap you; he will never tell the true ending (where does illegal sex lead?). He knows that the more we see it, hear it and consider it, the more likely we are to give in to it. A good example of the use of gradualism is Humanism. Forty years ago it was very mildly given to people mainly by pastors and teachers. People considered it and accepted it because it was given by people they trusted. Not considering what was the basic theory behind it (worship of self - therefore idolatry), people allowed this theory to so invade them that now we cannot recognize it for what it is. Many of us say we are against it but we live by it instead of the Bible.

We do not recognize God's provisions for us. We think our life should have no problems or privations. We are not grateful to God for all. **Deut. 28:47-48, Because you did not serve the Lord your God with joyfulness of heart and mind in gratitude for the abundance of all with which He had blessed you, therefore you shall serve your enemies whom the Lord shall send against you, in hunger and thrust, in nakedness, and in want of all things; and He will put a yoke of iron upon you neck, until He hath destroyed you.**

This verse presents some interesting ideas 1. Are you having problems because you are ungrateful to God? 2. Do you know which problems are from God to help you learn to endure to the end or which ones are brought on because of being ungrateful? 3. Which ones have you invited by yielding to temptations of the enemy? If you will know the answer to these questions, you will have to seek God. He has promised to give wisdom to all who ask for it not wavering (James 1:4-8). If you ask God for wisdom and He gives you wisdom, you must not waver following His wisdom. For example: if you have been one to look at dirty magazines, God's wisdom tells you this will lead you to want to do what you see; then you must stop it. You may need deliverance for the demons you have let in plus you must change your habits. No one can change your thought life by casting out your demons. Casting out your demons is one of God's escape routes. To deliverance must be added by the deliveree, discipline of mind and action.

The best attack against habit, and the attempts of demons to trick you and get back in that I found was 1. to tell them to leave in Jesus' name once and 2. immediately take control of your mind. I would do it this way: I would tell them Jesus has given me authority over you (Luke 10:19, Matt. 28:18-20), therefore I command you to leave me now. If I did not sense they were gone, I would say, "Since you are still here, I would like to read to you about what Jesus Christ has done for me." I would open the Bible to Matt. 26-28, Mark 14-16, Luke 22-24 and John 17-21 and read it aloud to them. Of course they did not want to hear of God's love and provision for me. The pressure they had placed on me and their thoughts were long gone but I would read on and bless myself in God's Word. Some times the pressure from the demons trying to get back in was strong enough that I would have to walk and read very loudly to them. I will still do this if I come under attack; it always works. After a time, you will be able to tell them the facts without reading it to them.

God also told me at this time that He had given it to my family. If I didn't have an attitude of gratitude about the house and furniture, He could easily remove them from me (Deut. 27:48).

My next attack was sent through people. When asked why I looked so much better and was losing weight, I would answer truthfully and say "I was delivered of demons and no, I was not dieting". If three people were present, you would get three distinct reactions. One would leave pronto, one would regard you as if you were radioactive, and one would grab your arm and want to know more.

Then you'd hear whispers - she had demons! They only talk about demons; do they worship them? They are fanatical; they believe there is a demon under every bush!

Next I was tempted to go back to some of my old habits of retaliation, etc. I must crucify the flesh - God said that vengeance belongs to Him (Rom. 12:19). I must not habitually sin or else I become the demon's house in that area again (I John 3:8-9).

Mental suggestions by the Devil must be put down. He will suggest a what if, could be or maybe. If this happens, what will you do (fear and more fear)? Unless you have facts to base your knowledge on, don't let the Devil play you along.

One of his tactics was to attack me about Marie: what if Marie can't adjust to her brother's death? Before deliverance, I would cringe in fear and worry. After deliverance, I learned to tell Satan that Marie can do all things through Christ who strengthens her; I can too!

You don't have to be perfect to give a word of encouragement, share an experience, help someone or even cast out a demon. If God demanded perfection, nothing would ever get done. I'm over fifty years old and I have yet to meet a perfect person.

You must have a total commitment to Jesus Christ. Rely totally on Him and His Word. Do these things and you will continue to get free and stay free. Don't be double minded: deciding and undeciding. Remember that a double-minded man is unstable in all his ways. Giver very careful study to what you read in THE BIBLE and carefully compare it to the thing you need to make a decision on. When you have judged it by the Biblical instructions, then don't waver.

I found a verse to put my temptations in prospective (Heb. 12:4). Begin reading at verse one which contains instruction on keeping pure. **It suggests we strip off and throw aside every encumbrance and sin which so readily (deftly and cleverly) clings to and entangles us, and let us run with patient endurance and steady and active persistence the appointed course of the race set before us. Looking away (from all that will distract) to Jesus, Who is the Leader and the source of our faith (giving the first incentive for our belief) and is also its Finisher, (bringing it to maturity and perfection). He, for the joy (of obtaining the prize) that was set before Him endured the cross, despising and ignoring the shame, and is now seated at the right hand of the throne of God. Just think of Him who endured from sinners such grievous opposition and bitter hostility against - reckon up and consider it all in comparison with your trials - so that you may not grow weary or exhausted, losing heart and relaxing and fainting in your minds. You have not yet struggled and fought agonizing against sin, nor have you yet resisted and withstood to the point of pouring out your (own) blood.**

If we are able with every temptation to resist to the shedding of our blood maybe, then we might have an acceptable excuse for failing to resist the Devil and him having to flee.

God will not make you over; He will work with you and help you. See Mark 16:20. A miracle is taking place as you go obeying The Word in the areas you have received instruction and deliverance.

A study of Matt. Chapter 5 will help anyone see just where they are missing it with their attitudes. It will inspire you to clear your mind of a lot of incorrect ideas and to broaden your understanding of the truth.

Earline's Testimony About Schizophrenia Deliverance

Schizophrenia means split mind (**schizein = to split** and **phren = mind**). I had a lifetime of mental and emotional tension. I was unable to decide what to do and see it through. I had many fears that something bad was going to happen. All of my life I had great fears of bad things happening: fears of failing and fears of people. I was often tense for weeks and I did not know why.

This is the earliest memory I have of going to school. I was so afraid of all the people I could not go into the school but hid behind the well house until my brother, Clyde, came and took me into the first grade. I was disoriented that day; strange feelings and fears tormented me.

I have very few memories from childhood below the age of nine or ten years. Generally speaking I lived in two worlds: home and away from home. I became very good at forgetting everything bad (parents' fights and my own troubles) that happened at home the minute I walked out the door. I felt more freedom and ease away from home.

At high school and college I had trouble with certain subjects like algebra and chemistry. They had things too similar for me to distinguish between them.

Both of these subjects ended in frustration and low grades for me. In my marriage I had some problems of accepting my husband as one who would provide for me, take care of me, and continue to love me. I was always expecting the marriage to end badly. After six years of marriage, we had a delightful son and two years later we had a beautiful daughter.

Double mindedness wears the person out, and frustrates and confuses him. Deciding, then undeciding stagnates a person. For example, my mom was here for a while; she couldn't be content for desiring to go home. When at home, she was pressed to stay somewhere else besides her home. When away from home, great fears filled her about the house. She was miserable and made those around her miserable (James 1:5-8).

Earline's Testimony About Deliverance From Indian Curses

What are the effect of curses? I had a heart condition which was unusual. It never occurred with regularity nor under any specific condition.

While taking a tread mill test, I experienced tremendous pain in the chest, arms and neck. Having been examined by a "heart specialist" in Minneapolis, who told me that my heart was good but he had written "death by heart attack" on many people's certificates like myself. These were people who didn't really have anything wrong with their hearts.

A year or so after my dad's death I found my heart acting up again. Sometimes one to five years would elapse between seizures. I began to ask God to show me why my brothers, dad, dad's brothers and his dad all had heart problems.

He showed me **Ezekiel 18 & Exodus 20**. He told me to repent for my ancestors and myself for the sin of idol worship in **Leviticus 26:40-41**. The curse of idol worship follows the blood line. I did these things and have been free for over eleven years. I was only the second generation from previous generations that sinned before God.

MARIE'S TESTIMONY
Earline's Testimony About Marie's Salvation

Some years ago, I had a scene flash through my mind. At the time of this revelation, I was thinking I was really serving God. I was so concerned with lost children. Many efforts and thoughts went into attempting to help others. Now, I know that God wants us to help others.

But the Devil is so clever in convincing us that if we'll help others, God will take care of ours. I have had pastors use this statement on me to get me to work in their vineyards - howbeit it was not God's vineyard. I awoke from my deception almost too late.

In this scene I was standing before God's throne. I was so proud of my life and expecting Him to really be pleased with me. I was standing there with a very large group of children I had been instrumental in bringing to the Lord.

I began to sense that something was very, very wrong. God seemed to be extremely dissatisfied with me. **I heard this question, "Where is Marie?"** I began to look for her feeling sure she was in the group. Finally I found her. She was not in the group. As she came around the edge of the group and looked up to God, I saw Him point the other way. (Parents, are you doing the right things with your children?)

I cannot tell you all the emotions I felt. All my pride was replaced with shame and failure. **I heard that Marie was the only person I had been given responsibility for.** She was given to me to love and guide but I had shunned what I had been given and had looked for something else to do. I was to have been her greatest rooter and one of her most important teachers.

I began at that point to repent (change directions completely and go the other way) and seek knowledge from God as to how I should perform on His job. I'd like to tell you that the problem was solved and that we all lived happily ever after, but that was not the case.

What was to follow was years of heartache and mental pain, but one day I noticed that things were just slightly beginning to get in correct order. A time period of probably ten years was needed for us following the leadership of the Lord to undo the works of the Devil in this area.

I had seen a glimmer of light and I was not going to let it go. My hand was on the plow never to let go again. **I looked up every verse in the Bible about mothers and daughters, and began to correct my thoughts and actions.** I must come into obedience to God if I was to see any change in our relationship. I also realized that I could no longer blame my failure as a mom on anyone but me.

These are some of the spiritual forces at work in this case: ignorance, dissatisfaction, rejection, irreverence for God, lack of natural affection, shirking God given duties, selfishness, lazy, arrogant, greedy for acceptance, generational gap, abandonment, bitterness and rebellion.

Our Testimony About Jesus Setting Marie's Broken Shoulder

One Sunday after going to church, we decided to get Marie's horse, King Fox, and go to the park. After enjoying an afternoon in the sun, we told Marie to ride back and stable the horse so that we could go to Sunday evening services. She rode thru the woods and we rode around the woods in our car.

When we got back to the stables, the horse was tied up and Marie was lying in a car. She had fallen off King Fox and broke her arm. Her face was white and her lips were blue. This shocked Earline and I, but we had the presence of The Holy Spirit, so we prayed for Marie; nothing happened outwardly.

After putting the horse in the stable and Marie in our car, we headed for home. We didn't know whether to take her to the hospital or to the doctor or to depend upon God for healing. As we rode back home, the Lord quickened this verse to my mind, **The steps of a good man are ordered by the Lord: and he delighteth in his way** (Psalm 37:23). I asked God to order our steps about what to do.

After we reached home, Marie sat in the car and felt the bones in her arm. She could feel the dislocated broken bones. We called our family doctor, but he was out and his backup was not to be found either, which was good because we sought The Lord about what to do, PRAISE GOD!

Earline said that one of us should be in the car with Marie. I said I would go and went back to my study to get the anointing oil. As I came out, Earline said, Go get your oil and pray for Marie. God had given us a Word of Wisdom, one of the nine gifts of the Holy Spirit, **For to one is given by the Spirit the word of wisdom; to another the word of knowledge by the same Spirit** (1 Cor. 12:8).

We were familiar with anointing with oil and praying the prayer of faith. **Is any sick among you? let him call for the elders of the church; and let them pray over him, anointing him with oil in the name of the Lord: And the prayer of faith shall save the sick, and the Lord shall raise him up; and if he have committed sins, they shall be forgiven him.** (James 5:14-15). I then anointed Marie's forehead, held her hand of the broken arm, and we all prayed again. **Her arm tingled and she could feel the bones moving within the arm, PRAISE THE LORD!**

We then took her to the hospital where she was x-rayed and attended by a bone specialist. He was very talkative and showed us the x-ray. He could see a complete break thru the shoulder socket. The bone was perfectly set and a chipped bone was perfectly in place. We told him about praying for her arm and he said that it was unusual to see that type of break and not have to set the bone.

He put a cast just past Marie's elbow and said come back in three weeks. Earline and Marie prayed that she would be completely healed by then. He examined her and took another x-ray to prove she was not healed. **PRAISE THE LORD, she was healed, the cast was taken off, and she rode King Fox three weeks after the arm was broken!** Any doctor will tell you that it takes six to eight weeks to heal an ordinary break and longer for complicated breaks.

We had memorized a verse in church the Sunday before the accident, **Behold I am the Lord, the God of all flesh: is there anything too hard for me?** (Jer. 32:27). The answer naturally is, No!

Since then I have heard of three other cases where God set the bones, I personally know two of the individuals.

The Lord taught us a number of lessons:
1. Anointing with oil is important to Him.
2. Pray The Blood Of Jesus over your family everyday.
3. He will heal injuries as well as sicknesses.
4. Be ready to pray at all times.

To God be the glory, honor, praise and credit for everything that was done!

Marie's Testimony About Experience With Demonic Objects

Some friends of ours were ministers who went to Haiti. One time they brought us some carved figurines as a gift. These statues caused us strife in the family. Our daughter, Marie, felt like there were eyes watching her as she walked across the room. The Lord finally got our attention and we destroyed the wood figures. The wood would not burn normally and finally I had to soak them in charcoal-lighter fluid. When they finally burned, a green flame came out and shot toward us. These dolls were probably made by Voodoo worshipers who blessed them so that they would be sold. After getting rid of the statutes, the strife left our family.

OUR TESTIMONY ABOUT PSYCHIC PRAYERS

This is a vivid testimony of a pastor, his wife and their church about what happened when **psychic prayers** were prayed for them.

This situation came about because the pastor taught the people about unforgiveness and entered into deliverance. The families would not forgive each other for past offenses. Some of the congregation did not want deliverance, and fled from the teaching and ministering of it.

After the people left the church, they went to other churches and prayer groups. There, they prayed for the pastor that God would make him get back into line and give up deliverance. **This is not a prayer to God but a prayer to Satan. Their prayers loosed demons on the pastor and his family.**

They were trying to control the pastor and his wife's wills. These were Jezebels that wanted the church back like they had it before. They had controlled the church and the pastor whom they called **"Our Little Boy"**.

The demons manifested and knocked the curtains off the wall of the pastor's house. One demon manifested and walked in front of our car as we were driving back home that night after this visit. The demon looked like a half man from the waist down. The purpose was to cause me to drive off the road and to kill us.

The Holy Spirit showed the pastor and his wife what had happened because of the psychic prayers. They forgave the people that had prayed against them (about eighty persons), broke the curses and soul ties, cast out the demons and sent them back to the senders, and prayed for the people to see what they were doing wrong.

Many things happened to the people that left and prayed against the church. **They suffered from divorce, family problems, sickness and death.** As you can see, it is dangerous to pray psychic prayers and fight against deliverance.

Gene's Comments

There are angels and demons around us. I can not see in the spirit world but I know that they are here. Can anyone see in the spirit world? If so, tell us what you see. **You don't have to see demons to cast them out.**

SECTION 18 - BALDNESS - BEARDS - HAIR
(PRIDE - EGO - VANITY)

CONTENTS
1. SCRIPTURE
    1. **Baldness**
    2. **Beards**
    3. **Hair**
    4. **Hoary Head**
2. PREFACE
3. FREEDOM OF CHOICE
4. JESUS CHRIST
5. REJECTION
6. BITTERNESS
7. REBELLION
8. INHERITED CURSES
9. DISEASES
10. PRIDE, EGO AND VANITY
11. FEARS AND INSECURITIES
12. WHIPSAW DEMONS
13. BEARDS AND BALDNESS
14. TRYING TO LOOK YOUNG
15. CHRISTIAN FANTASY
16. FALSENESS
17. FEMININE PREACHERS
18. WOMEN
19. ASK YOURSELVES SOME QUESTIONS
20. PERSONAL PREFERENCE

SCRIPTURE
Baldness

Lev. 21:5 Priests shall not make baldness on their heads.
Deut. 14:1 God's children are not to disfigure themselves in mourning.
2 Ki. 2:23-24 Bears destroy the children that mocked Elisha.
Isa. 3:24 The judgments which shall be for the pride of the women.
    15:2   The lamentable state of Moab.
Jer. 16:6   Do not make yourself bald for the dead that are punished.
    47:5   The destruction of the Philistines.
    48:37   Moabites shall be bald with beards clipped.
Eze. 7:18 The mournful repentance of them that escape.
    27:31   And they shall make themselves utterly bald for thee.
Amos 8:10 I will bring baldness upon every head.
Mic. 1:16 Micah exhorteth to mourning.

Beards

Lev. 19:27A repetition of sundry laws.
2 Sam. 19:24 Mephibosheth had not trimmed his beard for mourning.
Ezra 9:3 Ezra mourneth for the affinity of the people with strangers.
Isa. 7:20 Ahaz is judged.

Hair

Lev. 14:8 The rites and sacrifices in cleansing of the leper.
Num. 6:5 The law of the Nazarites.
1 Ki. 1:52There shall not an hair of him fall to the earth.
Job 4:15 Job's hair stood up at the nearness of God.
Isa. 50:6 They plucked out the beard of Jesus.
Jer. 7:29 Jeremiah exhorteth to mourn for their abominations in Tophet.
Eze. 16:7 God's extraordinary love towards Jerusalem.
Matt. 5:36 What it is to swear.
Luke 21:18God can protect every hair.
Acts 27:34 All came safe to land.
1 Cor. 11:14 Long hair is a shame to a man.
1 Cor. 11:15 Woman's hair is her glory.
1 Tim. 2:9 How women should be attired.

Hoary Head

Lev. 19:32 Honor the elderly and God.
Prov. 16:31 If it be found in the way of righteousness.

PREFACE

Either I coined a term for us or the Lord spoke into my spirit, **God's Little Trouble Makers**. I took the Dale Carnegie Course which teaches you how to win friends and influence people. Then the Lord gave us a ministry which is unpopular and controversial; exactly the opposite of winning friends and influencing people. We stir people up to help them. We have caused many Christians consternation because of their lack of belief in deliverance and how they interpret the Bible. This lesson will touch the lives of many people because of their vanity and weaknesses. Most preachers want to give you the good news of what God is going to do for you. We tell you what will happen if you do not follow the Bible. Sin will reap its harvest. I have not fully researched this lesson but you can see that the ramifications are far reaching in the ways that our lives are affected. Think about why people treat their hair the way they do, why people dress the way they do and why people act they way they do. Think about this lesson in the spiritual, mental, physical and material realms.

FREEDOM OF CHOICE

God gives us a freewill to choose our course in life. As such, we must give others a freewill to do as they please in things such as dress and hair styles. It doesn't matter whether it is our personal preference; it is not our life. Even if it is contrary to the Bible, the person still has a right to choose between the world and the Word of God. They will reap the good or evil from their actions.

JESUS CHRIST
Isa. 50:6: Jesus Christ looked like the other people of his day and probably had long hair and a beard. We don't have any pictures of Him but we have the customs of His day retained in history. They did have razors in those days and it was probably easier to shave than to trim their long hair.

REJECTION
If a person can not accept themselves as God made them and as they grow older, their problems probably are rooted in rejection. Many times the roots start with their parents. Most of women's rejection can be traced to how they have been treated by men in their lives: grandfathers, fathers, brothers, husbands and sons. **The fathers have the strongest influence on their daughters' lives.**

BITTERNESS
If a person has become rejected, they will tend to become bitter against those who rejected them. When a person becomes bitter, they will tend to become rebellious against those who rejected them or against society.

REBELLION
A common sight nowadays is a boy or man with long hair like a woman. Sometimes this is a sign of vain glory. Most times it is a sign of rebellion. Many times you can recognize why the person has long hair. If the person is in rebellion, check to see if they were rejected, became bitter and then entered into rebellion.

INHERITED CURSES
Baldness can be a curse that has been handed down through the generations. Some people say that baldness comes through the mother. If you see a family that has generations of men with premature baldness at an early age, that family probably is cursed by the sins of their ancestors. Check for familiar spirits if there is no disease and treatment such as cancer with radiation treatment which causes a loss of hair.

DISEASES
Some diseases can cause loss of hair on the head. If a person has a disease in this category, **take the person through deliverance and then pray for healing of the disease and baldness.** God is known to do creative miracles and may completely restore the body and hair.

PRIDE, EGO AND VANITY
Prov. 6:16-19: The driving force behind many of the actions of men and women is self or pride, ego and vanity for self. God hates pride because it causes so much trouble for the human race. It interferes with our relationship with God because we want to be Gods or to have our own way. Earline said that we should call this lesson **Vanity.**

FEARS AND INSECURITIES

For God hath not given us the spirit of fear; but of power, and of love, and of a sound mind (2 Tim. 1:7). Repeat this verse three times; it will make you feel stronger. God gave us spirits of power, love and sound mind. All fear comes from Satan.

Many people in the ministry and in public life are driven by fears of different types. Fears of ministers mainly deal with retaining their positions or ministries. Fears of the congregation mainly deal with retaining their jobs in their companies. Psychiatrists have cataloged at least 210 phobias which are fears.

Insecurities are found in many areas such as inferiority, self pity, loneliness, timidity, shyness, inadequacy, ineptness, etc. When we are insecure, we are looking for something to make us feel all right in that area of weakness.

WHIPSAW DEMONS

There are emotional demons that cooperate with each other to whipsaw the person from one extreme to another. For instance, take pride and insecurity. The demon of insecurity will drive the person to do some act to be prideful. Then the demon of pride will cause the person to feel insecure. The whipsaw goes back and forth and the person is never allowed to fell all right for long.

BEARDS AND BALDNESS

Many men have beards because they are going bald. They think this helps to make up for lack of hair on the top of the head. **This probably indicates insecurity or vanity** brought about by feelings of not fully accepting themselves or trying to impress others by being something that they aren't. If the Holy Spirit wanted all men to grow beards, there would probably be a general impression to that effect at least in the Christian community.

TRYING TO LOOK YOUNG

Another one of my objections is that the men preachers have to look young and act young to maintain their positions of leadership. Women have to follow suit to maintain their husbands and their respect. There is much pressure in the world of advertising for looking and acting young. This is ridiculous before God and in the Christian community.

Lev. 19:27 and Prov. 16:31: I believe that the Bible honors the grey-haired man who has wisdom and understanding to impart to the members of his congregation and is living a righteous life. Therefore, I don't believe in dying the hair to hide the gray strands to look young.

CHRISTIAN FANTASY

Deliverance brings you into the ultimate reality of God's truth. **God is total truth and there is no fantasy in God.** One of the problems we have in charismatic circles is Christian fantasy which is really lies in the guise of Christianity. I would like to paraphrase Jack Harris, **Sheep in wolves clothing; watch their tracks.**

FALSENESS

I object to anything that is false such as playacting, put on, theatrics, affectation, pretension, sophistication, etc. When you try to change your body and be something that you aren't, then you are entering into some degree of falseness.

One of the problems that women have is trying to be super spiritual so that they will be accepted and feel good about themselves. Women tend to have problems with accepting themselves as women because they think that the men have a better life. This can lead to fleshly prophesy out-of-the-mind, wanting to lead, mouthing spiritual sayings that are not Biblical, etc. to be noticed and to be seen.

We have had some experiences with women who have done a lot of prophesying in the church and to people. A friend of mine got into a position where she had words for people. At one point, she told her husband that he would die before the year was out. He did not die but was in good health. When her words began to fail, she asked me what should she do. I told her to come up to Lake Hamilton Bible Camp and we would all stone her. That was the prescription for making a false prophecy in the Bible. In the Old Testament they were told to stone a prophet if his words did not come to pass and also not to fear them. If we thought about the serious responsibility a prophet has, we would not say anything in prophecy unless we had no doubt God said it. God does not like falseness.

Why do women think they are not as good as men? When we go back to Genesis, we find that the woman took and ate. When she gave to her husband, he took and ate, and then all the bad stuff happened. Adam blamed it on Eve. If you take notice, the bad stuff happened only after he ate. In I Tim. 2:14, we see that Eve was deceived but not Adam. This means Eve was sure she was making the right decision. Adam knew the true state of their action and chose to do wrong. From there until today, women have been the brunt of men's jokes. This is still so strong in some countries today that if people have a girl child and they don't want it, they let it die or kill it. We have come from a long line of rejection so we are conditioned to reject ourselves. When you find yourself doing things a little out of line, give some thought to what your motive is and what are you hoping to gain.

FEMININE PREACHERS

Some men preachers sound, look and smell like women; this turns me off. In the Bible, the man and woman clearly have different roles and should look like different sexes. Men should be masculine and women should be feminine. The pressure of humanism and the new world movement is turning men into women and women into men.

WOMEN

Isa. 3:16-24: The following is the Moody Paraphrase based on the experiences of deliverance ministers. **The daughters of Zion are haughty. The Lord will smite with psoriasis. He will discover their secret parts with female diseases and burning. He will take away their bravery and give them fear. Instead of a sweet smell there shall be the stink of cancer and rotting flesh. Their clothes will be sackcloth and torn; their head shall be bald.** See Isa. 3:24, 1 Cor. 11:15 & 1 Tim. 2:9.

I Cor. 11:3-15: Paul reproveth them, because in holy assemblies their men prayed with their heads covered, and women with their heads uncovered. The woman's hair is given as a covering. Some people believe that a woman should have a scarf or hat on her head when she is in church and especially when she is ministering to the congregation.

The covering in this passage is not the husband but an actual covering for the head. It is a covering to show that the woman has chosen to submit to her husband. You realize, of course, that the covering is not proof of proper submission, but proper submission is a choice of the heart and mind of the woman.

Pat Forman had this experience once when she was to speak with Reggie Foreman. She was in the shower getting ready to go when her head become frozen looking up at the ceiling. She asked in prayer what was going on and was impressed that she should wear something on her head as a sign of submission to her husband. They looked up these scriptures and decided she would wear a barrette in her hair as a sign that she was choosing to submit to his leadership.

1 Tim. 2:9-15: These passages discuss how women should be dressed and what manner they should conduct themselves. 1 Pet. 3:1-6: Peter teaches the duty of wives to their husbands. The Bible clearly teaches that it is not the outward part of woman that is important but the inward part of her soul and spirit that God sees. The same could also be said for the man.

Our daughter, Marie, worked as a waitress while she was in college to help pay for her education. She noticed that the women in business had problems with loosing their hair in baldness.

Likewise, ye husbands, dwell with them according to knowledge, giving honour unto the wife, as unto the weaker vessel, and as being heirs together of the grace of life; that you prayers be not hindered (1 Pet. 3:7). God made women weaker physically and spiritually than the men. The men are to be stronger and provide for the women.

When a woman tries to usurp the role of her husband or tries to act like a man, she opens herself up to masculinity problems and demons. She may begin to have problems of baldness which is common to man but not woman. She may begin to look, act, talk and have the mannerisms of a man. She may grow excessive hair on the face while losing hair on the top of the head.

Some women preachers try to act like the men preachers to gain acceptance. They begin to take on the characteristics of men preachers. It is readily apparent when a woman is masculine. The woman is not sure whether she really fits into the role of preacher in the predominately man's world. She tries to compensate and become one of the boys and get accepted into the men's club.

Many times the profession of the woman stems from trying to please her father who wanted a boy or having a husband that didn't properly provide for her or having other men mistreat her. A woman ends up in a man's profession frequently because she has not been properly treated as a girl and then as a woman.

Women need to be very careful and watchful over their motivations. God does not look at the outward show but He reads what is in the heart. You may sit in this congregation and do all the correct outward actions but God is not impressed unless the heart and mind are correct.

Women wearing make-up comes from the occult. The women in Egypt were expert in the use of make-up. It was a part of the life of the women at the time of the Tower of Babel. Today women make their eyes in the same manner as the Egyptians. The Hebrew women then did not use make-up; even today they are modest in it's use. Women usually wear make-up because they hope to gain some advantage, manipulate somebody or because they feel rejected.

I suffered from rejection for many years of my life. I was often manipulated into doing things I didn't want to do because I wanted someone somewhere to like and approve of me. If your purpose for your manner of dress is to attract followers, you are in witchcraft. This is true also for you fellows.

II Kings 9:30-35: Jezebel was a beautiful person on the outside and she must have kept herself very beautiful. She has suffered through the sentence placed on her husband her children, and she is now alone in the castle. Jehu has been anointed to destroy her. She hears him coming, thinking she will just do her usual thing (seduce him). She paints her face, beautifies her head and looks out the window hoping to stop God's sentence against her.

Jehu was not impressed and carried out his instructions. She was thrown out the window, run over by horses and eaten by dogs. Once we had a young lady begin to scream, **Stop the horses, stop the horses.** She was holding her head in her hands and trying to protect herself. We thought this strange and looked this scripture up, II Kings 9:30-35.

Our motives will show up in our reasons for what we do and this is what God sees.

ASK YOURSELVES SOME QUESTIONS
Why do you need to hide the wrinkles? Why do you need to look better? Apparently, you feel like you look better (younger) and feel approval (about yourself). Earline and I have a tendency to examine everything. Was it the Holy Spirit or another spirit that talked to you?

PERSONAL PREFERENCE
I never have been impressed by long hair or beards on men. I prefer short hair which is easy to maintain. I don't like the beards which scratch and have to be cut periodically.

SECTION 19 - DRUNKENNESS AND GLUTTONY

CONTENTS
1. LIST OF SCRIPTURES
2. KEY SCRIPTURES
3. GENERAL
4. AMERICANS MUST CHANGE THEIR EATING HABITS!
5. EARLINE'S TESTIMONY ABOUT EATING
6. GENE'S COMMENTS
7. CONCLUSION

LIST OF SCRIPTURES

Gen. 9:20-25	Drunk - Naked - Cursed son
Lev. 10:9	Priest
Lev. 17:10-11	Do not eat blood - blood sausage.
Num. 11:4-6	Lust for food, hated God's manna
Deut. 29:18-21	God's great wrath - disobedience curses
I Sam. 25:36-37	Very drunken - paralyzed - died
I Kings 20:12, 16	Drunk kings - lost battle
Job 15:27	Fatness of face and flanks
Psa. 69:22	Trap
Psa. 75:4-8	Wine
Psa. 78:29-31	Slew the fattest.
Psalm 104:10-18	Wine
Psa. 106:14-15	Leanness of soul
Prov. 9:1-6	Wine
Prov. 20:1	Mocker
Prov. 23:2, 21	Appetite - Gluttony
Prov. 23:29-35	Sting like snake
Prov. 25:16	Vomit honey
Prov. 31:4-7	Dies
Ecc. 10:16-18	Drunkenness of Princes and King
Isa. 5:11-13	Inflamed
Isa. 5:22-23	Wicked
Isa. 24:9, 11	Judgment
Isa. 28:1-3	Pride
Isa. 28:7-8	Tables full of vomit and filth
Eze. 44:21	Priest shall not drink wine.
Hosea 4:11-13	Whoredom and wine caused them to err.
Joel 1:5	Howling and weeping for wine
Nahum 1:10	Drunken as drunkards
Hab. 2:15-16	Drunkenness for sex
Matt. 24:48-51	Drunkenness and gluttony - not aware
Luke 21:34-36	Surfeiting and drunkenness - not watching
John 6:26	Seeking Jesus for food not for worship

Rom. 13:11-14	Rioting and drunkenness
I Cor. 6:9-13	Drunkards shall not inherit the kingdom.
Gal. 5:19-21	Drunkenness and other works of the flesh
Eph. 5:15-20	Drunk with wine
Phil. 3:18-19	Whose God is your belly
I Thes. 5:4-8	Drunken in the night - thief will rob
Titus 2:3-5	Be sober - not given to much wine.
I Peter 4:1-3	Excess of wine and banquetings

KEY SCRIPTURES

Lev. 17:10	Boudan sausage is made with blood.
Num. 11:4	Lust for food.
Job 15:27	Fatness of face and flanks.
Psa. 69:22	Table is a snare.
Psa. 78:29-31	Slew the fattest of them.
Psa. 106:14-15	Leanness of their souls.
Prov. 23:2	Put a knife to your throat.
Prov. 23:20-21	Poverty for drunkard and glutton.
Prov. 25:16	And vomit it.
John 6:26	Seek Jesus, not food from Jesus.
Phil. 3:18-19	God is belly.

GENERAL

I am a serious person about the Lord. This is a serious lesson. I will try to start off on a humorous note. **Fools rush in where angels fear to tread.** Earline and me rush in where preachers fear to tread. We have discussed starting an organization called **Cowards for Christ**. We could even have a chapter called **Cowardly Preachers**. We could have millions of members.

Now back to a serious vein. Paul said that he declared the whole truth to the people in his day. That is what we should do in these modern days. How many of you believe that you should avoid the hard sayings of the Bible? I want to talk to you about an area that most preachers shun. It is hard on men of God as well as women in general. I don't have the preachers' problems about you leaving the church if your ears are not tickled or quit giving to the church if your toes have been stepped on. **One of the hard sayings of the Bible is that drunkenness and gluttony are the same!** You will either love or hate us.

AMERICANS MUST CHANGE THEIR EATING HABITS!

Jeanne Paul, Nurse Anesthesiologist, sent us the following horrible statistics about illnesses that are happening to modern men, women and children because of the way they eat. **Do you live to eat or eat to live? You can not eat like the Devil and live like the Lord.**

1. 80 million Americans are overweight. 30 million are obese (20% above ideal weight). 30 to 50% of these are Christians. 50% of males over 30 and 75% of females over 40 are overweight.

2. Some chronic conditions comparing normal to overweight people follow:
   Cholesterol gallstones are 300% more frequent.
   Toxemia of pregnancy is 700% higher.
   Infection of urine collecting part of the kidney is 500% greater.
   Diabetes Mellitus is 400% more common.
   There are more maternal deaths.
   Infections are 200% more frequent.
   Postoperative mortality is 250% greater.
   High blood pressure is found 250% more frequently when you reach age 45.
3. Over consumption of meat, fats, sugar, cholesterol, salt and alcohol have been linked with a higher incidence of six of the ten leading causes of death in the U.S.: heart disease, cancer, strokes, diabetes, arteriosclerosis and high blood pressure.
4. Turn of the century Americans were eating 4 pounds of sugar a year; today we consume 130 pounds per person per year - some statistics put it as high as 200 pounds because of the different type sugars being added to most prepared foods.
5. Readers Digest, September, 1987 stated that Americans eat 3 million gallons of ice cream per day and 3,000 tons of candy per day.
6. 20% of the American diet is now sugar. At the turn of the century there were very few diabetics; now there are 10 million with 600,000 new cases annually.
7. 20 years ago they never heard of hyperactive children; now there are 1 million.
8. Many pre-school children have rotted-off teeth.
9. At the turn of the century, people died most often from bacterial-type disease. Now they are dying from degenerative disease: diabetes, cancer, heart disease and strokes. Then 1 in 13 had cancer, now 1 in 3 and by 1990, 1 in 2. The age of chronic disease onset is much earlier.
10. The annual death rate from hardening of the arteries and degenerative heart disease in the U.S. for men age 50 to 59 is the highest in the world. Many accident victims and young men killed in Vietnam had the arteries of 55 to 60 year olds. The most common surgery in men under 55 is coronary by-pass surgery:
    2 to 5% die on the operating table.
    42% are back in two years for more heart surgery.
    47% are dead in 5 years.
11. There are now more children born with plugged arteries and children having heart attacks by age 5 to 6 years.
12. In 1912 the first heart attack was reported. Now 1 million Americans have heart attacks per year and spend 5 billion dollars trying to recover. Heart disease is not world wide. South Africa has to import American doctors to teach them how to treat tourists who have heart attacks.
13. Metropolitan Life Insurance Company has shown that a man 45 years old, who increases his weight by 25 pounds over standard weight, reduces his life expectancy by 25%, i.e. he dies at age 60 instead of 75.
14. Every pound of fat you add to your body forms and must nourish approximately 3/4 mile of blood vessels and flush them with blood every 5/6th of a second. The extra burden on the heart has statistical results as follows:
    70% of the new cases of hypertension are directly attributed to weight gain.

For every 10 pounds a man puts on, his blood pressure raises 6.5 points systolic (top number).

30 million Americans have high-blood pressure.

15. The American Cancer Society says that at least 60% of cancer is diet related. 90% of colon cancer could be avoided with fiber. Breast cancer can be greatly reduced by lowering sugar, fat and caffeine consumption.

16. The American Heart Association suggests the percent of calories from fat must not exceed 25 to 30%. The average for Americans now is 40% and some think much higher.

17. People are misled by the polyunsaturates in margarines and oils. You must look for hydrogenated on the label which is simply eating plastic. The only way the body can handle this is to deposit it in the arteries.

18. 30% of American women have osteoporosis and that is a world record. Many factors are involved such as low calcium intake, birth control pills, less weight-bearing exercise and higher consumption of phosphoric acid (the fizz in pops). The onset of this disease is much earlier after the 30's and even some men are developing it.

EARLINE'S TESTIMONY ABOUT EATING

1. I was sitting on the couch after eating a good breakfast. I had this urging to go and get more food, but I was not hungry. I asked The Lord why and He forced the demon within me to say, **My name is I Like To Eat, go and get me some food.**

2. After casting out the demon, **I Like To Eat**, I told God how I had tried dieting and I knew that was hopeless.

3. I was told **Obedience is better than sacrifice, and I knew how to eat but was not doing it. Plenty of fresh fruits and vegetables, not much meat and very little sweets is the basis of a proper diet.**

4. **Asked if I'd do what I was told, I assured God that I would. He said that food can be divided into two groups: God's and Devil's. Devil's foods include sweets to excess, junk food, and liquids which are mostly empty calories.**

5. It's not bad manners not to eat sweets or any other food when you know your body has not used up the last meal. I was intelligent enough to know if I truly needed food.

6. **Here are the rules in summary:**
   a. Eat fruits and vegetables; include leafy greens.
   b. Do not eat much meat - three or four servings weekly.
   c. Don't eat unless you truly need to.
   d. Don't let others stuff you.
   e. Seldom eat sweets.
   f. Almost never eat junk food.
   g. Remember those whose God is their belly.
   h. Cook all foods simply.
   i. Use little fat and cut fat from the meat.

GENE'S COMMENTS

1. Earline lost about seventy pounds and weighed less than she did when we got married and before she had two children. She weighed 100 to 110 pounds which was less than Marie, our teenage daughter, who had not had any children. It was like having a new wife!
2. Do you realize that the body has enough energy for you to fast for forty days? Marie fasted for forty days on water taking only vitamins, minerals and supplements.
3. You must take care of your spirit, soul and body. You can not neglect any part of your tripartite being and be in health. You can not neglect your body and expect God to take care of it or heal you everytime that you pray. One of Earline's sayings is, **If you don't brush your teeth, God will let them rot out of your mouth.**
4. Healing and deliverance go hand in hand. You can get healed by anointing with oil and praying the prayer of faith, or by casting out demons of infirmities. The Lord told me to take a person through deliverance and then pray for healing. You have a double possibility of getting the person healed.
5. Sometimes the demon of infirmity manifests as it is being cast out and you know that there was an infirmity demon in the person. If the infirmity is there because of sin, you won't get healed by the prayer of faith, because the demon has a legal right to be there. You must take away the legal right and then cast out the demon.

CONCLUSION

You can be healed by God or cured by a doctor. You can mentally discipline your body. Your demons can be cast out in the name of Jesus. You can ask God to help you control your weight. **There are no excuses (mentally, physically or spiritually) for being overweight in the Bible!**

Printed in Great Britain
by Amazon